JULIE RUSSELL

Secrets, Surprises and Love

My Childhood Journey

 FriesenPress

One Printers Way
Altona, MB R0G 0B0
Canada

www.friesenpress.com

ISBN
978-1-03-912340-3 (Hardcover)
978-1-03-912339-7 (Paperback)
978-1-03-912341-0 (eBook)

Biography & Autobiography, Personal Memoirs

Distributed to the trade by The Ingram Book Company

For my siblings Charlie, Chris, and Barry.
Precious memories spun together in our journey of life.

Acknowledgements

I appreciate all the support in bringing to fruition my book, Secrets, Surprises, and Love.

At FriesenPress I would like to thank my efficient Editing team, Design Team and a special thank you to my Publishing Specialist Emma.

To my parents, Bill and Laura, and my siblings, Charlie, Chris, and Barry many thanks for sharing the amusing, sometimes scary and lots of heart-warming experiences that inspired my book. I am grateful to my siblings Barry and Chris for providing a few of those missing details in my recollections.

A special thank you to many others – to my granddaughter, Jacey who throughout my writing would eagerly read, impart wisdom, and cheer me onwards with reassurances that I had an interesting story to tell and to my children, grandchildren and family members who avidly listened, encouraged, and eagerly journeyed along with me to bring my childhood stories to life. My heartfelt thanks to my dearest friend Linda and daughter Carrie for tramping hither and thither through the thick foliage, briars, and brambles in search of the perfect background setting to shoot my Book Cover photo. Special thanks to daughter, Carrie who survived precariously teetering on a stool to get the right angle for my Author photo and spending numerous hours enhancing photos for this book. And finally, I owe a huge debt of gratitude to my husband, Dave who listened to my stories over and over and over again, and diligently dug deep to enthusiastically issue yet another positive comment.

And most important thanks to God for giving me such a wonderful family, a small town full of loving people and for watching over me every day of my life.

Please note some of the *names* in my story have been changed.

Part
One

Mother and Father
1937 to Mid-1940s

Chapter 1

Love: Mother and Father:

I now pronounce you husband and wife echoes in Laura's mind as she gingerly clinks down the steps of the magistrate's office in her moderate high heels. Laura and Bill are married.

Stepping into the sun's blinding rays, the small troupe stumbles outside to feel the warm heat rise up from the wooden sidewalk. It is unusually hot for this autumn day in 1945. Laura sighs loudly and pulls at her wedding dress–much too big for her tiny frame.

Wedding dress shopping last week had been a disaster.

"We need a dress that is big enough to be worn for several months!" her mother expressed firmly to the saleslady. The words cut like a knife within Laura, tears sprung into her eyes, and she was overwhelmed with an emotion of shame mingled with anger. She felt the eyes of the saleslady glance down at her tummy. Laura cringed. *She might as well have told the whole world: my daughter is pregnant.*

This is not the wedding dress of my dreams, Laura muses as she yanks at her full-sized garment. Noticing a camera lens aimed in their direction, she smooths the strands around her face. Laura stretches her five-foot one-inch frame upwards alongside Bill who is tall at six foot and places her head on his chest. She smiles in happiness regardless of her *two-sizes-too-big,* basic knee-length frock.

Laura hopes the photographer will capture the essence of the moment. She reminisces on their engagement snapshot. The picturesque photo relives a happy memory where love leaps right out of the picture.

Laura exudes a stunning presence with sparkling big blue eyes, hair swung upwards, and looking elegant in a borrowed black tailored suit sporting a shiny satin collar. The stylish suit fit to a tee—it would be much too snug now.

Wrapping his arm around her waist, Bill looks strikingly handsome with his gentle brown eyes and dark hair.

Bill and Laura engagement photo

His muscular body is framed in a contoured medium grey suit, a debonair vest, and a two-toned blue and white tie.

It is true that a picture paints a thousand words. The photo portrays two sets of twinkling eyes and joyful smiles. An image of a dashing young couple in love.

Love culminating in marriage is a dream come true, Laura reflects. However, weighing heavy on her mind is the anxiety of her condition, and the judgment of family members.

Chapter 2

Homesteading:

Eight years earlier, in the spring of 1937, it is a journey into the unknown! Dreams of a better life entice the Nelsons and Allen's to homestead in Weekes, Saskatchewan.

Weekes is a bustling pioneer town. It is situated in the middle of the dense bush in the northeastern area of the province. Hitching posts are situated sparingly on both sides of the street to accommodate horses and carts. Wooden sidewalks do not appear until five years later. A Canadian National Railway station is situated next to the railway tracks. Palfenier's General Store/Post Office on Main Street is a homey shop which is stocked with shelves and shelves of dry goods. It is customary for Mr. Palfenier to sell his goods in exchange for eggs, butter, and lumber. A new Hardware Store is erected by Ivor and son Archie Stigen. In 1938 a one-room schoolhouse was built and a single teacher, Mr. Frank Germaine, instructed grades one to eight. That same year Harry Wing's Café opened, and the Pool grain elevator was built to become the skyscraper of the town.

The Allen's arrive with Bill, an only boy, and youngest daughter, Evelyn. Three older girls have flown the nest and are in the working world. Bill labors side by side with his dad on the land, four and a half miles out of Weekes, while Evelyn helps her mom. Charles and Mabel believe that boys perform the outside duties and girls complete the inside housework. The first item on the agenda is a home. A log cabin must be constructed.

Battling thick brush and mosquitoes, Bill studies the trees to choose the straightest trunks. The quiet air is broken by the thud of the axe and the rhythmic swishing of the saw during the process of chopping down the trees. Together they tackle the tree trunk and at the tipping stage shout a warning.

"Timber!" shouts Bill. The words echo and reverberate into the quiet, still forest. The tree crashes to the ground with a thunderous racket.

Attacking the tree with a saw and axe, Bill and his dad trim the branches and cut the tree into logs of the same length. Bill strips the bark away to prevent the tree from rot while his dad notches the ends of the log to enable interlocking at the corners. Laying the logs end to end on top of one another creates

The Allen's log house

the walls. In order to *chink* the walls, a concoction of straw and mud are mixed and plastered in between the logs to fill in the gaps. The completed log house is spacious, measuring 15 x 20 feet. In addition, it has a loft accommodating two bedrooms. To eke out a living, Charles and Bill begin to farm, and they set up a small sawmill.

Two years later in 1939, a disaster occurs at the neighbors. Mrs. Hamilton dies during childbirth delivering baby Gordon. Mabel and Charles come to the rescue when father, Frank, is unable to tend to a baby and care for his other children.

"We will care for the baby," Mabel and Charles generously offer, and they happily foster baby Gordon. Charles refers to him as *my buddy*; thus, his nickname becomes Buddy.

Charles William is a mild-mannered man who proudly displays his English traditions. Charles immigrated in early 1900 from Yorkshire, England to Sedalia, Missouri, USA where he met and married Mabel Hill. She is very generous and caring in nature; however, she is also a no-nonsense woman with high standards.

Bill's legal name is John William but he's known by his nickname, Bill. He is, like his dad, kind, caring, easygoing and on the quiet side. When words are spoken, it is to impart words of wisdom.

Bill is a strapping young lad of seventeen whose life turned topsy-turvy at the age of twelve when his Dad had a catastrophic accident. As rumor goes—a horse and wagon loaded with goods caught Charles off-guard. He heard the horses clatter down the street and out of his peripheral vision noticed the outfit barreling towards him. He swiftly scrambled to escape. Unfortunately, unable to move out of the path of the wagon, it knocked him roughly and uncontrollably to the ground. The sharp steel wheel crushed his right leg just below the knee. The tragic outcome was that Charles lost his lower limb and was outfitted with a wooden leg making it more difficult to work. Therefore, Bill sadly quit school in grade six to fulfil his responsibilities. Upon arriving in Weekes Bill is at home dutifully working alongside his Dad.

Bush surrounds the entire area of Weekes. The major roads are crudely constructed with cordwood, which are short-length pieces of debarked trees laid side by side on the ground, with mud used as a compound. The one-mile span between the Allen's and Nelson's is just a trail, with cord-wood laid down in the swampy parts. In the winter, the roads are better because the trails are frozen with hard-packed snow. The Nelsons' home-stead is near the railroad tracks; therefore, it is easier to walk the tracks two and a half miles to Weekes.

Laura arrives with her parents—Cornelias,

Weekes 1938

nickname "Kelly," and Christina Elsie, assumes "Elsie"–along with older brother, Earl, and younger sister, Rose. Her six older siblings are married, in a career, or at war.

They arrive in the autumn of 1937 just before the onslaught of winter. Two huge tents are erected to become their first dwelling. One tent contains a heater where the cooking, eating, and visiting transpire. A chimney is rigged into the roof, however the room is in a constant haze from the smoke. The other tent is for sleeping. Throughout the extremely cold winter months several layers of clothes are always worn. At the first sign of spring, the trees are tackled to transform into logs to build their log cabin.

A firm and upright man, Kelly holds many positions over the years– Justice of the Peace, mayor, councillor, police officer and school trustee. Elsie is on the quiet side. She reads from the Bible faithfully and teaches her children to live the righteous life.

Laura is outgoing and friendly. She chats to everyone, anywhere. Occasionally her abundant kindness and generosity can get her in trouble. At eight years old, Laura eagerly accompanies her mom to Palfenier's General Store/Post Office for the mail, where she will spend the twenty-five cents clutched in her tiny hands. She was gifted the coin from Tom Speedy, a conductor on the railway car. He often threw gunnysacks of clothing and candy from the train alongside their farm for the family. As a thankyou her Mom, Elsie baked a pie and Laura delivered it to the station. Tom gifted Laura with a quarter coin. This is a windfall. Thus, at the store Laura immediately spends it all on a small mound of candy.

"Who would like some candy?" she asks the patrons of the store with a big grin. The candy quickly disappears, and she is soon left with none for herself. On the way home, her mother angrily scolds her for being so foolish. Nevertheless, Laura is happy–she prefers to bless others. This is a life-long trait, where Laura prefers to give rather than to receive.

Laura is a smart cookie–she coasts through grade three and skips grade four.

"I want to become a nurse," Laura reveals to her teacher at the completion of grade eight. Her teacher, Miss Prestlic, solicits Laura's parents on her behalf and explains Laura's aspiration to continue her education.

"No, I need her to help on the farm and in the bush," her dad firmly responds. Unfortunately, Laura is the only child available to work since Earl went away to war and she is now the oldest child remaining at home. Rose, being the baby of the family, is given a lot more leeway in work responsibilities.

"Please …," Laura sobs desperate and disappointed.

"No!" is her dad's snappy retort, cutting her pleading to a sudden halt. It is like a cloudburst of rain dousing a forest fire. She motions frantically to her teacher, but to no avail. The decision is final. Laura is devasted that she is unable to continue her desire of a nursing career. Laura is forced to leave school—she is only twelve years old!

*****

The following winter Laura toils at the logging camp in the dense bush with her dad. The cold, bitter wind chills her to the bone. She stamps her boots on the ground to keep her feet from freezing. It is back-breaking work, as she attaches a downed tree to the horse's ropes. Laura audibly groans while pulling on the reins to drag her horse to the sleigh. She uses all her strength to help heave the logs onto the sleigh. She sighs. *This is hard work; I would rather go hunting*! Hunting for food with her dad is an easier task. Hunting the smaller animals—rabbit, prairie chickens, or grouse—Laura uses the twenty-two rifle. Her dad goes after the bigger prey—deer, elk, or moose. Laura grows to become an excellent markswoman.

Summer work is just as tough! Preparing the land for crops is challenging work. It is hard enough to pick roots left over from the cut trees, but more annoying is the horde of mosquitoes, relentlessly biting. Swatting them away with a tiny twig does little to stop them, therefore, on several occasions Laura builds a smudge fire. A smudge is created by tossing green leaves onto a fire to create clouds of smoke which will keep the pesky critters at bay. At day's end, Laura's body is filled with sore and throbbing muscles. Thankful for the arrival of evening, Laura falls into bed where she rubs her arms and legs to alleviate the aches and pains. It is a harsh life for a young girl.

Duties occur inside and outside her home! Other responsibilities extend to assisting her mom with the tasks of canning, cleaning, and cooking. Laura staggers with exhaustion while cleaning the supper dishes; her one saving grace and tranquility is to listen to her mom's nightly Bible reading.

She daydreams and prays while doing dishes—imploring God to miraculously arrange for her to return to school and pursue a nursing career. She gazes out the window into the yard at the trees outlined in the moonlight and imagines the Gates of Heaven. She knows God watches over her. Attending Church held in various homes with her mom and sister, Rose, is a pleasurable outing. Prayer is a way of life for Laura and her faith in God deepens.

Laura believes it is an answer to her prayer, although in a different way, when she is given the opportunity to live with her sister, Marie, in Saskatoon and find a job.

"I am so excited," blubbers Laura upon hearing the exciting news. Laura arrives in Saskatoon and quickly applies for a job. She is hired at the Dell Café and is soon working as a waitress. The work is easy, and she enjoys interacting with the customers. In addition, she earns a whopping thirty-five cents an hour. *This is like a vacation,* Laura happily reflects while laughing and talking with the customers. Life is pleasurable.

Several months later, her heart sinks and she is downhearted to be summoned back home to help her parents on the farm. Reluctantly, Laura explains to her boss that she must quit her job and return home. Her boss is sad to see her leave, telling her that she was his best worker. Laura despondently returns home.

Chapter 3

Dating:

Love is in the air. Bill and Laura begin to date. A movie is their first outing. It is a double date with Laura's brother, Raymond, and Bill's sister, Evelyn, who are married.

Bill and Laura embark on a steady courtship. Summers find them walking or doubling on a bike. In the winter, Bill arrives with a team of horses in an open sleigh. Laura can hear him long before she sees him—signaled by the horse's bells jingling in the cold, crisp air. They often go ice skating for entertainment.

Their love blooms quickly. Bill and Laura become engaged, and they have a photo taken to commemorate the occasion. Later, she will look at that picture and her heart will overflow with joy. The engagement photo is a precious reminder of their memorable day.

Bill's mom, Mabel, has a different attitude about the engagement. Her outlook is that *she's not good enough for Bill*. Mabel does not hide the fact that she considers Laura to be of a *lower status* due to her ancestry and not a suitable wife. In contrast, Bill's dad, Charles, is easygoing and approves of the engagement. He is not prejudiced.

Laura is proud of her ancestry. Dating back to the 1770s with immigrants from Scotland, England, and Ireland, her ancestors arrived in Canada and inter-married with the indigenous people.

Laura is perplexed–she loves her Gramma Jemima Halcrow whose father is native. However, at any mention of her Indigenous roots, Mabel's face becomes stern, and her eyes glare coldly. Laura shrinks under her scrutiny, knowing that, *she thinks I am not worth a hill of beans.*

Laura visualizes Mabel placing a want ad requesting a suitable wife for Bill:

> *Wanted:*
> *For Marriage. Upper-class female for handsome and respectable young man. Willing to relocate to an Up-and-Coming Farm in Saskatchewan, Canada. Reside with in-laws in luxurious two-bedroom 600 sq. ft. log cabin. Must have high standards and impeccable background. No Indigenous need apply.*

Laura in her mind adds, *Mother-in-law not willing to share her boy.* Laura is not eager to start off married life living with her in-laws. She takes a stab at an alternative plan by approaching her mom and dad.

"Can we please move into your house?" Laura addresses her parents in a pleading voice.

"Your place is with your husband in his home," her dad replies. He is determined to do *the right thing.* Elsie, Laura's Mom, relies on her husband to make most decisions; he has the final word.

Later that evening Laura implores Bill in a persuasive voice, "I really do like your parents, but can we get a dwelling of our own?"

"We will only stay with my parents for a short time," Bill replies, as he crushes his cigarette out on the ground and gives her an understanding look.

"Okay," Laura murmurs quietly. Her face expresses uncertainty as she jams her hands in her pockets. She hopes their love will conquer all obstacles.

Married Life:

Wedding plans are concluded. Laura was not consulted about the wedding dress or the ceremony. Instead, both sets of parents took charge of the date and location for the marriage vows. Bill, at twenty-four years old, is very easygoing and complied with the plans. Laura had little choice—at fifteen going on sixteen years next month, her parents' still treat her like a child. In spite of the nine-year gap between Laura and Bill they are very compatible due to Laura being very mature for her age. They are in love and are excited to be married. Thus, the wedding ceremony is performed at the magistrate's office in Tisdale, two and a half hours from home.

Abruptly, Laura is startled, standing in front of the magistrate's office, by a horse and carriage clattering noisily down the street. She realizes that the wedding photo has been taken.

"Congratulations," her parents' murmur. They are dressed in their Sunday best and smile in approval. Laura's brother, Lloyd, whom she adores, leans in to give her a warm and tight hug—he is the witness to sign for their marriage.

Laura is eagerly anticipating her marriage and coming baby; however, she speculates that the living arrangements will be challenging. Laura sighs quietly and worries in silence concerning the situation of residing with Bill's parents!

The small group moves as one towards her dad's Model T Ford for the two-and-a-half-hour return trip to home. The second-hand vehicle, nicknamed *Tin Lizzie*, earns its name by being prone to constant repairs. They encountered two flat tires on the road to Tisdale. Laura had worried they would miss their allotted time to take their vows.

"Are we going to be late for the wedding ceremony?" Laura had worriedly inquired of her dad.

"They can't start without us," he had candidly replied.

The sun's rays are scorching. Upon opening the car door, a blast of hot air gushes forth. Laura moans upon entering the sweltering vehicle. Her hair is damp against her neck and a bead of sweat appears on her forehead. Bill rolls down the back windows to let the small breeze waft throughout. Laura begins to feel normal—well, as normal as can be expected, considering she is expecting.

Laura and Bill snuggle. Laura's dad pushes the pedal to the metal and the Model T Ford springs into action. The vehicle, with twenty horsepower, hits its top speed of forty-five miles per hour. The brisk wind whistles through the open windows, tossing Laura's hair gently in the cool breeze. The tires crunch against the gravel on the gritty road to produce a billowing dust cloud in the rear. The trees glide by with the leaves in a vast array of colors—green, yellow, red, orange—signifying the season is fall, soon to be winter.

Home, Sweet Home. Laura visualizes their arrival at her in-law's house where she will be able to retreat for some privacy into their own bedroom. As if reading her mind, Bill grins and pulls her in close. Pulling into the lengthy driveway—or rather a very wide grassy path typically used by horse-and-buggy, Laura feels a flutter of anticipation and squeezes Bill's hand tightly.

She is shocked to see people gathered in the yard. Her breath catches in her throat, and she gasps in exasperation. "Why are all these people here?" Laura utters, and stares in amazement. Of course, Bill is clueless.

It is a surprise reception party! Laura is pleased to discover that her in-laws have arranged a surprise wedding celebration upon their return from the marriage ceremony. The agenda is snacks, a few games and gift opening. It is a joyful event and Mabel is a wonderful hostess. Laura is thrilled and speculates that *maybe Mabel has come around and accepts me as a daughter-in-law.* The evening culminates with a presentation of a group gift: a set of dishes!

"Thank you. This is exactly what we need," Laura enthusiastically expresses with a smile. She is full of gratitude and contemplates that this is one step closer in preparation for their own abode.

The guests have finally departed, and the clean-up is almost done.

"Time to sneak out," Bill whispers into Laura's ear as she is drying the last dish. She smiles at his words and feels a warm tingling as his arms encase her body. They stroll, smiling radiantly, hand in hand through the combined kitchen-living room to the steep staircase leading up to the bedrooms. Eagerly, Laura grips Bill's hand as they tread carefully on the stairs knowing that one or two might squeak. They do not want to advertise their departure.

Laura jolts to a sudden stop! At the top of the landing, she gapes in astonishment towards their bedroom.

"There is no bedroom door," she cries in a loud whisper. She remains stock-still. Hands clenched tightly, Laura stares in frustration at Bill. Concern flickers across his face as he quietly ponders the situation. He had not foreseen the open door a problem while single, however, now that he is married it immediately dawns on him that this is a problem!

"I have an idea," he speaks softly in a low tone.

Screech resounds throughout the room. Bill with his brute strength nudges the four-poster bed; it emits another loud *screech*. Each sharp push scrapes the floor, generating a loud skidding racket. Bill and Laura glance at each other and grin while attempting to stifle their laughter. They work together as a team and soon the bed is situated to the side of the room out of sight of the door opening. Clumsily they hang a towel from the top of the opening. It resembles a mini-Band-aid over a massive wound! They collapse onto the bed in silent hysterical laughter.

The next morning, Bill requests a door for their room.

Mabel frowns, however, father-in-law Charles grasps the situation.

"They are young, and they need some privacy. I will rig something up," he sympathetically suggests. Later that day, Charles moves a tall, heavy dresser abreast of the door opening, thus, creating some privacy for the newly-weds. Laura is pleased, knowing that their personal space has been respected.

Chapter 4

Mother-in-law:

Laura bends over backwards constantly trying to please her mother-in-law with the household duties. What a difficult task! It is impossible to meet her mother-in-law's standards.

Feelings of failure occur straightaway. Laura recalls their first dinner together, which ironically in her home they call supper. Setting the silverware on the table, she was promptly reprimanded:

"The silverware is not placed correctly," Mabel scolds. She has high standards and expects everything to be done in a certain manner. Head spinning, Laura is perplexed. *Does it really matter?* Next, Laura stares in astonishment as Mabel dishes up all the plates with food before setting them on the table. At home, the food is put on the table in bowls, and everyone digs in to serve themselves. Laura sighs. *I need to learn a new way of doing everything!*

The food looks delectable! Her plate has a mound of mashed potatoes, peas, and fried chicken. Hungrily, Laura picks up her piece of chicken with her fingers and promptly raises it to her mouth.

"Fingers are not for eating–we use utensils," Mable admonishes in a low voice.

Laura glances keenly around the table, to observe Charles carefully slicing his chicken with knife and fork in his hand. Laura, with blue eyes flashing, resentfully stares at Bill; he holds his knife and fork in mid-air, motionless, as if ready to dive into his food. Bill smiles candidly at Laura and at the same time lays his knife and fork gently on the table, scoops up his piece of chicken with his fingers, and raises it to his mouth to chomp a healthy bite. A tight-lipped Mabel frowns and visually shoots daggers at Laura.

Bill is an only boy, however, he is not tied to his mother's apron strings, reflects Laura. *I will try harder for Bill's sake.* Nevertheless, complaints from Mabel pound away at Laura like tiny angry jabs–it is an unbearable situation. On many occasions, Laura darts away and dashes to her parents' home.

It is a Monday morning in early spring and Laura is hanging clothes on the clothesline. Laura glances up to see Mabel, stern-faced with cold eyes, briskly strutting with a purpose towards her. Laura moans inwardly, thinking, *Now what is wrong?* She soon learns the problem!

"The pants should be hung up by the waist. The rule is if you wear it on top hang it from the bottom. If you wear it on the bottom, hang it from the top," informs Mabel. Laura cannot believe what she is hearing, in her estimation the pants would dry faster with the waist down. Her patience is at its limit. She storms angrily away in the opposite direction–striding swiftly towards her parents' house.

Laura stomps madly her frustration into the ground. Traversing the well-worn path of a mile to her parents' house, Laura's body expels her anger, and she soon begins to feel calm. Her mind analyzes the situation. *This not a good idea–my parents will not be happy.* She slowly clomps up the porch and stresses her dilemma to her parents. She is right, she is met with expressions of disappointment.

"You are married. You will have to go back," her dad instructs. Laura, close to tears and upset, throws her hands up and trudges back to the front porch.

She sits quietly and miserably on a stool. Tilting her head with her ear aimed toward the road, she listens for the far-away jingling of bells–the constant *ding-a-ling* that emits from the ornaments adorning the horse team. The sounds that signify, before she can even see him, that Bill is on his way to get her.

Bill arrives. He realizes the tense situation needs to be resolved.

"I have a solution. We can convert a granary into our home," he announces. Sliding off the stool, Laura runs to him with outstretched arms. She is ecstatic. It has been a long five months residing with her in-laws. At this point a tent would be a welcoming home! Laura knows that regardless of the small size it will be their home where love dwells.

Within a week, a section of land is rented a mile and a half north of Weekes on the Smith quarter. The location is approximately three miles from Bill's parents and four miles from Laura's parents. A granary is transported to this location for Bill and Laura to transform into their first home together.

Chapter 5

First Home:

Moving day arrives. It is humble beginnings in their one-room, fourteen-by-twelve-foot granary. Their brand-new cook stove is proudly installed at the end of the stark room. The remainder of their furnishings are second-hand, consisting of a table with up-turned nail kegs for chairs, a bed, and cardboard boxes to house the new set of dishes. The floor consists of wood boards which are hard to sweep, and the walls are missing insulation. The air is quite chilly, but the cookstove keeps the room remarkably cozy. Although it is a small, crowded home, the ambience is homey, not cramped. They have a new home to begin creating new memories.

Grampa Charles, Buddy, Gramma Mabel

Their first visitors arrive. Laura is surprised to glimpse Mabel, Charles, and Buddy strolling into the yard. She is apprehensive, but with a friendly smile she invites them in for coffee. Charles inquires in a soft voice how Laura is feeling, how the pregnancy is coming along, and questions Bill on the farming aspects of the land. Mabel tends to focus more on how the house appears, and to give advice to prepare for the coming baby, along with a list of Bill's favorite foods. Laura wishes Mabel could be as caring and generous to her as she is to others. Mabel is well-known in the community for giving a helping hand and giving to those who are in need. She was also instrumental in organizing the Weekes Ladies Aid in 1938 and is a valued member who takes part in planning events. One endeavor was to organize a Busy Bee for yard clean-up and beautification for the new school. At project end a photo was taken of the Ladies Aid group. Dolly Tyacke belongs to the group and her heart goes out to Laura being such a young bride. Therefore, Dolly takes Laura under her wing – she mentors her with compassionate listening and gently offers valuable advice. Laura looks up to Dolly and seeks out her opinion many times. Laura relies on Dolly's friendship and guidance - they are friends for life.

Weekes Ladies Aid: 1938
Back: Dolly Tyacke, Mrs. T. Tyacke, Aunt Evelyn, Mrs. Arlint, Annie Bebault, Mrs. Jessop. Front: Gramma Mabel, Gramma Elsie, Mrs. Louison, Corinna Inglis

In the meantime, Charles and Mabel dote on Buddy. He is the apple of their eye and Bill now takes a back seat. Bill and Laura continue to take on the responsibility of providing the needed monetary and emotional support to Bill's parents and Buddy. Bill keeps the financial provision private and does not complain. Together Bill and Laura forge ahead. There is hope for a happy and bright future.

Judith:

"Baby will arrive soon," Laura remarks with a look of exhaustion. Laura and Bill are wrapped together as one and Bill reaches over to feel the baby *kick*.

"We will need to arrange for you to stay in Tisdale, two-and-a-half hours away, to be close to the hospital," Bill remarks worriedly.

"I don't want to live in Tisdale. I will get lonesome," Laura replies dismally.

Regrettably, with no car there is no choice. Arrangements are made to stay at Mrs. White's Rooming House, where a room and meals will be supplied for a lower rent in exchange for light housekeeping. Mrs. White's Rooming House is a well-known, respectable place to rent at a reasonable price when away from home.

Several days later, an unhappy Laura arrives at Mrs. White's Rooming House. She is expected to do chores from morning to night—a far cry from her perception of "light housekeeping." She washes dishes, peels potatoes, makes beds, and cleans the house. Her energy wanes—the work is non-stop, all day.

Laura escapes at the first opportunity by obtaining a ride home with friends. Without a vehicle, Bill is unable to visit, and he is in the process of seeding the land which is a necessity for the upcoming crops.

"I am too lonely and she works me too hard. My feet swell and hurt," she informs Bill.

"We don't have a car and it is over two hours if you go into labor—please think of our baby," he soothingly remarks as he pulls her into his arms.

Laura returns to Tisdale. She is still just a kid of sixteen herself and being lonesome escapes to go home a few more times. However, when her labor begins Laura is in Tisdale. Mrs. White walks her to the hospital—when the spasm of a contraction starts, they come to a halt.

Dr. Wright is a general doctor at the Tisdale Hospital. He is kind and caring and reassures Laura that everything will be okay. He checks in on her periodically to chat in a calm manner. Nurse Lucy is the head nurse;

she is very experienced and has been at the hospital for many years. Nurse Lucy oversees Laura's progress.

Laura is situated on a gurney in the birthing room. She has been in labor for many hours and is tired and scared.

Dr Wright realizes her distress; he speaks to Laura in a kindly manner, saying, "Nurse Lucy will take good care of you, and she will call me when you are ready to birth." Nurse Lucy remains in the room to monitor Laura's labor situation.

"It hurts! I am scared!" Laura utters in a pain-filled voice. She has endured many hours of never-ending hard labor.

"Please be quiet—it's not that bad," Nurse Lucy brusquely replies.

The pain intensifies, shooting sharp, stabbing spasms throughout Laura's back. She sobs in agony.

"Help me!" cries Laura, moaning loudly.

Suddenly a resounding smack cuts through the air. Laura, in shock, reflectively grabs for her stinging cheek.

"Shut-up!" Nurse Lucy shouts as her hand retreats from the blow. Fear grips Laura's heart and tears roll down her cheeks. She grits her teeth to avoid shouting out.

Years later, Nurse Lucy gets married—but she never has any children.

Eventually Nurse Lucy leaves the room to retrieve Dr. Wright. Laura does not remember Dr. Wright returning because she passes out with the pain. When she awakes, she is in her hospital room with her legs spread and propped up, with a heat lamp on—she is in great pain from the perineal tears that occurred during childbirth. Ignoring the pain, Laura calls out for a nurse and asks about her baby.

Judith Mae is a healthy baby girl born on a warm spring day when new life is emerging everywhere.

Upon arriving home, Laura is in agony—an infection has developed in the stitches from the perineal lacerations caused during childbirth. Laura gets sicker and sicker and sicker, until finally she is rushed to the hospital. She is full of infection and develops *milk leg*, later known as Phlebitis. Dr. Wright explains that this is inflammation of the legs with the formation of a clot that blocks the channel of the vein—a condition that often occurs shortly after childbirth. Laura's legs are swollen, and they throb and burn. Her body shudders and trembles. Immediately, her frame is packed with ice bags, and she is administered antibiotic needles every two hours.

Judith

Laura is not only in pain; she is disappointed that she is unable to nurse Judith because of the infection. In addition, she is overwhelmed with the extreme throbbing of milk-filled breasts. At the time there were no available treatments for this predicament. Upon arriving home from the hospital, Laura is in a desperate need for relief from the pain.

"Please, draw the milk out," she implores Bill. He complies and diligently draws the milk and spits it into a bucket. He continues until the pain subsides.

Judith is a beautiful, contented baby girl. Bill and Laura are surprised at how their love expanded exponentially at her birth. They grasp precious moments to snuggle with baby Judith. However, farm work is never-ending, and they both resume required duties.

A couple months after Judith's birth, Laura organizes her supplies to begin preserving food for the winter months. Sugar is required for canning her fruit and jam preserves. It is World War II, when bacon, butter, and sugar are rationed. To ensure adequate supplies for the military and civilians, every person is given a ration book with coupons. Laura will therefore use her sugar ration coupons to purchase sugar.

"My sugar rations are missing," Laura cries in frustration to her mother, upon discovering her coupons missing from her ration book. Laura is distraught—she needs sugar. She moans, "It is inconceivable … but I wonder if Mrs. White has taken my sugar coupons!"

"Take some of mine, I do not need all of them," her mother replies, coming to the rescue. Instantly, a feeling of relief floods through Laura's body, knowing that she will be able to prepare their winter supply of provisions.

23

Two-bedroom house:

A new house is in the process of being constructed for their growing family. Laura dwells upon this dream-coming-true event while canning and preparing food for the winter.

Their new home will be a spacious two-bedroom house. Ruberoid Fibre Cement siding in a light blue color will cover the exterior of the house. This Ruberoid Fibre house siding is manufactured using cellulose fibres along with cement and sand, making it long-lasting and durable. Bill and Frank Hamilton are in the process of constructing the 900-square-foot home on their newly purchased Millsap quarter of land, one mile from town. Neighbors rely on one another. Today, for example, Frank helps Bill build his house and over the past year Bill while working at Frank's sawmill loaned his tractor to Frank to operate the sawmill.

Judith is three months old when they move into their newly built house.

Bill sets to work clearing the land of bush; it is back-breaking

Bill bringing in a load of threshing with horse team Major and Blackie

work. Roots are pulled and rocks removed. The ground is ploughed using a horse team. Their first horse team is Major and Blackie.

Laura works attentively to transform their house into a home. Every evening she gestures with eagerness at her latest achievement.

"Look at the cupboards I built from wooden boxes, and I lined them with brown paper for our new dishes," she proudly points out. Or happily comments, "The linoleum is so easy to sweep—so different to the wood floors in our last home." In a short time, their house is shaped into a home.

Chapter 6

Heartache:

Life is grand! Laura rocks baby Judith in a second-hand rocker while Bill smiles lovingly in their direction.

"We are so blessed—with a healthy baby, our own house, and our own land," Laura says, overcome with joy. Bill beams a huge smile and dips his head in agreement. They are unaware that disaster is just around the corner.

Autumn brings in a bountiful harvest, with the granaries bulging with grain. Bill builds shelves in the cellar for the jars of fruit and jam that Laura has prepared for the winter months. It has been a laborious year, however, they can see the fruits of their labor. November arrives with battalions of chilly north winds, shuddering the trees and rattling the windows—a clear indication that winter will soon descend upon the land.

In mid-November, the winds abate and a calmness settles over the farm. In the wee morning hours Bill tiptoes over to the crib; a deep feeling of love overwhelms him as he stretches down to pick up six-month-old baby Judith. Suddenly, the air is broken with a deep cry of anguish that reverberates throughout the house.

"No, no, no," Bill moans loudly, in deep distress.

Their world turns upside down. Laura dashes to Bill's side and is horrified to observe the un-moving body of baby Judith. Shocked, Laura freezes–riveted to one spot staring at the motionless bundle enfolded in Bill's arms. It takes a moment to sink in and then, shrieking at the top of her lungs, she streaks out of the room, out of the house, down the highway, straight to her parents' house.

"She's gone. She's gone. She's gone," Laura blubbers, crying profusely. It takes several minutes for her parents to grasp the situation. They wrap a traumatized Laura in their arms. Their immediate concern is to return quickly to baby Judith. In a frenzy, they rush to harness the team of horses. Laura is hysterically and uncontrollably wailing. *Why Lord? Why?* Swiftly, they tuck her into the wagon and force the horses into a gallop.

Inside the house they gather as one beside Judith's crib–a small, distressed group, sobbing, weeping, moaning as they wait for the police to arrive. Visibly upset, the policemen conduct their investigation. It is a teary-eyed officer who bundles baby Judith carefully in her favorite pink knitted blanket to transport her to the Regina hospital.

The autopsy concludes: No visible signs for cause of death. It is determined to be a crib death. The death certificate states simply, "God's Will."

Judith is buried in the Weekes cemetery and engraved on her headstone are the words: *Heaven is one angel more.*

The town of Weekes has recently set aside and organized an area for burials. The Weekes Cemetery is on the edge of town and borders the Gough quarter. In order to build the Cemetery, the town raised money by pre-selling burial plots. Laura and Bill were one of the first to

Heaven is one Angel more

purchase their burial spot. Judith is buried alongside their plots and is one of the earliest to be laid to rest in the Weekes Cemetery.

Laura is depressed. It is seven months later, and her hand tenderly strokes Judith's tiny shoes, that were silver-plated to commemorate her short life. She reaches up to caress Judith's gown–the shiny silk material so delicate, so soft. So many months ago, yet it hurts like yesterday. Laura mourns for baby Judith.

Shortly after Judith's passing, Laura's parents move to Vancouver Island, British Columbia, seeking an easier life. Laura's grief is compounded by missing her parents and feeling abandoned in her time of need. Bill also grieves, but directs his grief into working long hours clearing the land for upcoming crops.

Laura and Bill struggle on their own. The future appears bleak and unfamiliar amidst their heartache. However, their faith and love bind them together. Little by little, their loss diminishes– but their love for Judith endures forever!

Laura and Bill relied on God for strength to carry on with life. Their hard work and love for one another enabled them to pursue their dreams of expanding their family and to be successful in building up their grain farming career.

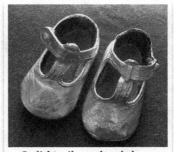

Judith's silver-plated shoes

I am honoured to call Bill and Laura my parents. I admire the strength of my parents in the way they pulled themselves up from the depths of depression to carry on with living life to the fullest. They relied on one another through thick and thin. They embody many wonderful character-istics–bravery, loyalty, generosity–and were industrious, responsible, faith-ful, loving, and kind. I am proud of my parents.

Part Two

Baby -Toddler Years
Julie 0 - 3 years

Chapter 7

Children arrive:

When the going gets tough, the tough get going, resonates in the lives of my mom and dad, Laura, and Bill. Farm life is very challenging and even more so when a tragedy strikes. The crib death of my sister, Judith Mae, at six months old, is heartbreaking–yet, as pioneers in the late 1940s, a busy life ensues, and Mom and Dad are resilient.

They must make hay while the sun shines. Thus, they cling to each other to mend their heartache and strive to work as one to rebuild their dream. With Mom expecting another baby soon, they are on their way to fulfil their dream of a life together.

Home life has more changes. Shortly after Judith's passing, it is with mixed emotions that my parents wave goodbye to Dad's parents and Buddy. They are moving to Kelowna, BC, to be close to their daughter, my Aunt Evelyn, and Uncle Raymond. To continue supporting them and send money regularly, Mom and Dad budget tightly and count pennies. Money is as scarce as hens' teeth!

*****

A crate of fruit is coming. With great excitement, my parents get the message that Aunt Evelyn and Uncle Raymond, who live in Kelowna, have shipped a crate of fruit by rail. Regrettably, Mom and Dad do not have the money for the freight charges; they decide, however, to walk to town and search the road for any wayward coins. They pray. Scouring the road, Mom on one side and Dad on the other, they scan the area for pennies. They are elated to find several coins along the one-mile stretch of road. Arriving at the train station, they hastily spread the coins in their palms and count. It is a miracle. They have collected the *exact* amount of money needed to pay for the freight.

The fruit is shared with the only family remaining in Weekes. Mom's brother's family–Uncle Earl, Aunt Kay, and children. Mom and Aunt Kay are best friends who encourage one another, share their ups and downs, and discuss their future plans.

One late afternoon, after spending the day canning fruit, Mom and Aunt Kay sit under the blazing-hot sun on upturned five-gallon pails with coffee cups in hand. Their feet are lowered into a square tub filled with cold water–desperately attempting to reduce swollen ankles. With expanded bellies, the handwriting is on the wall: *babies are on the way.* Their love and family is expanding.

Chapter 8

Charlie:

It is just over one year after Judith's passing when my brother, Charlie, emerges into the world via forceps on a blustery cold winter day. This instrument cradles his head to pull and guide his tiny frame through the birth canal during a very difficult delivery. He is a blond, blue-eyed, robust, roly-poly baby. He has the prestigious honor of being the first baby boy born in the new Porcupine Plain Hospital which was officially opened in October 1947.

His name is predetermined. The tradition in the English Allen family is that the firstborn boy takes the name Charles William or John William, whichever name comes next down the line. My Dad is John William; thus, my brother's preordained name is Charles William.

*****

It is Christmas Eve. Mom and Charlie are released from the hospital. They embark on many modes of transportation for the twenty-five-mile trip to Weekes where Dad will meet them for the final leg of the journey home. Mom walks from the Porcupine Plain Hospital to the railway station. Charlie sleeps bundled up in Mom's arms, listening to the rhythmic crunch of her boots on the snow. He is content with the jostling and cyclical sensation as they embark on the short hike.

They board the train. During the fifteen-mile ride to Caragana, Charlie is lulled to sleep listening to the hum of the vibrating wheels. He sleeps through the ear-splitting sound of squealing brakes and the shrill train whistle as they pull into the station. A friend greets them and hustles them into a cozy, warm car where they ride in comfort for the ten-mile drive to Weekes. Charlie slumbers serenely.

Dad awaits their arrival in the bitter cold weather. He stamps his feet to keep warm while standing next to their final means of transportation: a six-foot-long toboggan, secured to their horse, Star. Dad quickly bundles Mom and Charlie into the toboggan and wraps them snugly in blankets to fend off the bitingly cold winter weather for the one-mile trip home. Climbing in behind Mom, Dad wraps his arms and legs around them, and gathers up the reins.

"Giddy-up!" he shouts and snaps sharply on the straps. Star moves forward at a brisk prance into the crisp and frosty air. Puffs of hazy vapor disperse into the atmosphere from each breath emitted by adults and animal.

Charlie sleeps. He slumbers tranquilly to the gentle, melodic humming sound of the toboggan as it skims over the crusty and icy snow. A mile later, they view the warm farmhouse at a distance. What a welcoming sight, to see the rooftop swelling with puffs of white snow and the chimney shooting twigs of smoke into the atmosphere. Home looks so peaceful.

Home is not so peaceful! Charlie is not a quiet baby; he is a needy baby! Confusing his days and nights, he is asleep all day; at night he comes alive. Charlie knows what he wants and wants what he knows. He wants to play, he wants attention, and he knows how to get it. Wrapping Mom and Dad around his little finger, Charlie brings them scurrying to his side at the utter of a small cry. Upon hearing footsteps approaching, Charlie stops crying. It is *his* game; but it is not a game to Mom and Dad.

Weariness etches into their faces with the dreaded apprehension that crib-death might hit again! Mom prays nightly for Charlie's well-being. Exhaustion sets in, yet they spoil Charlie and cater to his every whim–that is, until I, Julie, arrive ...

Chapter 9

Julie:

I am difficult from the get-go! My slow, slow, slow entry into the world in the early winter is just eleven days short of being a year from Charlie's birth. Anesthetic is administered to an exhausted Mom after too many hours of hard labor. I am a beautiful blond baby with big blue eyes. This is where my story begins.

My chosen name evolved from a serious discussion. I resemble Judith–an exact replica of my dear departed sister. My Dad, therefore, compassionately proposes that my name be *Judith Mae*, in remembrance of my sister. Worry flickers across Mom's face–she is convinced that it might be tempting fate. Aunt Myrtle, Dad's sister dismisses the idea right away and convinces Dad to allow his baby girl, me, to have my own name. My name will be *Julie May*–not the same name but similar to Judith Mae.

On a freezing, blizzardy winter day, Mom and I depart from the Porcupine Plain Hospital. Dad arranges a ride for us with Tony Baich, due to not owning a vehicle and needing to mind Charlie. Dad and Tony are close friends, having worked together in the bush at Baich's sawmill. Tony arrives and shuffles us into his vehicle. With a loud roar, the sedan springs to life and we set off for home. The steady hum of the vehicle lulls me to sleep; like Charlie I sleep peacefully on the ride home.

Arriving home, I am still sleeping serenely in Mom's arms, so she lays me gently in the crib. Instantly, a loud wail radiates from my lips! Mom quickly leans over the crib-rail to grasp me in her arms. She rocks my vibrating body softly to and fro, to and fro, to and fro. She prays. Worry is written all over her face

I am not Judith. My parents slowly discern that I, Julie, might look like Judith and possess a comparable name, but that is where the similarities end. She was relaxed, I am not! I have colic! I howl incessantly for hours on end, non-stop, and disturb the whole household. Mom and Dad have their hands full, striving to comfort me.

Many remedies are explored. Mom discovers two solutions.

"The cookstove must burn day and night so I can put diaper cloths in the oven to warm and wrap Julie in the folds," she advises Dad. The second solution is for Mom to hold me in her arms all day as she completes her chores. It is a never-ending task, and she staggers with exhaustion.

Dad is not exempt. After completing strenuous work in the bush all day, he eats supper hastily in order to give Mom a break to walk and rock me in his arms. I am calmed with the warmth from their bodies, along with the rhythmic movement as they walk to and fro. Contented I peer out of the blankets at my caring and loving parents.

With little sleep, Mom and Dad struggle alone together reliant on one another. We survive, we all survive—three months of colic, three long months! God gave me the perfect family.

Chapter 10

Visitors:

Mom is leery of strangers. We are secluded, living a mile from town with the closest neighbors a quarter of a mile away. Mom feels vulnerable when Dad is away especially when unexpected, unknown visitors arrive on the farm. Mom's past affects her future.

*****

My Mom, Laura learns to be suspicious of outsiders, due partly to growing up next to the railway tracks where the hobos walked daily. A hobo is a less fortunate traveling worker–not a tramp, who only works when forced to, and not a bum, who does not work at all. Most hobos are friendly, but the odd person is dangerous.

A hostile confrontation transpires. Laura encounters a threatening situation travelling to school via the railroad track. A hobo unexpectedly appears next to her on the parallel track. He is shabbily dressed in dirty, tattered clothes. Laura's sixth sense kicks into high gear and she shivers at the look of malice on his wrinkled face, dark from the sun. A chill zips up her spine. Walking with a slight limp, the hobo skulks sneakily over to Laura's side of the tracks. As his arms extend to seize her, Rover, her dog, snarls aggressively and wedges himself in between them. Rover continues to snap and bare his teeth ferociously until the hobo moves back to the other side of the track. Laura knows God kept her safe–however, she developed a real fear of strangers.

*****

Fear is embedded within Mom's psyche. Mom, home alone with Charlie and me, is therefore overwhelmed with fright upon hearing a commotion outside our farmhouse. The house doors were already shut and locked and the curtains drawn, to keep out the oppressive heat from the blazing hot sun. This enabled us to munch on homemade bread spread with peanut butter and preserved jam in a relatively cool house.

Our quiet lunch has been broken. The loud, rowdy voices of men in the yard erupt into the quiet atmosphere. Startled, Mom swiftly creeps over to the window to pull the curtain slightly to one side and lean into the opening, peeking through the tiny slit. She frowns upon seeing a group of men huddled in a cluster, raising beer bottles in the air and chatting loudly to one another. With an expression of distrust, Mom hurriedly shuffles Charlie, two and half years, and me, one and half years, into the living room. With finger flicking to her lips, she gestures *silence*.

The room erupts with a rapid pounding from the front door. The pounding reverberates, deafeningly, throughout the room. Fear

Charlie and Julie

flickers over Mom's face. She glances in our direction and again indicates silence with finger touching at her lips.

We become mute statues. Frightened, our tiny bodies tremble. Mom slinks stealthily to the window adjacent to the door and gently lifts the window a crack.

"What do you want?" Mom whispers nervously through the slit in a strained, yet friendly, voice.

"Can we drink down by your dugout?" asks the closest male, garbed in a red and once-white checked shirt and stained coveralls.

The dugout is a huge cavity where dirt has been removed to a depth of eight feet and a circumference of thirty feet long by fifteen feet wide. It is filled to the brim with run-off water. The water provides a variety of farm uses, including drink for our animals and crop spraying.

Mom contemplates the stranger's question and timidly mumbles, "Yes."

We remain motionless. Mom goes back and forth between us and the window, peering out at the rowdy men. The dugout is in plain sight, about fifty feet from our house. The men continue to sit, talk, and sip beer, and occasionally toss a stone into the water. I notice Mom with her eyes closed and mumbling; my young mind nervously wonders, *Why Mom pray? What bad thing happen?* We are glued to the sofa, a small group huddled in distress, until Dad arrives home. Dad immediately turns to stride to the dugout. Mom peeps out the window and sees Dad sit down and join the men for a beer. An hour later he returns.

"They are friends of mine and they mean no harm. They just wanted a place to sit and have a beer," Dad informs Mom with a chuckle.

Dad introduces Mom to his friends. They have a good laugh over the trivial incident. However, Mom remains distrustful of strangers–a benefit in the far distant future.

Visit incident:

That same summer we receive a surprise visit from Grampa and Gramma Allen from Kelowna, BC. The visit goes awry.

Gramma Mabel decides to have some fun with me; her plan backfires. With a slightly imperious air, Gramma attempts to amuse me.

"Julie," she calls. I lay my dolly on the floor beside me and tilt my head upwards in her direction. Gramma opens her mouth and I innocently await her words. Suddenly my heart skips a beat when her teeth jump out of her mouth and waggle at me in mid-air! A chill rips through my body and I leap to my feet to run as fast as my little legs can churn. I scurry under my bed into the shadows in the uppermost corner and scrunch into a tiny ball.

Mom is puzzled. Unaware of the incident, Mom hunkers down by the bed and attempts to coax me out from my hiding spot. I am skeptical. The vision of Gramma with her translucent skin, tiny creases around her eyes, and her teeth jumping out at me is terrifying! I think she is a monster! I do not budge! I am frightened of Gramma Mabel.

I remain under the bed. Grampa Charles with twinkling baby-blue eyes smiles sympathetically in my direction. However, Gramma Mabel's face flushes in frustration.

"She is a spoiled brat!" she snaps sharply. I am confused. *What is a spoiled brat?* However, I do know all about monsters! Eventually I emerge from my hiding spot; I stay clear of Gramma. During their one-week visit Grampa is very kind and enjoys the antics of Charlie and me. Gramma fusses about the house, helping Mom. I am pleased when they return to BC.

Chapter 11

Farm Life:

Farm life is demanding. Mom and Dad unite to face the harsh and demanding rigors of grain farming. The grain is stored in granaries until it can be hauled to the elevator for shipping. Throughout all the challenges of farming they learn patience, love, hope, faith, and endurance.

In 1949, the purchase of a 1946 Twin City tractor with the big steel wheels succeeds in making life much easier. The tractor replaces the horse team to plough, seed, and harvest the land. Farming takes its toll with floods,

Dad on 1946 Twin City tractor

rape beetles, early frost, and hail. Nature plays a huge part; during the spring, summer, and fall, therefore, many prayers fervently drift to the heavens. Keeping faith in God guides them forward.

Better yet is the purchase of a 1936 Chevy pickup truck whose road-worthiness is questionable; Mom and Dad are, however, over the moon with their *treasure*. On the positive side, the truck appears solid with a heavy-duty body and solid running boards. On the downside, it has glass-less windows in the doors, no windshield wipers, ineffective headlights, plus numerous mechanical problems.

Dad deals with the problematic vehicle. He cleverly removes the silver paper from a cigarette package, crumples it up, and inserts it into the light socket. Voila—the lights work. Apparently, the spring in the socket wasn't making contact so the foil bridged the gap.

Once during a cloudburst, the road became distorted due to the rain pouring down in a cascade. Without windshield wipers, Dad solved the problem.

"Poke your head out the window and direct me," he instructed Mom. She pushed her head out into the pouring rain and in a matter of minutes her hair was drenched.

"A little to the left. Going straight. Now a sharp right," she directed Dad. This created wails of laughter during the downpour!

The truck brings joy. Regardless of all the problems, they are delighted with their new-old posses-sion. Several times a week along with Charlie and I they proudly hop into their truck to drive the couple of hours to Tisdale.

On one of their outings to Tisdale, a friend

In front of '36 Chevy truck is Aunt Kaye with Blaine and Carol, Mom with Julie and Charlie

laughingly confronts them in a playful manner. "You are always here–don't you do anything at home?"

Mom and Dad glance at each other in silent communication and grin gleefully. They are proud of their old rattletrap of a truck that brings them so much pleasure.

Chapter 12

Sister or Brother:

"I have exciting news," Mom exclaims on a scorching-hot summer afternoon. It is wash day and Charlie and I are playing with wooden cars in the dirt. I lift my head in anticipation. *What could be exciting news?*

Mom smiles while bending over the big square tub perched on the front step and rubs clothes viciously upon the surface ridges atop the scrub board. She uses a lot of elbow grease, and we watch her jerky movements. Up and Down. Up and Down. Up and Down. Finally, with a sigh, Mom stretches and grasps the pegs for the clothesline.

"I will just hang these clothes on the line and then sit with you for a minute," she informs us.

Under the heat of the sun the clothes will dry within an hour. Washing clothes outside on the step is an easier task in the summer months. In the winter, it was an arduous chore. The clothes and diapers would be scrubbed inside the house and then pinned on the clothesline outside in the cold weather. The items froze as stiff as a board, and it was a struggle to drag the rigid garments into the house. The clothes would be strung around the living room on twine and, as the dampness escaped, the steam would rise hazily into the air. The house would become very humid.

Presently, it is strenuous work. Mom's knuckles appear bruised and red, with beads of sweat dripping down her face. Despite this, she sits and chats amiably with Charlie and me. "I have some very exciting news," Mom, repeats and continues, "I am going to have a baby soon. Do you want a girl or boy?" I look at Mom with shock – it is a super surprise!

"I want a girl," I answer quickly, envisioning a playmate.

"A boy," Charlie answers. I am quite puzzled. I wonder why he would choose a boy; after all, he should want another sister like me! I will pray for a girl.

"I am going to the hospital," Mom announces several days later. Dad pulls the truck up to the house and we all clamber inside. On the journey to the hospital Charlie and I are dropped off at two different friends' houses. We will stay there until Mom comes home with our new baby.

We are separated and will stay with neighbours and close friends of our parents. Charlie goes to Frank and Lena Hamilton's, where there are several children. I go to Ralph and Thelma Berg's, who live a quarter mile away and whose children have grown up and left home. Their home borders Highway 23 where they constructed Berg's Corner Store which is a service center with gas pumps and store selling bakery and confectionary items. Thelma dotes on me lovingly—a bath every night in the kitchen sink, she brushes my hair each morning and ties it with ribbons. She enjoys fussing over me. I am well taken care of; but I am a homebody—I like to be at home! I miss my circle of love at home.

Chapter 13

Christina:

Weekes is a bustling town and has been growing like a weed since the start of the Second World War and it now boasts a population of three hundred. It is at this time that my sister arrives in the autumn – a beautiful dark haired, brown-eyed baby. She is named after her two Grammas, - her name becomes Christina Ruth. Mom is delighted to get her wish of a baby girl who looks just like Dad.

It is a pleasant, picturesque day with the trees bathed in an array of color when Mom and Christina are released from the hospital. Dad arrives with the '36 Chevy pickup truck. Blankets are tucked snugly around Christina to protect her from the air gushing in through the glassless windows. Arriving home, placing Christina gently in the crib, all is blessedly silent. She is a happy baby.

I am positive I want a baby sister. She arrives. I change my mind; I do not want her! I am not thrilled at the age of one and three-quarters to be replaced as the baby of the family. In fact, when Dad lifts me up to view my new baby sister, I am shocked. *Why she in my baby carriage?* Resentment burns within. Upon being set back down on the floor, I glance around and spy a stray shoe in close proximity. I pick up the shoe and raise my arm to chuck it aggressively at the intruder lying in my baby carriage.

I cannot be trusted. After that violent display I am sent swiftly back to friends Ralph and Thelma, where I am expected to stay for a week to give me time to adjust to my new baby sister. I am not pleased! However, Ralph and Thelma love having me and grow quite attached—so much so that they ask Mom and Dad if they can adopt me. Of course, Mom and Dad will not even consider the idea and after my week's stay, I am established back home.

Both sets of Grandparents arrive within weeks of each other to meet baby Christina.

The first visit is a pleasant encounter. Grampa Kelly and Gramma Elsie, Mom's parents, arrive from Vancouver Island, BC. Gramma Elsie cuddles baby Christina and does errands around the house, which gives Mom much needed help. Grampa Kelly builds

Grampa and Gramma Nelson

new kitchen cupboards. Thrilled with her new kitchen cabinets, Mom swiftly places her dishes inside and tosses out the temporary dwelling of wooden boxes. A couple of weeks later, it is with a sad heart that Mom says goodbye at their departure.

A week later, a not-so-pleasant visit is in store. Grampa Charles and Gramma Mabel (Dad's parents) arrive from Kelowna, BC. They step into the house, anxious to see baby

Grampa and Gramma Allen

Christina. She resembles Dad, unlike Charlie and me, with very extraordinary dark skin and brown eyes.

"This is not your baby!" blurts Gramma Mabel, as her eyes observe baby Christina. "They got your baby mixed up," she spoke in a rapid and perplexed tone.

Mom cannot believe what she has just heard. As the words sink in, Mom is horrified and wonders. *How can she state such an outrageous notion?* Mom lovingly gazes at her baby and feels the familiarity of love deep inside. She gathers baby Christina tightly and snugly into her arms as if to protect her from the world.

Gramma Mabel is a proud woman and refuses to acknowledge history. A dark-versus-light skin is due to Indigenous and Scandinavian ancestry. Mom focuses on her family. Although, she discerns that her mother-in-law will soon accept and love baby Christina; it is a relief when their visit ends.

Usurped:

"Here is your dollar," Dad says, as he places a dollar into Charlie's hand. Harvest has ended on a high note with a bountiful harvest of wheat, oats, and barley! Dad, with a heart full of love, wants to share and celebrate our good fortune. He turns with a huge grin to place a dollar in my hand. I am thrilled to bits, and I cling tightly to my precious money. With a loving gesture, Dad positions a dollar on baby Christina, sleeping in *my* baby carriage, and utters soothingly, "This dollar is for you, Christina."

My blue eyes sweep over the scene, and I frown. Perplexed my thoughts run wild. *Why give to her? What she do with dollar? She don't know dollar.* I am not happy, obviously still a little put out by this new baby usurping my spot. Pulling down my bottom lip, I pout!

Two weeks later, the earth is frozen and covered in mounds of snow. It is an early winter. Unfortunately, the potatoes are still in the ground, and they need to be harvested. Mom settles baby Christina, asleep in her crib, and assembles objects to amuse Charlie and me. Mom ventures out to dig up potatoes on her own. Dad has returned to work at the sawmill in the bush.

It is laborious work. Removing the snow is easy, however it takes brute force to bury the spade into the frozen ground under the potato hills. With the cold, bitter wind howling from the north, Mom is chilled to the bone. She struggles and toils valiantly until the potatoes are all hauled into the potato bin in the cellar. Thankfully, baby Christina sleeps peacefully all the while—and miraculously, Charlie and I do not get into any trouble.

Christina is a calm baby! Mom and Dad are elated to discover that baby Christina is a pleasant and relaxed baby. At every diaper change Mom takes the time to snuggle for a precious moment, thus creating precious memories. With such a busy household, it is a blessing that baby Christina does not demand a lot of attention.

Chapter 14

A Caregiver:

Our little household is bulging at the seams. Life is thrown into turmoil several months later when Grampa Charles, Gramma Mabel, and Buddy return from BC to move in with our family. Gramma Mabel has developed heart trouble and is too sick to care for herself. She is no longer a monster—in front of my eyes she has morphed into a sick old lady. We are very cozy, tucked into two bedrooms. In one bedroom, our grandparents use the double bed while Buddy sleeps on the floor. In the other bedroom, our parents have the double bed, Christina is in my crib, while Charlie and I sleep on the floor. It is like camping!

Mom becomes a caregiver and lovingly takes on this responsibility despite their past issues. Mom is a very understanding and forgiving type of person and will always give more of herself in every situation. In the blink of an eye, Mom is transformed into Gramma's nurse. Gramma is a bit cantankerous and complains a lot—she sits upright in her chair with a slight superior air. Every morning Mom tucks Gramma's thick grey hair into a bun, drapes a knitted blanket over her knees, and administers the daily needle. Gramma's piercing brown eyes shoot daggers, and she whines as Mom dispenses the needle.

"It hurts me to give you the needle, however it is a necessity," Mom explains gently, trying to pacify Gramma. Mom has a lot of patience and extends a lot of compassion in the most exasperating moments.

Gramma's weekly check-up is difficult. At the Porcupine Plain Hospital, Gramma bitterly grumbles to the nurses and points a bony finger at Mom, accusing her of being mean. The nurses just nod and smile—their hearts go out to Mom, fully aware that the comments are unwarranted. Gramma Mabel is not an ideal patient.

This *sandwich* stage of life—taking care of parents and children at the same time—is very stressful. Mom is caring for elderly parents, young Buddy, and her family of five all at the same time and in a small two-bedroom house.

Charlie, Christina, Julie

The biggest load lands on Mom, although Dad is very supportive and helps as much as possible. They willingly and lovingly provide the love and support that is required at this stage of life.

Training Tots:

Our full house is just *a-rockin'*. It is a hectic household with my grand-parents, Buddy, and us children—the three of us under the age of three, in diapers, and all on the bottle.

Mom vigilantly tries to potty train Charlie–no success. She tries to remove the nightly bottle–no success. Charlie cannot fathom the idea of potty training or having the bottle removed.

It is my turn, and I am a fast learner. I am quickly potty trained and give up the bottle–Charlie follows suit! I set an example for Charlie.

"Julie, you trained Charlie!" Mom claims.

Chapter 15

Snow Days:

The day begins innocently enough–the air is crisp and cold, with snow-flakes gently drifting to the ground. Mom hooks our horse, Star, up to a long, narrow toboggan for our trip to town. There is plenty of room for our trio - Mom, Charlie, and me. Our 1936 truck is unreliable; transportation for our entire family of five, therefore, is with Star attached to a sleigh or we travel by tractor. We must bundle up warmly to fend off the fierce wind that whips bitterly at us in the cold open air.

Mom, Charlie, and I snuggle cozily into the toboggan. We skim speed-ily over the snow, creating a melodious swishing sound floating into the silent space. Getting restless, Charlie begins to squirm and wiggle until his tiny frame is free of his blanket. Suddenly his body tumbles over and out of the toboggan. He rolls swiftly into a snowbank, generating a cloud of billowing, puffy snow sailing into the air. He disappears!

"Whoa," Mom yells at Star and pulls on the reins to turn him around. Charlie crawls out of the snowdrift with a huge grin on his face. He thought it was great fun; Mom did not! We arrive without further incident at the store and purchase our groceries. We hustle into the toboggan for our return trip home.

Squirch, squirch, squirch, echoes eerily into the air. Mom focuses on the noise, attempting to decipher the weird sound.

"Whoa," Mom shouts to Star. She glances at Charlie, to find his mouth drawing fiercely on a nipple typically used atop of a baby bottle. In addition, in his fist he grips tightly to a bundle of nipples! The baby bottle nipples were taken undetected from Parchewsky's General Store which sold groceries, household supplies, novelty items and confectionary goods. Immediately, we turn around and return to the store. Mom explains the situation, pays for the nipples, and issues an apology. That eventful day we learned one of the ten commandments: *Thou shalt not steal.*

Snow House:

The next day, Mom plays several games with Charlie and me. *All work and no play makes for a dull day,* is Mom's motto.

"Follow me," Mom shouts as she tramps through the snow. Soon we create a Fox and Goose game. Mom is not very good at the game–we can catch her very easily! Mom shows us how to make a snowman using a carrot for a nose, sliced carrot for eyes, twigs for arms–an old hat tops his head. We are elated with our creation. Next, we learn to make snowballs. Soon the snowballs are flying through the air–none of us have great aim. Next activity has me super excited, however Charlie is not filled with enthusiasm.

"I am building a snow house," Mom explains as she wields a shovel and swiftly removes snow from a huge snowdrift. I love it–my pretend home. There is a doorway with snow chairs and a snow table inside the room. I proudly serve snow cones to my "visiting friend," Mom. Charlie does not want to come into my snow house–he would rather use his shovel to dig holes into the snowbanks. I do not care–Mom plays with me! I learn that we all like different things and that is okay.

Chapter 16

Wood Stoves and Danger:

Our parents attempt to watch us children like hawks. Due to farm duties, however, giving us a great deal of freedom is a necessity. Farm life is our Adventure Land. We are risk-taking children and some of our games are downright dangerous. Accidents transpire …

"Help! Help! Help!" yelps three-year-old Charlie. He is stuck under the kitchen cookstove. Charlie had been playing make-believe and in his imagination a cave existed beneath the cookstove. His adventure took a turn for the worse. Now he is firmly wedged underneath the stove. He wiggles, he jiggles; he cannot move his little body one inch! He is trapped.

"Will you lend me a hand?" Mom inquiries to Aunt Kay, who is visiting. Aunt Kay is married to Mom's brother, Earl, and is her best friend. They set about to rescue poor Charlie. Thankfully, the cookstove is not lit, however it is very heavy. Normally it takes several men to shift it. Mom and Aunt Kay position themselves on either side of the stove, clutching the edge of the black cast-iron top. Together they chant, *One, two, three, lift.* The stove does not move! Mom's heart is pounding to the beat of drums!

"Let's try again!" Mom shouts. They chant, *One, two, three, lift.* Uttering a silent prayer, they exert their muscles into one huge, powerful heave. "It's moving," shouts Mom, as the stove shifts upwards a couple of inches. Mom continues to scream, "Charlie. Crawl out. Quick!" Charlie scrambles like a mouse out from under the stove.

Unbelievably, Mom and Aunt Kay miraculously developed supernatural strength! Mom maintains that, "The Lord gave us the extra power."

The Black Cast-iron Heater:

Trauma begins on a peaceful winter day. The sun is shining brightly outside creating dazzling brilliant diamonds atop the mounds of snow drifting into the horizon. Streams of smoke from the chimney billow into puffy clouds floating into the atmosphere. Inside our tight house the kitchen cookstove and living-room black cast-iron heater distribute radiant heat, keeping us snug and warm.

"Don't play near the stoves," is a frequent warning we hear from our parents; we avoid the stoves like the plague. We are especially aware of the danger due to Charlie's recent incident of being trapped under the cookstove. Eying the stove, I skip from the living room towards the kitchen. Suddenly, I trip! Tumbling forward out of control, my smallish two-year-old body propels violently into the air. I land sideways with a harsh thud against the searing hot metal of the heater. The skin on my arm shrinks like crumpled paper and the smell of burning flesh erupts into the air. I bellow a blood-curdling scream.

The pain is excruciating. I scream and scream and scream at the top of my lungs. Within seconds Mom and Dad are towering over my limp body, sprawled in agony on the floor. Mom picks me up quickly yet gently, being mindful not to touch my burning limb.

"Get the butter, quick!" Mom yells in a shrill, hysterical voice. There is very little butter in the butter dish. Dad flies out of the house in his woolen socks, ploughing through the deep snow to snatch a slab of butter out of the wooden box. The butter is stored with other items in an enclosed box outside in the snow, to keep everything frozen.

Dad, with snow-covered wool socks, returns with the butter. He is unmindful of his footsteps, sprinkling clumps of snow throughout the room. Mom gently pats the frozen slab of butter on my incredibly painful exposed burns. In the meantime, Dad retrieves snow, and they gently sprinkle snow over the injuries. The throbbing eases a bit.

This is how Mom learned to treat burns. She was taught that slathering butter all over the affected area would relieve the pain, prevent infection, and speed up healing. In reality, it made things worse!

Actually, the grease will slow the release of heat from the skin and cause more harm. In my case, the frozen butter felt cool against my skin and the snow eased the pain, however it probably contributed to some of the damage to the outer layer of my skin. In hindsight, it is obvious that butter is better on toast!

The burns leave large circular scars extending in a row, like stair-steps, from the back of my right hand to the top of my arm. The marks grow fainter each year, but I have very visible identification marks throughout my childhood. The scars become a natural part of my body.

Chapter 17

Logging in the bush:

The stoves are an integral part of life. Dad retrieves firewood in the frosty forty-degrees-below weather while Mom scrunches paper to squeeze amongst the sticks in the cookstove. Flames shoot from the wood, showering the room with warm rays of heat. In the mellow radiance of the coal oil lamp Mom dumps three tablespoons of ground coffee straight into the percolator and sets it on the back of the cast-iron cookstove. It is five o'clock in the morning and pitch-black outside. Dad strikes a match to the kerosene lamp mantle which bursts into a glowing red then changes to a white brightness emitting a brilliant glow around the room. The coal oil lamp is now unnecessary therefore Dad turns the wick down into the burner until the flame is extinguished.

Snap, crackle, pop emanates from the fire along with the fragrant aroma of coffee perking, penetrating our sleep. In addition, we wake to other delightful sounds and scents: the metal spoon stirring the pancake dough and the bacon exuding aromatic smells as it sizzles and sputters on the griddle atop the cookstove. The radio is dialed into the Prince Albert station, and words drift into the room with chit chat, news, and music.

Sounds and aromas are the best alarm clock. We eagerly rise in time to watch Mom make Dad's lunch and prepare his coffee to go by six o'clock. Dad is on his way to the logging camp in the bush. Dad grabs his lunch, gives Mom a hug and a kiss, and departs the house.

Chug. Chug. Chug. The murmurs of morning is broken by the tractor as it roars to life and pierces the universe. Glancing out the window into the pitch black, we wave at Dad's shadowy frame, outlined in the reflecting beam of the tractor lights. The tractor is a luxury compared to earlier days when the mode of transportation was a team of horses. In the cold weather, Dad ran alongside the horses to keep his frozen feet warm. Attached to the tractor hitch is a caboose, which is a tiny little shed on skids, housing a small bench and wood heater.

It is bitterly cold to work at the logging camp. The caboose has a heater in it, however there is never time to fire it up. The crew stops for lunch and everyone is more aware of the harsh wind whipping around their bodies and whistling shrilly through the trees. Dad consumes frozen sandwiches and icy coffee. When a person is hungry and thirsty, everything tastes good.

Upon Dad's return from the bush, Charlie and I scramble to grasp the jar of cold coffee.

"It hurts my throat," I utter as I sip the cold, icy coffee. The frozen liquid is frigid on my throat—it's a slushie in the making.

"This morning, why put hot coffee in jar with spoon? Why it froze when Daddy come home?" I childishly implore Mom. I am puzzled by the procedure of preparing coffee to go.

"The spoon inside the jar prevents the sealer from breaking as I pour in the hot coffee. A sock over the sealer keeps the coffee warm longer. However, by day's end the cold weather freezes the coffee," Mom replies. I am confused. *Why put in hot coffee if it freezes anyway?*

Mom is unaware that she has discovered iced coffee decades before it's time!

Chapter 18

Grandparents gone:

It's a heart attack! Gramma Mabel's heart fails in the month of June at age fifty-seven. She does not survive. Mabel is buried in the Weekes cemetery. Gramma's parting creates a huge void in Grampa Allen and Buddy's hearts.

A two-room log cabin is purchased – it is perfect for Grampa Charles and Buddy. They move in together in their new abode in the town of Weekes. Several months later, Frank, Buddy's Dad, arrives unexpectedly with upsetting news.

"I've come to take Buddy home to the farm," announces Frank. He had remarried and is worried that Grampa Charles at age sixty-eight is too elderly to care for Buddy.

Gramma Allen's Funeral
Back: Uncle Irvin, Aunt Evelyn, Dad, Mom, Aunt Annie, Aunt Elsie, Grampa Allen. Front: Gary, Aunt Hazel, Aunt Myrtle, Aunt Ethel and Buddy

"I have raised him from a baby, and he is only twelve years old," Grampa Charles replies, pleadingly. The concern over Grampa's age is paramount, thus Frank insists on Buddy returning home to live with him. There is no choice. Buddy departs. Grampa understands the reasoning behind Buddy leaving, however his departure creates an emptiness in Grampa's inner soul and a hollowness surrounds him in the log cabin. He has lost two loved ones at the same time. Mom and Dad visit often and bring him to the farm to try to help ease his hurt; it is, however, a heartache no one can heal. In the meantime, Buddy misses Grampa, but adjusts and thrives in his family environment.

Grampa Charles' heart continues to ache for his wife, Mabel, and foster boy, Buddy. He misses them both until his passing two years later in 1953.

Chapter 19

Out of Black Waters:

I am not a hero, muses Mom upon reading the startling newspaper head-line. A violent shiver reverberates up her spine as she ruminates. *I did what I had to do!* Her hands tremble holding the newspaper as she recalls the traumatic event. She still suffers nightmares!

*****

A death trap looms within sight. Mom is only twenty-three years old. She is devoted to us children. Christina is one and a half years, a tranquil baby, Charlie is four years, a mischievous lad, and I, Julie, am three years, a determined child. Mom uses eagle eyes to keep us out of trouble amongst the many hazards on the farm. One such safety risk lies within walking distance of our house.

Our dangerous venture begins unexpectedly on one of the hottest days of the year. The sun's heat is scorching hot, and there is nary a breeze in the air. The weather, whether it is blazing sun or biting cold, does not stop farm work. The weeds in the vegetable garden must be destroyed in order to have a bountiful harvest in the fall. The garden plot is situated on the edge of the field, a fair distance from the house, and Mom's weapon is a hoe.

A farm woman's work is never done. Anticipating the searing sun and biting mosquitoes, Mom dons a pair of beige cotton pants, a long-sleeved cotton shirt, and a beat-up straw hat. She bundles baby Christina in a bright yellow sunsuit, with a wide-brimmed bonnet to keep the sun at bay. Toys are tossed into the baby carriage along with a blanket. Charlie and I are outfitted in play clothes–Charlie garbed in brown durable coveralls, and I, sporting a ruffled blue sunsuit. Both of us exhibit bare feet.

"You must stay in the front yard to play," Mom tells us, prior to going to the garden. Charlie and I nod our heads in agreement.

"I have an idea," utters Charlie, "let's play swords." I love my brother and we are great pals.

"Ok Charlie," I reply. We pick up sticks and swing them through the air banging them together shouting *Yahoo!* It is great fun; however, I soon tire of the game.

"What else to play, Charlie," I ask.

"Let's make mud pies," Charlie suggests in an excited voice.

"How to make mud pies, Charlie?" I inquire with a puzzled expression.

"It is easy, take some dirt and mix it with water," Charlie explains smiling confidently.

"Charlie, how that make mud pies?" I ask. I am perplexed. Of course, my little mind is visualizing one of our mom's delicious pies. I especially like her rhubarb and strawberry pie.

"Let's go to the dugout and I will show you," suggests Charlie. I ponder Mom's recent words. *Stay in the front yard. I* only

Julie and Charlie

think about it for one second and then her lingering words go in one ear and out the other!

"Okay, Charlie, let's go," I answer quickly.

We run to the dugout. As I mentioned earlier, our dugout is a huge cavity in the ground about eight feet deep, thirty feet long and fifteen feet wide. It is full of run-off water which is used for our farm animals and crop spraying.

Charlie demonstrates. He picks up his miniature pail to stride to the side of the dugout. He flings the pail towards the surface, plunges it into the water, and swiftly drags it through the liquid to haul up a full pail of water. Charlie struts to his mound of dirt. The liquid slops out of his bucket at every step; he pours the remaining water onto his dirt pile. He picks up a long, sturdy stick and stirs the concoction swiftly. I am intrigued, as I watch in awe to witness the final act. Charlie scoops up a chunk of mud and shapes it into a small, flat, round shape.

"Here's my mudpie," Charlie says, as he extends his hand holding the lump of mud and smiles broadly.

How will it turn into Mom's delicious pies? I wonder. However, this is right up my alley–I can do this! *After all*, I figure, *whatever my brother can do, I can do.* Picking up my little toy truck with the open windows, I have my own makeshift bucket. I stroll excitedly to the edge of the dugout and lean over the water to push my little toy truck upside down into the water. I pull it up gently and carry my precious water towards my pile of dirt. Unfortunately, as I transport my valuable cargo the water flows rapidly out of the open windows in a steady stream to the ground. By the time I arrive at my designated spot I discover there is no water left to make my mud pie. I am confused!

An idea rings a bell within my mind. I have a hunch. I must put *extra* water in my little toy truck. I zip back to the dugout to push my truck under the surface. Upon pulling it out of the water, I notice the liquid spill rapidly out of the open windows. My quick-thinking mind lights up like a lightbulb. *The obstacle is the water*. I need the water further from the shore! The deeper water will stay in my little toy truck. I stoop down on my knees to stretch my body way out over the water, to reach as far as my smallish arm can extend. I dip my little toy truck down, down, down to get the deep, deep, deep water. My body begins to slide slowly forward, forward, forward. I slither into the black waters! Everything goes dark.

Meanwhile, it is peaceful at the vegetable garden with Christina sleeping quietly in her baby carriage parked near the long row of peas. The atmosphere is soundless, aside from the whacking thump of Mom's hoe as she forcefully chops the weeds.

Suddenly, shattering the silence, Charlie's terrified screams reverberate into the air.

"Mom, Mom, Mom," Charlie frantically yells, running towards the garden. His arm stretches out with his tiny pointer-finger aimed at the dugout.

"Julie, Julie, Julie," he shouts. Mom's head jerks upwards—something is wrong, she can hear it in his tone. She flings the hoe into the air and takes off like a shot. She observes Charlie's extended finger and gasps. She does not need to ask what is amiss—with her maternal sixth sense, *she knows.*

Mom's heart is racing. Galloping at a super pace she swings around the corner of the dugout, and her eyes dart frantically over the water's surface. Her breath comes in short, panicky spurts as she speedily scans the water and sees no visible sign of her little girl's body. Her heart is pulsating at an irregular rate and her stomach is tied in knots. Dashing to the edge of the dugout, she stares wildly about, praying to God. *Please help me!* Suddenly, she spots a faint, tiny tuft of hair floating at the surface in the middle of the dugout.

Mom cannot swim! Cold fear wells up within her! Despite her fright and without hesitation, she plunges into the inky blackness. She feels a cold dread wash over her as the cool water hits her trembling frame. Rushing headlong through the depths, she wades in until the water floats in a grip around her neck. Terror fills her soul—she is out of her comfort zone and out of her depth. Only one thought prevails. *I need to get my little girl.*

Out of arm's length. Filled with horror, she stretches her arm over the surface, desperately trying to grasp the small, floating string of my wavy hair. Frustrated and in despair, she creeps forward until the water covers her chin and once again stretches out her arm; my tiny stringy hair is just out of reach. Only seconds have passed. She shuffles quickly ahead, bit by bit, until the liquid begins to seep into her mouth. She spits out the water, closes her lips, and breathes through her nose. She tries to shout my name, and water pours into her mouth again; she gags, sputters, and rapidly spits the water in a stream to shoot over the surface. Holding her breath, Mom gives a gigantic thrust of her arm.

She seizes a small wisp of hair. Clenching tightly, she swiftly yet carefully yanks on my minute tresses. Mom drags me quickly towards her and snatches the ruffle on my sunsuit. Thrusting my head above water causes her to wobble and she struggles to maintain her sense of balance.

Time stands still. Unsteadily, Mom holds me upright, keeping my head over the water surface. She is scared, vulnerable, and her motherly mind screams, *Please Lord, I've lost one child, I can't lose another, please help me.* Mom leans back to keep us stable as she gently edges her feet backwards. Seconds seem like hours. Stepping back several steps, she turns around to face the shore. She moves swiftly to wade up the slanted slope of the dugout. She emerges with water pouring in a torrent from her clothes.

I am rigid, unmoving, and not breathing. Hysterically, Mom lays me flat in her arms, and begins to violently shake me up and down, up and down, up and down. Mom is in a frenzy, standing by the dugout crying, with tears tumbling from her eyes.

"Julie, Julie, Julie," she shouts and viciously jolts my small body.

Why in Mom's arms? Why shaking me hard? I momentarily come to my senses.

"She is breathing," Mom gasps in a breathless whisper. I am in a hazy world, but I hear Mom shout desperately to Charlie, "Go get Ralph and Thelma."

Charlie moves. He dashes down the driveway and hits the secondary road, his feet flying as fast as his little four-year-old body can muster. Mom launches into a mad dash towards the house with me bopping about in her arms. I do not remember anything from that moment on, until I dazedly realize I am bundled on the couch with blankets tucked all around.

What is happening? At my first lucid moment I view the door being pushed open and Mom wheeling the baby carriage into the house. There is worry in Mom's eyes as she looks at me. I glance questioningly at her, pondering, W*hat is going on?* In an instant, Mom is by my side and hugging me tightly. I lean into her; I feel tired.

Charlie is back–with Ralph and Thelma. They are friends of my parents, neighbors who live a quarter of a mile from our house. Upon Charlie's message, they immediately jumped into their motor vehicle, and hurtled hastily to our house. Ralph, Thelma, and Mom huddle together speaking intensely in low tones in the kitchen.

I feel small. Ralph and Thelma are towering over me and I feel uncomfortable with everyone ogling me. W*hy looking at me?*

"Julie has pulled through and appears fine," Thelma murmurs. They stare down at me and talk about me as if I cannot hear them. "Let's continue to keep a close watch on her," continues Thelma as she embraces Mom. They keep Mom calm and praise her actions, "You are a very brave young lady to enter the dugout when unable to swim."

"Throughout my ordeal the Lord was by my side," Mom replies.

Charlie drops into the seat beside me. I feel much better. I am still trying to decipher what is happening–it is all a blur. I sense that Mom is upset, however I am too young to realize that she is in a state of shock. Ralph and Thelma stay to comfort Mom and monitor me until Dad arrives home. He is working on one of the quarters several miles away and is expected home at any moment for dinner.

Dad returns at noon, as expected. He was ploughing the land with the cultivator and dirt covers his clothes, his hair, and his face. Mom lurches into his arms, unmindful of the dirt and dust. She is uncontrollably sobbing. Listening to our life-threatening incident, Dad glances at me and his eyes well up with tears. He consoles Mom, draping his arms around her and holding her tightly.

"Laura, for the children's sake you will need to learn to swim." Dad speaks softly. He continues with a faint tremor in his voice, "There will always be a dugout on our farm."

"I will. I was terrified that we might lose Julie!" Mom's voice breaks as she replies softly. Mom is so traumatized she cannot discuss the incident until many, many years later.

News travels fast. The near-drowning incident occurred on a Sunday and the following Tuesday a newspaper article appears in the Regina Leader-Post announcing, *Child Rescued From Deep Pit*, and on Wednesday the Saskatoon Star-Phoenix announces, *Mother Rescues Tot From Dugout*. The article mistakenly calls me Judy, spells our surname wrong, and states Charlie at six years instead of his four years. However, Charlie did use his middle name Billie up until he started school.

The news story proclaims, *Weekes woman risks own life* and elicits praise for Mom's brave act in saving her three-year-old daughter, Julie, from the water-filled dugout on a farm in the little town of Weekes, Saskatchewan. Mom feels so much attention focused on her is unwarranted, because she knows that she did what any mother would do! Regardless, my mom is a hero!

— THE LEADER-POST, REGINA, TUESDAY, MAY 27, 1952 —

Weekes woman risks own life

Child rescued from deep pit

WEEKES, Sask. (Special).— A Weekes district farm woman, Mrs. Bill Allan, Sunday risked her own life to save her three-year-old daughter Judy from drowning after the child had fallen into a deep water filled pit at their farm one mile north of here.

While Mrs. Allan was in her garden her two children, Judy and a six-year-old brother Billy wandered away from the house to a deep, water-filled pit nearby. While reaching into the pit for a can of water the little girl lost her balance and tumbled in.

Summoned by the screams of her son, Mrs. Allan rushed to the scene and though unable to swim plunged into the water.

After wading out until the water reached her neck, she was able to grasp the child by the hair as she was sinking for the second time.

Pulling the unconsious child from the water Mrs. Allan then called neighbors to help. The child, however, recovered consiousness before they arrived and artificial respiration was not needed.

The girl's father, Bill Allan, was not at home at the time of the accident.

Part Three

Early Childhood Years
Julie 4 – 6 years

Chapter 20

A baby crib:

Winter has descended on the farm; activities are created inside the home.

"Can I get crib for my baby girl?" I eagerly ask Mom, who is constantly on the go!

"Yes, we can make one together," replies Mom. She grasps every opportunity to spend time with us and often enfolds us tenderly into her ample bosom for a loving hug. We feel special and important. Mom affectionately attends to all our needs even though she is bone-tired.

We prepare to build my crib. Mom rummages around to pull out a wooden box that once housed

Charlie and Julie

Christmas oranges. I gaze at the box and recall the succulent taste of sweet, juicy oranges. This will be my crib-in-the-making. The Sears and Eaton's catalogues are dragged out to take part in the miraculous transformation. These catalogues are my dream books where I amuse myself for hours, flipping pages to admire and wish for the beautiful clothes and toys.

Pictures of baby dolls, baby carriages, bottles, and baby clothes will adorn my crib. I choose many wonderful pictures from the catalogue and Mom cuts them out for me. Next, Mom pours flour and water into a cup. My job is to stir the contents to make the glue. Wildly, sloppily, I whip the spoon around, causing little white globs to become airborne; I am unaware of the mess, as I continue to stir crazily until the mixture is smooth and resembles glue. Enthusiastically, I slather glue haphazardly on the back of my pictures and slap the images firmly in a higgledy-piggledy manner onto the sides of the wooden box.

Mom hands me the button jar. There is a vast array of buttons: big ones, little ones, square ones, and all the colors of the rainbow. I choose the pretty, small pearls. My crib is taking form and looks very promising! A scrap of brightly colored cloth is transformed into a bag on the Singer treadle sewing machine. I gaze in amazement at the speed of my mom's foot rocking swiftly back and forth, back and forth, back and forth on the bottom pedal of the machine. Simultaneously her work-worn hands skillfully shifts the cloth under the fast-moving needle.

I stuff the mattress. Mom passes me the bag along with a bundle of rags. Determinedly, my little hands clumsily stuff the scraps into the pink-flowered bag. When the bag is full, Mom, with nimble fingers, quickly stitches up the open end and voila, we have a crib mattress. I am ecstatic.

A look of wonder flows over my face as I observe the prettiest baby crib ever! The glimmer of light from the gas lamp reveals a tender expression on Mom's face and casts a warm glow over my baby crib. Gently, I clutch my treasured dolly and lay her softly in her precious bed. It is at that precise moment that Mom leans over to put her lips against my ear.

"I have a special secret to tell you," Mom whispers quietly. She shifts her body to look me in the eye and with a look of delight she says in a soft

71

voice, "We are going to have a new baby in our family." My mouth drops open with astonishment; I am surprised and excited. *Maybe it will be a girl!*

A boy:

Whispers, tears, and dead silence overtake the house. Mom returned from the hospital several days later, looking woebegone and lost. There is no baby.

"It was a boy," Mom speaks softly to Dad in a sad tone. "Dr. Wright said it will be too dangerous for me to have any more children." Mom and Dad are sad. There is no close family remaining in Weekes to commiserate their loss. Mom's best friend/sister-in-law, Aunt Kay, moved with her family to BC. I feel a sadness in the house, as if something is missing.

Mom and Dad rely on their faith, and one another for support. They lean on their friends who rally around to give encouragement and comfort. There is no language for loss. Life continues in their busy world on the farm.

Chapter 21

Sibling pals:

"Julie, come to the house. We are going to town," Mom calls from the steps of the house. Our horse, Star, is hooked up to the wagon, eager for a jaunt— our summer transportation.

"I don't go," I reply. Charlie and I are building a fort in the shop; I do not want to stop our fun.

"Okay, Charlie, you can come," Mom replies. In a flash, without thinking about me, Charlie darts towards the house.

"I'm coming, I'm coming, I'm coming!" I bellow, and take off at a run, close behind Charlie. I do not want to miss out. In the end, we both go to town. We are very close in age and have a tight rela-tionship. I follow Charlie everywhere. Whatever Charlie does, I must do—we do everything together, work and play. My brother is my lifelong buddy.

Charlie and Julie

Soldiers at Play:

Some of our escapades are downright hazardous. The farm is our playground and Charlie and I invent our play.

"I have an idea. Let's play soldiers," Charlie announces.

"Okay. How do we play?" I ask excitedly.

"It's easy," he replies and reaches for a shovel. "This is my rifle." He passes me a long, heavy piece of wood, with the command, "This is your rifle." With a flourish, Charlie whips the shovel over his shoulder. "Follow me," he utters. Awkwardly, I raise my rifle over my shoulder and step up close to march behind him.

Hup. Hup. Hup, rings out in the tranquil air as Charlie shouts and demonstrates a soldier's walk.

I follow his example and we loudly bark a strident, "Hup. Hup. Hup," in unison. Tramping in harmony with our knees rising sharply to the sky, I imitate his every move. If Charlie halts to a standstill, I halt to a standstill; when Charlie advances to a march, I advance to a march. Whatever Charlie can do, I can do! It is immense fun. Together we traipse briskly around the yard, mimicking the game of Follow the Leader.

Suddenly, Charlie transfers into a soldier's spin. Abruptly, with a sharp left-hand turn, Charlie rotates his body in a wide arc. With a piercing, final *Hup*, he spins into position. I catch a sudden movement in my outer vision, but before I can modify my stance, Charlie's rifle whacks me dead-on to the upper front side of my head. Pain explodes through my skull.

Bright red blood gushes forth like a waterfall. It streams in ribbons down my face. My mouth opens and pierces the air with a blood-curdling scream. I peer through the haze of fluid that flows in a cascade over my eyes, and I gag on the disgusting taste in my mouth. I vaguely see my Dad through the rivulets of crimson liquid, sprinting across the yard at a rapid run towards me! I feel faint and dizzy. I sway slightly off balance and Dad sweeps me up in his arms. He runs and I feel the rush of wind blast against my body.

"It hurt. It hurt. It hurt," I moan, as Mom swiftly shoves a hand towel snugly against my head wound. She pulls me onto her lap and whispers words of comfort in a calm voice. The towel quickly turns scarlet and seeps relentlessly. Dad plops a clean cloth atop the previous one and holds it tight against my wound. Worry is etched on their faces. Finally, the fluid begins to congeal, and they can assess the damage.

I sustain a deep gash on the top right side of my forehead. Dad reaches for the white tin with small black and gray letters, along with huge red letters spelling *BAND-AID*. Visualizing the familiar tin, I instantly feel better–I know that a Band-aid heals wounds. Lifting the hinged lid, Dad withdraws several Band-aids and Mom gently covers my wounds. I feel like a wounded soldier.

Charlie sits nearby, looking woebegone. Later he informs me that we will never play that game again–we never do! I heal, however a scar remains for a lifetime.

Chapter 22

Bath or Play:

"Julie, come in for a bath," shouts Mom from the front door.

"I don't want bath," I whisper quietly to myself. My young mind silently argues. *Why have a bath? The sun is shining, and it is not dark. I want to play.*

I run off to play. *Do not touch,* pops into my mind when I spy the bag of seed grain. I am aware that the forbidden bag is off-limits for play; I am tempted to check it out.

Step by step by step, I saunter slowly in the direction of the bag of grain. I peer at the bag; the top is untied and loosely open. Furtively, I glance around and observe Dad, busy repairing the combine machinery. No one else is nearby. I noiselessly plunge my hand inside the bag of grain. The texture is like any old grain. Grabbing a handful, I study the kernels and am dismayed to discover that it is not any different to regular seeds. I conclude, *It is not special grain.*

This not-so-special grain wants to play, and I have an idea that might be fun. Compressing the grain tightly into my fist I raise my arm swiftly, open my clenched hand, and toss the seeds high into the air. With my head tilted upwards, I watch the kernels fall like raindrops all around me. The seeds splatter haphazardly and sting my face sharply. It hurts. I decide to try a different strategy. After throwing the seeds into the atmosphere, I jump out of the way quickly to avoid the plummeting seeds. I am lost in my wonder-world of fun.

"Hey, get out of the seed grain!" orders a firm voice, penetrating the atmosphere. My fun game is interrupted amidst seeds in mid-flight. The words jar me to my core. I rotate my little body and glimpse Dad moving fast in my direction. I might be little, but I know *I am in trouble.*

I react! In a split second I dash away from the bag with my little legs spinning as fast as they can go. I zip around the combine, imagining Dad in quick pursuit. Hearing no footfalls behind me, I quickly crane my neck to glimpse backwards. Dad is not behind me; I gaze around and see him on his knees gingerly scooping up the grain, shaking the dirt out, and returning it to the bag.

My mind works double-time. I pick up my pace and run to the house, to sprint up the four steps into the porch.

"Mom, I am ready for my bath," I shout. Mom is pleasantly surprised.

"Julie, you are such a good girl coming in for your bath," she remarks. Mom has drawn a bath in the square tub, and it is perched on a bench in the front porch. Gratefully, I lower myself into the fresh, warm water. I feel safe.

Dad appears at the porch door. Mom is busy scrubbing my body and I slink down as low as I can go into the water. I hold my breath! Dad begins to relate the story about Julie and the seed grain. I slink further down in the tub and avert my eyes. Mom interrupts, however, before Dad can finish his sentence.

"Look what a good girl Julie is for coming in for her bath," she exclaims excitedly. They exchange a knowing glance and Dad raises an eyebrow, nods, and smiles.

Dad fixes me with a steady eye and with a confidential grin addresses Mom, "Yes, she is a very good girl."

I feel the love and forgiveness from my parents. I feel sad inside for disobeying. It is a lesson learned–I have good intentions to never play with the precious seed grain in the future.

Bath Day:

Girls first! It is Sunday and bath day. A square tub is situated in the middle of the kitchen floor and filled with very warm water, heated on the kitchen cook stove. The kitchen is *off-limits* at bath time. I bathe first, being the oldest girl. Us girls bathe before the boys. Stepping into the tub, I relish the very warm, clean, and refreshing water. Sunday night is always a special night in my mind, instilling pleasurable memories of the ambiance of warm heat emanating from the cookstove and sinking my body into a bathtub of hot water. The atmosphere is luxurious. To this day I love taking a bath!

*****

Water is a precious commodity that we can't live without. In the summer, water is supplied from a well. A pail and rope are used to draw up the liquid which is then deposited in the water barrel, next to the cookstove. In the winter, water is procured in a different way. A patch of clean snow is scooped out, shoveled into a large pail, and deposited into either a tub on the cookstove to melt or into the water barrel next to the stove. When the snow is deposited into the water in the barrel it creates chunky pieces of icy snow. Scooping up these icy bits delivers a very cold, refreshing drink. Our friends always request a glass of water at our house, murmuring as they drink the cool liquid, "This water is so refreshing. It is like an icy drink." We are unaware that it is a forerunner of a Slushie drink!

Chapter 23

Homesick:

Life is harsh, so visiting becomes an important diversion. Neighbors are an integral part of pioneer life to provide entertainment–visiting or playing cards. Or to provide support–lending a helping hand, giving sound advice, or commiserating on the unforeseen ups and downs of farming.

Communicating with one another entails visiting in person–no one has a telephone. The telephone exchange office is in the town of Weekes. Dolly Tyacke is the telephone operator–she manually connects calls with cords inserted into a telephone switchboard. Dolly receives messages and either delivers the news or dispatches a messenger to deliver the news to those in the area.

Social interaction involves community dances, Fowl suppers, Christmas entertainments, Church activities, and neighborhood gatherings.

Neighbors are friends who rely on one another. Ralph and Thelma live within walking distance, a quarter mile away. Thelma and Mom enjoy and value their coffee visits together. They discuss news of the world, family happenings, and exchange recipes or ideas to make their workload quicker and easier.

Our other neighbors are Frank and Lena Hamilton. They live three miles from our house. It is a fun time—we children are thrilled to play with the older Hamilton children while the adults visit or play cards.

Once I was having a marvelous time with the older neighbour girls, and I asked if I could stay with the girls overnight. Energetically, I waved goodbye to my family—at bedtime, however, it was a different story.

That is the night that I glean an insight into my inner being at the age of four years old. I am homesick. I refuse to go to bed. I stand at the window and stare in the direction of our house, which is two miles across the field as the crow flies. I am homesick! I want to go home! I stand at the window like a soldier on guard duty; ramrod-stiff, I do not budge, I just stare out the window into the darkness. Anxiously I silently pray, *God, let me go home.*

"Julie, come with me. I will tuck you into bed," Lena the matriarch of the Hamilton household speaks in a soft and gentle voice as she crouches to my level.

"I want to go home," I mutter sadly. Defeated, Lena turns to her daughters, Clara, and Fern.

"Julie is homesick. You will have to bundle up warm and take her home." The girls are upset with me. It is a bitter, cold evening and they do not want to take me home! However, the girls unhappily don their winter gear, and we strike out across the field. The cold takes our breath away; each puff disperses misty vapor into the air. It is a full moon, and we can see for miles. The moonlight bathes the snow in shimmering cut diamonds and the crystal stars glitter brilliantly overhead to display a dazzling light show. Snow drifts rise in mammoth mounds.

I am too small to tramp over the snow. If I crunch through the top crispy layer I will disappear! The girls take turns to ride me *piggy-back* style. I listen to the rhythmic scrunch of their boots on the snow as I jostle about to and fro. Occasionally, I plunge down abruptly when their legs plummet through the snowdrift and I feel the sharp edges of snow-ice scratch my legs.

The girls are cold and frustrated with the task of taking me home on such a frigid evening over humungous snowdrifts.

"Why are you homesick? Why couldn't you just stay the night? Why do you need to go home?" they complain as we traipse through the deep snow.

I am silent. Meanwhile my eyes frantically peer over the dazzling snow drifts in search of our house lights. Suddenly, appearing like tiny specks in the far distance, I glimpse the radiant beam of lights shining brightly. Smiling inwardly, I am aware that I will soon be home. I continue to stare at the lights coming closer and closer and closer. The gas light casts a glow, warm and cheery.

Several minutes later we clomp up the four steps and gather, nestled in a small group, on the landing. Fern raps sharply on the door. Mom's eyes widen in astonishment, but she immediately swings the door in a wide arc and swiftly hustles us inside into the warmth of the house. Mom serves hot chocolate and homemade oatmeal-raisin cookies to the girls and me.

"I am so sorry you had to bring Julie home on such a cold night. She is such a stay-at-home girl. Thank you so much." Mom addresses Clara and Fern in a sympathetic tone.

"Oh, it's okay—we didn't mind a bit!" Clara answers. Her response shocks me to the core. I stare at her. I am confused and surprised.

"Was it difficult to carry Julie over all those snowdrifts?" Mom asks.

"Oh no, it was easy for us," Fern replies convincingly, avoiding my eyes. I cannot believe what I am hearing. I clasp my hands together and compress my lips tightly. I remain silent—I am home! I am amazed at how uncomplaining and gracious the girls are despite the struggle they encountered piggybacking me home.

This is my first insight into being diplomatic and stretching the truth in order to please others.

Chapter 24

Barry:

Fate is unpredictable. Mom had been told that she could not have any more children, however, God has different plans. It is with great eagerness I learn that a baby is on the way! Maybe it will be a girl!

I love my sister Christina. For a while, our sister bond was on rocky ground. However, my nature is to prefer harmony; it was not long, therefore, before I adjusted and grew to love my sister. She is our baby girl to nurture. We are playmates and friends.

It is harvest time. On Thanksgiving Day, Mom waddles to the combine to help with the harvest even though she is due any day! Mom has all three of us children positioned either on the combine with her or on the tractor with Dad.

Farming is a part of our life from birth onwards. During seeding and harvest time, we children ride on the machinery. As babies, snuggled into a pillow, or as toddlers, propped between pillows until we can sit on our own. It is a normal way of life for us, and we revel in the moment.

I love to partake in my favorite pastime, riding the tractor. I run to the field and wave to Dad to stop, motioning madly my intention to ride—we cannot converse due to the reverberation of the tractor. I wedge myself nimbly between the wheel hub and the gearshift. The tractor springs to life with a loud *chug-chug-chug* and at the same time a thick swirl of dust sweeps up, in and around me. Dad is using the cultivator, where the machine's teeth pierce the soil, tilling the land in preparation for a crop the following year. This is called summer fallowing, where a quarter of land is left without sowing for one summer, allowing the land to recover and store organic matter while retaining moisture. The cultivator churns up the dirt, hurling a flurry of dust into the atmosphere. I breathe in the flying particles and daydream to my heart's content. This is my happy place!

We are in the midst of harvesting the crops when surprise visitors arrive, mid-afternoon. It is Mr. and Mrs. Gough, come to check on how Mom is faring with her pregnancy.

The Gough family live on a farm at the edge of Weekes. Mrs. Gough is an older woman who took Mom under her wing when Mom's parents moved to BC. Mrs. Gough willingly and lovingly took over the role of a parent and became like my mom's second mom. Mom relies on Mrs. Gough for questions regarding aspects of food preparation, child rearing, or life in general.

Mom is therefore excited and greets the Goughs with a warm welcome. Mom stops combining and returns instead to the house, to prepare a Thanksgiving supper. During the meal, Mom is a little under the weather and expels a loud sigh.

"Wouldn't it be funny if your baby is born on Thanksgiving Day?" Mrs. Gough jokingly remarks. She predicted it! Baby decides to come into the world that night. Dad rushes Mom to the

Charlie, Chrissy, Julie, Barry
ready for Sunday School.
In background '51 Chevy truck

hospital in Porcupine Plain in our new truck purchased in 1951. Labor is normal for Mom. *Rough!*

Our *miracle* baby is born – my brother is born on Thanksgiving Day, three years after Christina's birth. He is a beautiful blond, blue-eyed baby boy. My brother is named Barry Nelson, after my mom's maiden name, Nelson. Barry is a happy and relaxed baby! He looks like me, however he has a better disposition.

Emergency:

Mom returns to the Porcupine Plain Hospital—under doctor's orders—for an operation to prevent any more pregnancies. During the surgery, the expected routine operation deviates into an emergency.

In Weekes, Dad is unaware of the dire situation. He is loading cordwood into a box car at the railway station. A phone call is received at the telephone exchange office and Dolly quickly dispatches a messenger to relay the important message to Dad. In the midst of shifting the cordwood, Dad hears his name being called—he glances up to see a young fella dash to his side.

"Bill, you are to rush to the hospital. Laura is not expected to survive," the messenger blurts out breathlessly.

It is an emergency! Reeling in shock, Bill, frantically seeks out Miss Cochan. "Can you watch the children? I need to go to the hospital." Desperately he ponders, *What is the quickest way?*

Suddenly in his peripheral vision he detects the train pulling out slowly from the railway station. Without another thought, Dad turns and breaks into a fast sprint. He reaches the train, bounds alongside and takes a running leap—hurtling his body into the boxcar. His frame hits the wooden floor with a resounding thud. Dad is oblivious to the instant pain radiating throughout his body. His is extremely worried about Mom.

The train wheels accelerate. Dad's heart accelerates. He wills the rumbling wheels to move at a faster pace. Time stands still. Finally, arriving at the Porcupine Plain station, he springs down from the boxcar, and dashes off the platform.

Dad is immobilized at the sorrowful scene that greets him in Mom's hospital room. Mom lies motionless, with eyes closed and looking like death warmed over. The vision sends quivers to the depths of his soul, his legs feel like rubber, and he steps forward shakily, sinking into a chair. Fear flickers over his face and his tears begin to stream down. He reaches over the coverlets to pick up her hand. He prays. Dad feels helpless. He does not leave her side. He gazes worriedly at Mom and his heart aches. Several hours later, Mom stirs and, feeling the eyes of Dad upon her, she cranes her neck to exchange a loving glance. Words are not necessary—they communicate in silence.

Later, Mom recounts her strange experience.

"I was going through a tunnel. I saw a bright light and it felt peaceful. I had the impression that I was entering Heaven." Mom paused. "Then I woke up to see your Dad sitting next to my bed and holding my hand." Mom ends her account, "I guess it was not my time to go. God knows I have small children at home that need me to take care of them. God is good."

Baby of the Family:

"I can nurse Barry," Mom exclaims in an excited voice. She places Barry gently into position, and within seconds he is suckling eagerly, adapting to nursing like a duck to water! Mom is thrilled to be able to nurse Barry, the only one of five children. Determined to nurse him as long as possible, it becomes apparent that too long is too much! The practicality of weaning him occurs to Mom after Barry toddles up at sixteen months while she is washing clothes to grab a teat and nurse. Instantly, Mom knows that it is time!

Barry is *our* baby, and we all spoil him! I take charge and am his little mother. At five years old, I willingly change diapers, feed him, and watch over him. Chrissy is easygoing and readily accepts Barry taking her spot of being the baby in the family. Charlie is thrilled to have a brother and watches over him with love. Barry is *our* baby; we all spoil him! He becomes a life-long baby in our family.

"Dudie, cut me bed," he asks as a toddler.

"Okay, I will get the knife, go to the bedroom, and cut you a piece of bed!" I reply in a teasing voice.

"No, Dudie, cut me bed," Barry stresses.

Eventually, with a smile, I willingly cut him a piece of homemade bread and spread it thickly with peanut butter and homemade cranberry jam. I like to take care of my baby brother.

*****

On a trip to town, we are *snug as a bug in a rug,* crowded in the cab of our truck. Mom holds Barry on her lap, Charlie, and Christina sit squeezed between our parents, and I stand in front of Mom. We are body-hugging!

"We can't have any more children," Charlie declares.

"Why can't we have any more children? "Mom asks in a puzzled tone.

Charlie replies in a serious voice. "Because there is no more room in the truck!"

Chapter 25

School:

"I want to go to school," I moaned bitterly in September when Charlie started school. "Why can't I go with Charlie?" I demanded, upset at being left at home.

"You are not old enough to go to school, and you are too little to walk the mile to school," Mom explained. School buses have not materialized yet; therefore, it is a mile walk in all kinds of weather.

"Please, let me go to school," I begged Mom constantly. Mom gave me a small box of crayons to play school. I appreciated the crayons, but my one desire was to go to real school, and I missed Charlie, my playmate.

*****

"I am going to school today. I am going to school today. I am going to school today," I singsong a year later. I am super thrilled, merrily dancing around the room. It is September and I am five and three-quarter years. I am going to school.

I am joyful; it is the first day of school. Charlie and I walk in the bright sunshine and listen to the crunch of our shoes on the gravel. Together, we enter the little white schoolhouse that accommodates both grade one and two.

Julie's first day of school with Charlie

Mrs. Smith directs me to a seat in the grade one side of the classroom. I am thrilled. I sit down and place my hands on top of my very own desk. I am anxious to start grade one.

School class begins and I learn the rules: 1. We must remain in our seat. 2. Sit quietly. 3. Listen to the teacher. 4. Raise our hand to ask permission to use the washroom. This is not what I expected.

I am naturally shy. I gaze around the room nervously to locate Charlie. I spot him over on the other side of the classroom, and I want to go to him, but I cannot leave my desk! I try to pray; without warning, I burst into tears and cry softly.

"What is the matter?" Mrs. Smith asks gently.

"I want to go home," I answer, with tears spilling down my cheeks. I realize, *I do not like school!*

"You are a big girl now. Big girls attend school." Mrs. Smith talks to me in low tones while crouching down by my desk. She is very understanding and caring. Her kindness makes me feel better.

I settle into the routine of school life. I discover, however, that Charlie is a wee bit mischievous, and a problem arises. When the teacher scolds him, I get so upset that tears well up in my eyes and threaten to spill over. I am distraught. When Charlie is disciplined, I feel it deep in my soul and I wish I could protect him. I contemplate telling Mom that it upsets me to witness Charlie being scolded. One thought causes me to rethink that idea: *If I tell Mom she will probably lecture Charlie for misbehaving in school.* I do not want to get Charlie into more trouble; I remain silent.

John and Joe:

Whether it was at school or in the community, I didn't like seeing my brother in trouble.

"Don't bury my brother in the snowbank," I shriek in anger at John and Joe, who on occasion babysit for our parents. We are walking home together from school because they live across the road from our house. On this particular frosty and chilly winter day they grab Charlie and position his body as though they are about to shove his head into the towering snowbank. All eyes are on me as I holler, "Leave Charlie alone!" I am upset, angry, and sad to see Charlie treated so roughly. This occurs several times and my insides tremble with anxiety.

"John and Joe were going to push Charlie into the snowbank," I tattle furiously to Mom upon arriving home.

Charlie
Grade two

"We were just fooling around. It was just a game," Charlie admits laughing heartily. I was totally unaware that Charlie was in on the scheme! I am surprised and wonder, *Whose idea, was it?* Obviously, this was all an act to get a reaction out of me–it worked splendidly! This is my first insight into the art of teasing, and I determine that a boy's idea of fun is different to a girls' idea of fun.

*****

A week later, our parents have an emergency, so they take Christina and I across the road to be babysat by John and Joe.

Julie
Grade one

"Can pay in cabooshsh?" Christina asks John in her little toddler voice. Joe fires up the caboose's heater and we are soon toasty and warm. Christina indicates for me to take her coat off; she cannot unzip her coat, and neither can I. John gallantly offers to help, and unzips her coat. My little mind is impressed by how gentle and kind John is with my baby sister.

"Would you like a baked potato?" John asks.

"Yes," in unison, is our immediate response. John wedges many potatoes amongst the coals. My mouth salivates at the aroma of the potatoes baking amongst the coals. Eventually, Joe grabs the poker and shuffles the potatoes out of the stove. Soon we are munching on a hot, yummy potato. It is delectable. My little mind thinks, *John and Joe are nice boys.*

Ride with Stranger:

In those days no one warned us to stay away from strangers. One day I am walking alone to school because Charlie was dilly-dallying—I left ahead in order to arrive at school on time.

Forlornly, I walk slowly, kicking at the snow. I want Charlie to catch up to me! A quarter of a mile into my walk I stop at the corner of Highway 23 to check for Charlie. I am exuberant to see him in the far distance.

"Would you like a ride to school?" A voice breaks the silence. I glance up to see a sedan has come to a stop and a man has popped his head out the window. I do not know him–he is a stranger.

"Yes but can you wait for my brother, Charlie, and give him a ride, too?" I reply promptly. I point my gloved hand to Charlie's figure, slowly progressing a long way back. Mr. Stranger agrees. He steps out of the vehicle, and we wait for Charlie in the cold, while snowflakes drift around us. The air is bitingly cold.

Charlie is dawdling. He feels no urgency to get to school. I wonder why he doesn't move faster and why he is making us wait for him.

"Hurry up, Charlie," Mr. Stranger shouts. It makes no difference; Charlie continues to walk at a snail's pace. Mr. Stranger and I wait impatiently for slow-moving Charlie. I think Mr. Stranger is a special person to stand in such extreme weather and wait for my brother. Time moves at a snail's pace until finally, Charlie arrives. When we are dropped off at the school, we utter "Thank you," in unison.

God watches over us. The Stranger is not a kidnapper. Mr. Stranger is Mr. Andy MacDonald who lives in the town of Weekes. He runs the elevator and is a good friend of our parents. Charlie and I are unaware of who he is, however, when we describe him and his car to our parents, they know exactly who gave us a ride. Our parents tell us that it was a very nice gesture of Mr. McDonald's to give us a ride and they will be sure to thank him for being so thoughtful. It is in later years that we are warned to not get into a vehicle if you do not know the person.

*****

Sports Day:

I am excited to go to the sports day which is taking place at the Weekes Sports Ground.

A sports day is a get-together of the community for food, fun, and games. Booths are set up, with ladies selling homemade pies, cakes, and other goodies, along with coffee, juice, and Kool-Aid. Another booth sells ice-cream and cool, juicy slices of watermelon. There are racing contests of many sorts: single racing, three-legged races, and sack races, where contestants climb into a flour sack and hop, jump, or hobble towards the finish line. Bingo is a popular game played by the adults. At the end of the day, several judges determine who has the best decorated bicycle. It is a day of fun and excitement for all ages.

"Win an ice cream cone," are words that thunder into the air and into my tiny brain. Puzzled I look at Mom.

"Julie, do you want to enter a race to win an ice cream cone?" she asks. Of course I do! This is my first memory of the sports day.

I can feel the excitement in the air, as I eagerly step up to the mark for my race with the fellow contestants in my age group. I envision the wonderful prize. My mouth salivates at the thought of a cold, luscious ice cream cone.

"On your mark. Get Set. Go!" rings into the air and I scurry off as fast as my small, short legs can churn. Out of the corner of my eye I notice my competitors fly by me, one by one! I struggle desperately to keep up, but drop back, along with several others to the rear of the group. I do not give up but determinedly charge ahead. The race is over–I finish the race, but I come in second last!

No ice-cream cone! Distressed, my bottom lip puckers into a pout. I did not win my ice cream cone! Tears spill out of my eyelids, and I look at Mom in despair. I am not sure what hurts me the most–coming in near last place or missing out on the coveted prize of an ice cream cone.

"The important thing is that you finished the race. You did not quit," Mom whispers, adding, "I will buy you an ice cream cone." Apparently, Mom assumes that the ice cream cone is the most important element of the race. I do not feel like I deserve an ice cream, however, since I lost the race. I continue to weep and am in a state of misery. *Why wouldn't my legs run faster?* I muse.

"All participants win and receive an ice cream cone!" is announced into the hot, dry air. I am puzzled. *Didn't a person have to be first to win?*

"You finished the race, and you get an ice cream cone," Mom says softly, with a smile. The implication sinks in and immediately my face transforms from a frown to a look of delight. I realize that it did not matter who came in first because we won an ice-cream cone if we finished the race! Zealously, I collect my prize–a vanilla ice cream cone!

Mom and Julie

As a young girl, I did not understand that I was short for my age group; my little legs just could not keep up to my opponents. In later years I discover that my strength surfaces in long distance running.

The lesson that I learned at this young age was that it is more important to *finish* the race than to win the race.

Chapter 26

Blossom, a docile cow:

Sometimes traumatic events happen innocently enough. We are at the neighbors, a quarter mile from home, where Mom and Thelma are enjoying a cup of coffee for a much-needed visit. Charlie and I enter the house after playing a game of tag. Christina is sitting by Mom, slowly flipping pages and eyeing toys in the Eaton's catalogue. Barry is resting quietly on Mom's knee.

"Charlie and Julie, please go home and fetch Blossom so she is ready to milk when I come home a little later," informs Mom. This is not an unusual request. It is our chore to bring Blossom in from the field to the barn for milking.

Yes," we answer in unison and nod our heads. Charlie is almost seven years and I, Julie, am almost six years. We strike out for home. We dilly-dally along the road, plodding at a slow pace, listening to the crunch of our boots on the coarse gravel and occasionally kicking forcefully at the tiny stones to send them flitting into the air. We are in no hurry to perform our typically boring task.

Blossom is a very docile cow. It is extremely easy to round her up and direct her to the barn shed.

"I have a great idea," Charlie announces.

"What is your idea, Charlie?" I ask inquisitively.

"We should tie our little red wagon to the cow's tail and go for a ride," he answers, with great excitement. The vision of Blossom pulling us slowly around the yard sounds like a lovely plan.

"How are we going to do that?" I question Charlie.

"Watch me," he replies. "It is easy." I watch in awe, as he grasps a piece of twine with his little hand and ties it in a firm knot onto the handle of our little red wagon. Blossom gazes at us with her big brown eyes as we drag her out of the shed and position her rear end facing our soon-to-be vehicle.

"Julie, climb into the wagon," Charlie instructs. I obey. I hop into the wagon and scoot to the front, leaving room behind me for Charlie. Meanwhile, Charlie deftly ties the twine to Blossom's tail. He makes a running leap to jump and sit behind me. Clutching the edges of the wagon, our fingers grip tightly, and with a shiver of apprehension we wait for Blossom to take us for our ride. Blossom remains stock-still.

"Charlie, how will Blossom give us a ride?" I ask in a puzzled tone.

"I have an idea," he says, with a twinkle in his eyes. Charlie leans precariously over the side and expertly grasps a small, but thick and heavy, stick from the earth. Straightening his body upright he initiates a powerful swing of his arm in a wide arc. Suddenly, Charlie pitches the stick straight at Blossom's rump.

Blossom bolts! Blasting like a shot out of a cannon Blossom jolts our little red wagon sharply and snappily and we lift off like a space shuttle. We hang on for dear life, frantically trying to keep our miniature bodies firmly in the saddle. Blossom gallops at the speed of light, sending us like a skyrocket through the atmosphere.

"Help! Help! Help!" we scream in unison. Charlie and I fly crazily into the air as if we're on a rogue magic carpet. We plunge straight to the ground, bounce, and rise sharply upwards to stop momentarily in mid-air, and plummet sharply down again, like a roller coaster. Blossom veers and makes a beeline straight for the bush; like a wild boar she plunges into the thick forest of trees.

We scream as one. Our little red wagon bounces solidly on the ground, jarring our bodies to the core, and then suddenly it sails rapidly upwards. Our tummies are fluttering weirdly as we bounce rapidly up and down with scraggly branches whipping cruelly at our face producing sharp stinging welts. In agony, we grit our teeth. We are terrified.

"Help! Help! Help!" we scream. No one is around to hear.

A tree stump looms in our path. Our little red wagon smashes into it with a loud, grinding thud; our cart ascends to the heavens. We scream. Losing our grip on the wagon, cold fear wells up within us as we are hurled out and soar helplessly into the atmosphere. The upward thrust stops sharply and for a moment our bodies hang, motionless. Abruptly, we drop, falling quickly to land with a tremendous *thump* in a pile of brush. Stunned, our breath comes in shuddering gasps as we lie motionless and silent. Surprise flickers over our faces—we have survived! God heard us.

Ouch. Ouch. Ouch! Without warning, tiny fingers of sharp, stabbing pain enters our bodies. Shattering the stillness, we generate an ear-piercing cry in unison. Our arms flail around us as we stumble rapidly to our feet. We are engulfed by angry, stinging bees! They were housed in the undergrowth we disturbed!

We scramble away swiftly enduring the stings of bees, the whips of willow branches, and the sharp, scrubby underbrush poking roughly into our shoes. Plunging out of the brush, we zip down the driveway and hit the main road at a gallop. We are howling hysterically, wailing, and shouting at the top of our lungs. Our destination, a quarter of a mile away, seems to endlessly retreat from us. The bees engulf our figures in a hoard and sting our tiny bodies ferociously. Our spinning legs cannot out-run them.

"Mom! Mom! Mom!" we shriek, louder than thunder. We charge like bulls down the road as the bees attack us relentlessly. Our high-pitched yelling shatters the air and we are heard before we are seen. Mom and Thelma instantly drop their coffee cups and careen down the driveway, hitting the secondary road at break-neck speed.

They assess the scene and act. They wave their arms to swat the bees away and begin to snatch madly at our clothes to yank them from our frames. Charlie's baby-blue coveralls are entirely covered in bees. Mom flings the bee-covered clothes into the air. Instantly frozen, we gape in amazement: bursting out from Charlie's coveralls is an object tumbling in a lump to the ground. It is a bees' nest.

The bees' nest had relocated itself! The bees had angrily joined us in our race, to fight for their home. They are still fighting for their home as they gather together like an army, hovering and swarming near their flattened beehive, lying squashed on the road. We need to escape. Half-naked, we dash away from the scene. We arrive safely home. Mom bathes Charlie and me in baking soda and water.

Blossom is waiting quietly in the barn shed with our little red wagon still attached to her tail. She does not produce any milk that evening.

We suffer from the bee stings; Charlie, however, experiences additional pain since the bees' nest was buried within his clothes.

Mom considers it is punishment enough. A good lesson learned the hard way. Our parents impress upon us that the farm animals are not toys.

Part
Four

Mid-childhood Years
Julie 7 – 8 years

Chapter 27

Character developed:

Our parents grow up together. Married young and with no family to guide their way, they jointly develop their characters. They are both well-liked and respected in the community.

Dad walks at a slow and steady pace. This matches his personality—steady, patient, and kind. He is slow to anger, and when he reprimands it is in a calm manner.

It is a well-known secret that Dad has a stash of black licorice in his bedside stand. His candy quickly disappears. Many times, the little ones sneak in and out of the bedroom, fingers clutching the delicious sweets. Dad never questions the disappearing candy, and the drawer is always full!

Dad loves and spoils Mom. He often tells her that he would give her the stars if he could. Mom works right alongside Dad—they are hard-working pioneers in a harsh land.

Mom compliments Dad in her positive attitude. She is loving, caring, kind, and always gives of herself. She is full of life and brings joy to all those around her. She stops and talks to everyone. We can always keep track of her location by her wonderful, loud infectious laugh that follows her everywhere.

In the summer of 1956, we purchase the Gough's house and farmland, a quarter mile from town. It seems fitting for Mom to be moving into the house of Mrs. Gough, her friend and mentor, who is like her second mom.

I am seven years old. The house is a two story, and since the attic is undeveloped it becomes our play area. A favorite game to play is *school*; of course, I am the teacher.

Dad's first mission is to dig a large dugout which is twelve feet deep, forty feet long, and twenty feet wide. The dugout is surrounded by trees blocking the view from the house a hundred feet away. The dugout will provide water for our livestock, crop spraying, and also become our very own swimming spot. Next, he builds several granaries to house the threshed grain. They stand in a row east of the house, along with two oblong buildings which have separator walls inside for the different varieties of grain. A large round-roofed building is erected to store the combine.

In later years, Dad has the second floor of the house removed and an angular roof installed. Prior to the renovation, Dad builds a small replica

granaries

sawmill

Our Farm   dugout

of how the house will appear. My dad is an excellent carpenter and can build anything with wood.

The yard adjacent to the house has a luscious lawn surrounded by a hedge of Carragana bushes–diligently dug up and planted by us children and Mom. There are various fruit trees in the back yard: cherry, apple, and honeysuckle. Our favorite is the big cherry tree that extends its arms for our little legs to climb. We skitter in and out of the branches–sometimes breaking a limb or two on the tree.

The farmyard is bordered by two areas of bush that become our adventure land. We build a tree house and organize our very own high jump by inserting nails into two adjacent trees and a skinny tree limb becomes the cross-bar. Together, we siblings clear out paths in the bush; one huge path, extending from one end of the bush to the other, is designated for our *short-cut* to school. We siblings bond in play. To add to our play, we adopt a dog from the Tycky family. They are neighbours who sold their farm and moved to the city. Francis was a friend of mine and she told me all about her precious dog, King. He is a black and white sheltie-type dog, very mild mannered and past the puppy stage. He is our protector, barking at everyone that enters our yard. He adapts well to his new family and new home.

It is our house, to be made into a home! Mom is always redecorating the house, either painting or moving furniture around.

"This will bring life into the home," she says. Our home is decorated exactly the way she envisions. Dad smiles and just goes right along with whatever idea Mom has.

Love is visible! Our parents are open with their love and often snuggle on the couch. They tease one another in jest–Mom makes a fist to knock gently on Dad's head, with the remark, "Anyone home?" which creates gales of laughter and ends in a tussle of tickling. Gaiety fills the room. Thus, along with having an ever-changing house, we have a home filled with love, laughter, and fun.

Reading is a passion:

I love reading! This is a joy I inherited from Mom and Dad, whose reading covers a variety of subjects. Dad's favorite subjects are science, history, war, and detective books. Mom's favorites are *The Farmer's Almanac* and the *True Stories magazine*. I find books

Pilgrims Progress

to be good company that fill my mind with vivid images and interesting adventurers. I quite often curl up in the little alcove behind the kitchen cookstove with a good book in the *Nancy Drew Mystery* series. I love reading and am the official reader to my siblings.

My favorite books are the *Pilgrim's Progress* and the *Bible* which are big measuring eleven inches in length, thirteen and a half inches wide and four inches deep. These antique books arrived with Grampa Allen from England. I read the intriguing stories to my siblings. In the summer, we gather under the canopy of the cherry tree with its delightful aroma. Quite often

Bible

our dog, King, joins our group. In the winter, we snuggle cozily on our girls' double bed. The ancient book is spread wide so we can all study the colored pictures as I read the stories of long ago. Tradition dictates that these special books will be passed down to the oldest boy in the family. Charlie is the oldest; he will inherit these precious books.

In the Bible I am fascinated with the list of family births, marriages, and deaths dating back to 1872. The names are written by my ancestors of generations and generations ago. My sister Judith's death is recorded in my mom's handwriting. I finger the old, yellowed

Births and Marriages

sheets and visualize my descendants of long, long, long ago touching these very same pages.

A coin collection also arrived along with the Bible from England. Younger brother, Barry, will inherit the collection. I study the coins and slowly turn them over in my palm to ponder about this country called England.

Deaths

Apparently, Grampa Charles who immigrated from England was to receive an inheritance. The story told is that his grandmother, Lady Shackleton, owned a large estate in England. Charles was due a substantial inheritance. However, as rumor goes, the lawyer who should have dispensed the money got drunk and lost the papers. The war arrived and the city hall burned to ashes; the papers could not be recovered. I often wonder if there is an inheritance, just waiting to be claimed.

Chapter 28

Surgery:

"It will be a family event," Mom informs Charlie, Chrissy, and me. She adds, "We will all have our tonsils removed." At the Porcupine Plain Hospital we are designated a "Family Room." A smallish crib will be Chris' bed. I am guided to my bed–it appears to be a large crib housing a single size mattress. I gaze at my domain in disgust. My mind is in a turmoil. *Why give me a crib?* Even though it is more than big enough for me, I believe *I am too old to sleep in a crib!*

It is my refuge, however, as it comes to my rescue when the nurse arrives to administer a needle. The nurse arrives, I zip under the crib, she whips to one side, and I scurry to the opposite side. She cannot catch me.

"Julie, you need to come out," Mom coaxes gently. I do not budge. This is a recurring scenario throughout our entire stay at the hospital. I avoid several needles.

"Play quietly," Mom instructs when she slips out of the room to visit friends in another room. We decide to build a stagecoach. Flinging all the blankets and sheets in, around, up, and down, we create a masterpiece in my huge crib. Proceeding to play that our stagecoach is being attacked, we hoot and holler. We do not know how to play quietly. During our playfight, Mom appears at the door–her visiting time has ended and so has our fun.

"After the operation you can have ice cream," Mom promises. I am excited. I hope it is an ice cream cone! The ether is administered, a mask is placed over my face, and I am instructed to count to ten. It smells strange. I count, *One, two, three.*

After the operation, I do not want ice cream. I did not expect to feel so sick. My throat is painfully sore, and I feel nauseous. I just want to lay still and groan. My initial expectation of an operation was that afterwards I would feel exactly the same way as I did before the surgery. I just learned that an operation is painful.

I am glad Mom, and my siblings are recuperating with me. I am not alone–I have family by my side.

Medicines:

Removing my tonsils was an exceptional experience. For our more mundane health needs, we have a different routine.

"Here comes the Watkins man," we echo at the sight of our travelling salesman. He sells a variety of food, medicines, and sundry items. The Watkins ointment is a popular item and used regularly in our household. Cuts and scratches appear on work-worn hands in the struggle to clear land for crops. Mom gently washes wounds and liberally slathers them with the Watkins ointment. We do not complain over simple ailments like a cough – we just expect the symptoms to subside unless it transitions into whooping cough.

Our typical health products besides the Watkins Ointment, consist of Vicks, camphorated oil, iodine, mercurochrome, and, of course, Band-aids! First-aid supplies are a necessary commodity.

Chapter 29

Organic Food:

Life on the farm is always preoccupied with preparations for the future.

"It is time to pick berries," Mom announces early in the morning. It is best to perform this job before the hottest time of the day. Berry-picking is seasonal when the wild berries are ripe. We gather a wide variety–highbush cranberries, pin cherries, strawberries, raspberries, and Saskatoons. We don long pants and long-sleeved shirts to avoid being scratched by the branches or thorns and to deter the mosquitoes. If the mosquitoes get too annoying, we break a willow branch with plenty of leaves and swish it around our body to drive them away. We are designated to pick amongst the lower branches while Mom gathers from the upper area. We do our best to pick only the berries and not any leaves or tiny twigs. I am not a fan of berry picking!

Mom plants a humongous garden. We often trek to the garden patch to eat raw vegetables. We pull up a carrot to clean with its leaves, pinch pea pods and beans straight from the vine. We are unaware we are consuming organic food and raw vegetables; these, along with some dip, will be a snack people pay good money for in the future.

Our winter supply of fruit and vegetables is prepared during the summer. Garden items are stored in the cellar or preserved in sealers. The canning process consists of filling the sterilized jars with prepared fruit or vegetables, adding appropriate hot liquid, sealing with sterilized tops, and inserting in the canner to process. Mom's hands are often scalded during the process of canning while extracting the jars from the graniteware water-bath canner. Once processed, the items can be stored up to five years in the cellar.

The cellar is an underground room. It is a huge hole under the house with wooden walls and a packed dirt floor. It houses a potato bin which holds all the potatoes/carrots/turnips for winter. There will always be plenty of potatoes remaining *with eyes* for planting in the following spring. The cellar has numerous shelves for all the jars filled with the jams, jellies, vegetables, various pickles, relishes, and all kinds of fruit. We eat healthily.

"Who wants to go into the cellar to get the fruit for our dessert tonight?" asks Mom. We have dessert every night. We can pick whichever fruit our heart desires. I always pick my favorite, peaches.

Fried Chicken:

It is a fun chore to feed the chickens. At the chickens' coop, hands toss and scatter grain to the chickens. The birds flutter about, pecking up the delicious kernels. We gather the eggs from the nests situated inside boxes. Eggs are bountiful and for a period we wash and sell this precious commodity to the grocery store in town.

"Dad is chasing a chicken," shouts Chrissy. This is a common occurrence, and we get excited—we know what is coming. It is comical to watch Dad spring after the chicken with both legs just a flying—he always wins! After killing the chicken, he skins it, and douses it in a pail of cold water.

"Fried chicken for supper," Dad shouts, as he approaches Mom with a big smile while extending the pail in her direction.

This is one of our favorite meals! Mom dips the chicken in a special flour/spice mixture and cooks the chicken pieces in hot lard rendered from our pigs in the fry pan on the wood cookstove.

It tastes better than KFC.

Fridge/Freezer/Food:

We do not have a refrigerator or freezer.

In the summer, items are kept cool by placing them in a pail that is then dangled in the water well.

In the winter, a wooden box is situated outside next to the house for our items to be frozen. Every winter, Dad orders a crate of white fish from up north which is shipped by train. This box is settled next to our wooden freezer box.

We enjoy one of Dad's favorite meals from his dad's home country–English fish and chips. Mom prepares the fish in a flour mixture and fries it until it looks light and crispy and mouth-watering. We chew the tasty fish carefully, in search of tiny fishbones, which we place gingerly on the side of our plate. It is our dream that one day we can eat fish without bones.

A few years later we abandon the winter freezer box and instead store our meat in the Lussier Locker plant which opened in 1953. It is a refrigeration and storage establishment consisting of quick-freezing equipment with storage lockers in a big walk-in freezer rentable for stowing food. In addition to renting storage space, they operate a meat business. In 1959 it becomes Blackmur's Locker plant, and they add a café at the front. Mom and her friends gather together often for morning coffee and a piece of homemade pie – Mom always orders lemon pie.

Food is plentiful at our house. We have an abundance of potatoes; we consume them at almost every meal. They are served in a variety of ways–mashed, boiled whole, fried, French fries, scalloped, and in soup. French fries are cooked in an interesting manner. Mom takes the round lid off the cookstove and puts in a round pot that is set in the hole, with the edge of the pan clinging to the stove top. The cooking fat, which is rendered pig fat, is poured into the pot and when hot the potato strips are inserted. We douse the fries with vinegar and salt–delicious! Fried potatoes is a favorite. The potato is thinly sliced and fried in the cast-iron fry pan until brown and crispy. Scalloped potatoes are thinly sliced potatoes and onions layered along with sprinkles of flour, salt, and pepper and then all is smothered with milk and baked.

Our table is set with the normal condiments like salt and pepper, however, we automatically include sliced homemade bread at every meal. Dessert comes with every supper. We enjoy many varieties of fruit from Mom's canning. In addition, Blossom, our cow, provides milk for chocolate or vanilla pudding, and our chickens provide eggs for custards or cakes. We always have plenty to eat at mealtime and it sustains us until the next meal–we never consider having a snack in between meals.

Bread-day Monday:

Monday is a traditional day of wash clothes, bake bread, and simmer beans all day in the oven. We will consume fresh bread for supper along with bean soup, and in the evening, slip into bed with fresh sheets.

Washing clothes is now a luxury with the purchase of a Wringer Washing machine. It has as tub with an agitator to move suds within the laundry. The clothes are fed through a wringer to squeeze out the water and dropped into a square tub of rinse water. Mom swishes the clothes by hand in the rinse water and then feeds them through the wringer a second time. Viewing the laundry on the clothesline it is evident that whites are washed first, then light articles and finally the dark clothes.

Mom is up at the first light of day to brusquely mix, punch, and shape dough for bread before washing clothes. *Snap, snap, snap* is an indication the bread dough is at its peak. The snap of bubbles is another exciting sign. It indicates that fried bread is on the menu for lunch. This delicacy is prepared by taking a small chunk of bread dough, stretching it into a circular shape, and then gently laying it into hot fat in the frying pan. It puffs up and rises into crispy golden-brown cloud-like mounds. As we gather around the table our mouths sink into the crunchy, tasty, airy texture. It is so delicious.

Baking is a challenge. This is because the temperature varies depending on how blazing the fire is in the wood cookstove. The fire is constantly monitored to attempt to keep the oven at a steady temperature. The baking bread, along with the coffee pot which perks year-round on the back of the stove, emit a pleasing aroma.

Memories of these Mondays conjure up feelings of love, contentment, and happy times.

Supper Guests:

It is a common sight for friends to pop in for a quick visit during supper time. There is no advance notice as we do not own a telephone.

"There is always room for one more," comments Mom, as she quickly sets an extra plate on the table, and we squeeze our chairs together to make room for our guests. We have an abundance of food with our own pigs, chickens, turkeys, and a cow. Mom always cooks plenty so there is ample food for unforeseen guests. "Come on in," resounds many times in our household. We learn generosity and kindness by our parents' example.

Be the kind of person you expect of others, is a motto our parents teach us. Mom and Dad extend a warm welcome to everyone in our home. We children are expected to model their standard. On one occasion, we are seated cozily around the kitchen table, six in total. A couple appears for a visit and Mom shuffles everyone closer together, using the corner of the table to add two more plates. I was sure there was no room, but Mom made it work; we were squished together like sardines!!!

Guest Outhouse:

If in need of the toilet, our guests know to head outside to the outhouse, which is a tall and skinny rectangular building that houses a bench with a toilet seat. The waste is dispersed into a hole dug into the ground under the building. In the winter, a five-gallon pail comes into the house for a toilet, so we do not freeze our butts off outside. The bucket is placed in the back room encircled by a curtain wall. These are necessities in our life.

"Keep the old catalogue for the outhouse," exclaims Mom.

It's our toilet tissue! The old Sears or Eaton's catalogue is used for toilet tissue!

Many an outhouse is tipped over at Halloween, which is a favorite trick for the pranksters.

Chapter 30

Creative Games:

Creating games is our special gift.

Charlie, Chrissy, and I assemble in the granary, sitting in a circle on the grain, contemplating our next game. I suggest a brilliant game called The Queen.

"I am the queen of the shop, and you will be my subjects, who must follow my orders," I announce in an authoritative tone. My mind is on the plums, waiting for Mom to preserve. I continue in a queenly expression, "My first command is to go into the house and bring me a handful of fresh plums." Mom has just bought and stored the plums for canning the next day. She is preparing our winter supply of fruit.

My subjects scramble to fulfil their duty. I sit regally, awaiting their return. A short time later I hear a commotion outside. I peek out a crack in the open window.

"What are you two doing?" Mom asks Charlie and Chrissy on the walkway.

"Nothing," they reply in one voice. However, I notice Charlie awkwardly flapping his arm up and down like a duck. He looks guilty! Suddenly, the plums come tumbling out of Charlie's shirt—caught red-handed.

"If you want plums just ask. Don't be sneaky!" Mom states and adds, "Why can't you be good, like Julie!" I wonder, *Is this a ploy to get my siblings to confess that I am in on the event?*

I recoil and wince inwardly, realizing I led my siblings down the wrong path! I comprehend that this is all my fault. Fortunately for me, they do not tattle—it is our sibling's secret. I determine to live up to Mom's expectation and be a better example to my siblings.

It is not a surprise to me that my siblings did not tattle—we stand up for each other through thick and thin. We are loyal to one another, love each other, and are best friends.

Firewood Transformers:

Farm children are expected to undertake jobs at an early age; one of our jobs is to haul firewood into the house. Firewood is a necessity to keep the cookstove and heater fired up.

Dad brings firewood home from the lumber camp. The slabs of wood are unused pieces of lumber. They are derived from sawing the outside bark from the trees to produce logs. The slabs are then cut into small lengths for firewood.

"I can carry the most wood," insists Charlie. This becomes a game, to see who can carry the most wood in one armful. Our tiny hands pile as many cut slabs as possible in our arms and we stumble clumsily to the porch. We stack the wood in a neat row as high as our miniature bodies can stretch. Mom constantly pops her head out the kitchen door to check our progress.

"Wow, I am surprised. You have hauled so much wood—great job," she exclaims encouragingly.

We get side-tracked. Our gigantic woodpile invariably becomes a playground.

"Let's make roads with the wood," Charlie suggests. We begin to lay the slabs in long, flat rows to make roads. We hunker down to resemble cars and crawl along our newly laid road. We play for hours; however, in the end, we transfer *our roads* into the porch where it transforms into firewood once again. We built our very own *Transformers*. We learn from very young that inserting play into our work makes the job efficient, fast, and fun.

As we get a little older, we unload the wood at night. After a scrumptious supper we step outside in either the pitch-blackness or in the bright, moonlit night.

At the Woodpile

"How much wood can a woodchuck chuck, if a woodchuck could chuck wood?" we chant into the shadowy, tranquil darkness as we toss the wood briskly into the air onto the woodpile. Once the last piece of wood is chucked onto the woodpile, we clamber down from the truck and throw ourselves onto the snow.

We lie on our backs and make snow angels in the snow and gaze up at the stars and converse about the important things in our life. We discuss our friends, school, favorite teacher, hockey, and most important, what exciting events is on the horizon.

Snow is a part of our playground. In the mid '50's we had almost six feet of snow – it was so abundant that it caused our road into Weekes to be one big snowdrift. The Regina Leader-Post headline stated, *Storm Plugs Saskatchewan Roads*, and *Bus, Air Services Knocked Out*. The Snowplow rammed forcefully into the snow over and over and over again to pile it up on each side of the road - the snow stacked up to almost reach the top of the telephone poles. What a wondrous sight! We children revelled in climbing and playing on this *mountain* of snow. This was a momentous and memorable winter.

Mom, Kate, Peggy

City trip:

It is with great excitement that we look forward to a trip to Saskatoon. Mom and Dad have farm business to take care of and we will stay overnight in a hotel.

That evening after supper, our parents decide to go for a walk, and we are instructed to play quietly. Our parents leave the room and Charlie has a great idea.

"Let's ride the elevator," Charlie suggests. He no sooner utters the word than we are racing for the door. We push several buttons and take in the wonders of a moving cage. We visit several floors when suddenly, the door opens, and we are staring at the attendants at the front desk. Their faces initially convey bewilderment, immediately replaced by comprehension. The sight of us four children huddled in the elevator explains why the elevator indicator display has been showing so many movements between the floors.

"Oh no, they might tell on us," I sputter nervously. "We better get back to our room." We scoot back to our room and devise a new game to play.

In the meantime, our parents are returning from their walk when they notice a huge crowd gathered on the sidewalk, looking upwards at their hotel.

"I wonder what is going on," Mom exclaims to Dad.

They join the crowd and look upwards. Outlined in the windows, ten stories up, they observe children playing on the windowsill.

"Oh my gosh," Mom whispers to Dad. "It's the kids–let's get up there quick."

We children were not playing *on* the windowsill, we were using the windowsill as our launch pad to jump onto the bed! As my body is sailing through the air, aimed at the bed, the hotel door opens. My eyes widen in astonishment as I land with a soft thump on the bed–I am caught red-handed!

Our parents lecture us on the perils of playing on the windowsill and inform us of the huge crowd gathered below. We hurriedly run to look out the window and, sure enough, there is still a small group staring up in our direction. We wait to be reprimanded for the elevator riding–it does not happen. We are secretly pleased that the front desk staff did not squeal on our escapade. Once again–sibling secrets.

Chapter 31

Bus Driving:

"Bill are you be interested in driving a school bus?" asks Mr. Wallace, the Co-op store owner, and president of the Weekes school board. Mom and Dad discuss the possibility and decide it will be a great idea. This decision replaces Dad's job of laboring in the bush in the cold winter months.

My parents discuss the pros and cons of purchasing a new or used bus. It is decided they will acquire a new bus from an Ontario company. Dad will take the train and drive the new bus home.

Charlie gets to go! He is the lucky one to travel with Dad to Brantford, Ontario to pick up the new bus from the dealership. Upon their return, Charlie entertains us with his rousing stories of his exciting trip.

Dad beside his big Bus

We listen in awe. Charlie regales us with his travels–this trip turns him into a storyteller. Charlie tells how they spent three days on the train where you can move from railway car to another railway car. He laughs while explaining an incident at a service station. Apparently, Dad sent him in with twenty dollars to buy a couple of bananas.

"I forgot to ask for the change," Charlie informs us with a frown.

"That's a lot of money–what did Dad do?" I ask.

"Dad calmy said, 'Oh well, it is too far to go back,'" replies Charlie.

That totally makes sense to me, Dad doesn't sweat the small stuff.

"The Mackinac Bridge is a suspension bridge, five miles long. It is known as the Big Mac," Charlie explains and stretches his arms as wide as they can reach. I can see it all in my mind's eye.

"The most sensational part of the trip was touring the Great Lakes of Ontario," Charlie announces. I am so envious! Charlie continues, "I brought something back for you," and he offers each of us a pop bottle full of sand. I open my bottle excitedly and slowly pour some sand into my hands. It feels gritty as I swirl it around and let it slip between my fingers into my other hand. I imagine what the Great Lakes look like, with sandy beaches stretching for miles into the horizon. I gently replace the sand into the bottle. This is the best gift ever.

The brand-new bus smells wonderful and is pristine inside. Bus driving becomes a career to complement farming. Dad is such an excellent bus driver that Mom is offered a bus run too. Both parents are exceptional bus drivers. My parents love kids, which is a necessity in driving a school bus.

We children are free to take the bus if we feel like it. Sometimes, after school, I walk home with my friends and other times I hop on the bus. We feel special because we are the only ones allowed to randomly ride the school bus. It was like a feather in our cap.

Mom beside her Stationwagon Bus

On one occasion when Dad left to take his bus run early in the morning, he was surprised that there were no children at his first stop.

Why are the children not waiting? Dad wonders. He is surprised when the house door opens and instead of children flying down the driveway, it is their papa.

"Good morning, Bill, you are an hour early," is Papa's greeting. Apparently, Dad read the time in error upon leaving home. Papa continues, "Come in for coffee. It will be our pleasure." Thus, Dad enjoys this unexpected visit with friends.

Mom and Dad generously make an exception for one boy who is not on a designated bus route. He has several miles to walk to school; Mom and Dad arbitrarily add him to their route.

Mom and Dad drive school bus for seventeen years, at which time my brother, Charlie, takes over the bus runs.

Chapter 32

Christmas:

"Here comes Santa Claus pulling on the reins!" A magical parade down Weekes' main street creates a lull in the air–everyone is mesmerized by the wonderous sight.

What a vision, to witness six small reindeer–their heads tilted up like royalty, eyes shining brightly like brilliant stars, and their legs prancing delicately up and down in a dance to the rhythm of Santa's sleigh. Bells jingle sharply and melodically into the frigid air, a constant *ding-a-ling, ding-a-ling, ding-a-ling*, signaling Santa is in town. Santa, large as life, sits gallantly in the colorful sleigh, holding the reins in a practiced and professional manner. I envision him flying through the air later this month on Christmas Eve! I

Santa's Reindeer (Mr. J. J. Dalke with his Deer team)

crane my neck and move closer to the path as Santa raises his voice and shouts, "Ho, ho, ho."

My skin prickles as I gaze at the magical scene. I am oblivious to the cold. I clap my mittens violently as the enchanted image rushes past me within a couple of feet. My child's eyes absorb the wonderment of the moment. I am on cloud nine and will forever cherish this wonderful experience.

For many years, Mr. J. J. Dalke from Carragana decorated his Deer Team and sleigh to bring Santa Claus to many towns spreading Christmas joy. In 1944 J. J. Dalke was Santa with his Deer Team in the movie *Road to Utopia* with Bob Hope, Bing Crosby, and Dorothy Lamour. Mr. Dalkie travelled throughout Canada and the United States with his Deer Team.

After Mr. Dalke retired his Deer Team Santa found a new mode of travel. We witness Santa arriving in a great substitute. Mr. MacNaughton volunteers his Husky Team and toboggan for the parade. Santa arrives,

Santa's Husky team
(Mr. MacNaughton's Dog team)

decked out in his red and white suit, seated elegantly in his brightly colored toboggan-type of sleigh, being pulled by a pack of four huskies. The huskies sprint in unison along to the resonating sound of the jingling sleigh bells. We gather along both sides of the street and with thumping hearts we stare in excitement at the captivating scene. I believe in magic and can envision Santa flying through the sky with huskies on Christmas Eve!

Santa Day parade comes along with a free movie in Siery's Theater. After the parade we troop excitedly into the theater to watch a family movie. Upon exiting we are thrilled to receive a bag of goodies from the Ladies Club. I open my bag to view a luscious Christmas orange and a wide variety of candy! We clutch our bag of candy like a bag of treasure. This is one of my favorite days of the year.

Delicious aromas fill the air. Mom prepares our Christmas pudding in jars and Christmas cake several months earlier. The Christmas cake receives a good shot of rum! A couple of weeks prior to Christmas our home is filled with Christmas baking—mincemeat tarts, chocolate marshmallow slices, peanut butter slices, and gingerbread men emitting their sweet, spicy smell.

One year I hid my gingerbread man in the Christmas tree and then was so disappointed when I could not find it in the tree. *Did one of my siblings find my Gingerbread man?*

Typically, Santa brings one gift on Christmas Eve. For example, Charlie receives a toy tractor, Barry a toy car, and Chrissy and I a doll—surprisingly both dolls have blond hair. I am curious. *Why are there no black-haired dolls for my sister?* It isn't until several years later that Chrissy receives her doll with dark hair.

Charlie, Barry, Chrissy, Julie

The Big Gift:

"Who gets the big gift?" reverberates throughout our grade-three classroom. Our party will begin after first period in the afternoon. All us students stare in wonder at the numerous presents under the tree, deposited by my favorite teacher Miss Elsie Wallace. She bought everyone in the class a present—such a touching gesture.

She is my favorite teacher. She does several special things for me, so I know she likes me too! Our class ogles the one *big* box nestled amongst the smaller gifts. We gaze in awe. *Whose could it be? What could be in it?* We wait with bated breath, half listening to story time—a long half an hour. Our eyes are like saucers, staring in anticipation at that humongous box.

Finally, the story is finished. Miss Elsie Wallace begins to pass out her presents. Eventually, she approaches the big box to gently pick it up and turn towards the class. We are all agog while holding our breath in wonderment. *Who is getting this big box?* She walks slowly down my aisle. My stomach is all-aflutter, and my heart accelerates. I pray, *Please God, can it be for me?* She stops just short of my desk, and I clasp my hands tightly—my stomach plummets in disappointment. It is not for me. With a mysterious smile, Miss Elsie Wallace bends over and promptly sets the big box *on my desk*! My heart soars with delight and I have a look of wonder as I reach lovingly for the sought-after box.

The room is buzzing with excitement! Everyone is anxious to see what is in the box. I can feel the blood pumping through my heart as I surge ahead with nervous energy. With trembling hands, I slowly tear the Christmas wrapping paper away. Suddenly, the box is exposed, and a label jumps out with large red letters stating, *Bake Set*! It is all I ever wanted—a bake set! In awe, I feel a joy well up inside me as loud murmurings erupt in the classroom. My bottom lip trembles, my eyes well up with tears, and I clutch the box to my chest. Miss Elsie Wallace keeps a close eye on me; we exchange a knowing glance and a secretive smile.

There is no need for words. She is my favorite, and I am hers!

Christmas at home:

At home we open our gifts on Christmas Eve. After our evening meal, Dad always leaves the house to take care of an errand while we are eating dessert.

"Ho, ho, ho," booms a loud voice, coming from the direction of the living room. Following this is the sound of rustling bags, which causes a huge commotion. Our eyes dart excitedly at one another—we know that

Santa has arrived and is distributing our gifts. We remain glued to one spot, waiting for the next big moment. Dad arrives and we dance around wildly.

"Let's go check out if Santa has arrived," Dad announces breathlessly. Scrambling into the next room we come to a halt, in awe of the presents. I spy two big boxes under our Christmas tree. *Is one mine?* I wonder. It is! I am ecstatic to receive another bake set, and I meld the two sets together to make a giant bake set. *A child can never have too many bake sets!* Chrissy also receives a bake set. In addition, Chrissy and I receive our very own package of Aunt Jemima pancake mix. We will be baking up a storm! It is a magical Christmas. Charlie receives a Meccano set consisting of various miniature pieces - metal strips, angle girders, wheels, axles, gears, nuts, and bolts. Dad helps Charlie build a workable Crane standing almost three feet tall. Barry receives an electric Lionel Sears train set. Dad and his friend Dave assemble the track into a figure eight, set up the station, crossroads, and other train items. They demonstrate to Barry, Charlie and Lorne, Dave's son, on how to manage the controls. I watch them all huddled around the moving train and think, *The men enjoy the train set just as much as the boys!*

The tradition of Santa arriving on Christmas Eve continues. We get older; Barry, however, is young, so we pretend for his benefit! We watch with delight as his eyes widen with wonder and joy! In later years, Dad dresses up as Santa Claus for grandchildren. Our parents become like children at Christmas and enjoy the season just as much as the little ones.

Mom and Dad celebrate Christmas to the fullest, keeping in mind the true meaning is not in the presents but, in His presence.

Jelly Roll:

"Which are Mrs. Allen's sandwiches?" is a question voiced at many events. Mom's sandwiches, prepared with homemade bread and quite often egg-salad filling, are always a hit! She is known for her cooking and baking talent. Her goodies are always welcome. Mom supplies delicious provisions to the Ladies Club who host many occasions, including weddings, wedding showers, baby showers, turkey suppers, and all money-raising events

Thus, whenever I have the opportunity, I encourage my mom to bake. One such opportunity arises in grade four, when our class is organizing our annual Christmas party.

"Who can bring snack to our Christmas school party?" my grade-four teacher, Miss Elsie Wallace, asks.

I raise my hand quickly and answer, "I can bring jelly roll!" This elicits an audible gasp from the classroom–they all relish this delicious treat. Mom will not be surprised to learn that I have promoted her baking skills and offered to provide jelly rolls to my class. Upon arriving home, I eagerly dash into the house with my important news.

"You need to bake several jelly rolls for my school party," I inform Mom.

"You will need to help me," Mom replies with a smile. I help mix the batter and watch as she slathers a thick layer of homemade jam on the baked cake and roll it up tightly. It looks scrumptious. A few days later, I proudly arrive to the party with the famed jelly rolls.

"Your Mom's jelly roll is so delicious!" Miss Wallace comments.

I beam! Thanks to Mom I am famous for a day!

Chapter 33

Fire:

It is a cool October day—Mom and Dad are driving their bus run. Charlie and I arrive home from school to a very chilly house. The living room cast-iron heater needs to be lit.

"I can light the heater," Charlie proclaims.

"Good idea," I agree eagerly, knowing that my brother can do anything.

Lighting a fire appears easy. We have watched our parents prepare the fire many times—a little wood, a little gas, strike a match, and voila, the fire is lit. Charlie stacks several pieces of wood atop each other in the heater and puts in a splash of gas, and then another splash of gas, and then another splash of gas.

"Isn't that too much gas, Charlie?" I worriedly question.

"We just want to make sure that it will light up quick," he replies with a grin.

"Stand back," Charlie instructs. We expect a small *pouf* when the match hits the gas. Charlie lights the match, tosses it into the heater, and quickly jumps backwards. It ignites and detonates with a loud explosion that rocks the room.

The heater jolts erratically. It is bulging at the seams and vibrating wildly. A horrific flash of fire blasts into the room out of the open heater door in a stream of red-hot scorching flames. The smokestack damper shows flashes of fire, flickering frantically in and out of the openings. The heat is excruciating, and the fire is out of our control.

We freeze. Stunned, we stare in a state of shock with worry etched across our faces. Simultaneously we shift towards the door–braced, ready to run! I shudder and feel a flutter in my tummy; but I am mesmerized by the antics of the glowing and dancing fire shooting out of the front of the heater. We gaze at the ferocious flames–drawn to the bright, vivid colors.

Charlie grabs the poker. He creeps stealthily towards the scorching-hot heater with his weapon poised–he slams the front door heater shut with a resounding bang. The fire is locked in! I am amazed Charlie is so smart! Eventually the fire returns to normal. Thanks to the Lord.

We exchange glances. Our eyes lock and in silent communication we vow not to utter a word. We do not discuss the accident, we do not tell our parents, and we do not tell anyone, ever! Without discussion, we know that we would be reprimanded for not being more careful in lighting the fire and lectured on the correct way and safety aspects. The house burning down would be the least of our parents' worries–their biggest concern would be that we put our lives in danger. We know that keeping quiet is the best option–more sibling secrets!

Fire hazards are a common risk. Because we are so young, we don't always have a strong grip on the risks of poorly lit fires. On another occasion, two of my siblings grazed tragedy with a reckless flame.

"Don't light a fire by the house," I order Chrissy and Barry. They ignore me and continue to pile sticks together to build their bonfire, butted up against the house. I know this is a dangerous activity and they could burn our house down to the ground. Sibling secrets fly out the window when disaster is imminent.

"Chrissy and Barry have lit a fire by the side of the house," I blurt out to Dad.

Frowning at my outburst, Dad hustles out the door ahead of me. Chris and Barry glance up to see the flash of anger on Dad's face as he rounds the corner, and immediately their faces turn a sickly white. Dad rushes over and madly stamps the fire out with his boots, shoving the remnants far away.

"Do you realize that you could have burned the house down with that fire?" Dad addresses Chrissy and Barry in an angry voice. They are surprised and puzzled to receive a spanking. It will be the one and only spanking they ever receive.

That night, Dad takes us all to the dugout to demonstrate on how and where a fire can be lit. We listen intently to his lecture on the danger aspects and proper procedures when dealing with fire. Afterwards, we sit around the fire and have a wiener roast for supper. Dad teaches fire safety by implementing an enjoyable illustration. Dad believes that children learn by example. The fire lesson is imbedded in our minds forever.

Treasure Hunt:

A pile of ash is our treasure chest. Charlie's chore is to distribute the ashes from the stoves onto a spot at the edge of the bush line. The ash pile is transformed into a *Treasure Chest*.

Shovels are just a-flying! Digging into the ashes, the soot rises in a hazy cloud around and above our bodies. The more we dig, the thicker the cloud develops. We are oblivious to our frames turning white from the powder and continue to burrow into the ashes looking for our fortune. Our dog, King, is right along with us digging in the ashes.

We are covered in white soot. Entering the house, we wear a blanket of white dust encompassing our entire body.

"Go for a swim and afterwards pin your wet clothes on the line," directs Mom, upon glancing up at our pitiful sight. "And take King with you," she adds, upon noting that the black areas of his coat have turned white. Our parents never discourage us from our many adventures–they allow us children to be children.

Chapter 34

Saturday night:

"It's time to listen to the *Big Red Barn*," Mom shouts as she twists the dial on the radio on a Saturday night to propel a blast of music through the room. And with a shout of "Let's dance," she grabs Barry and swings rhythmically to the beat of the music. The living room is a hub of activity. Mom eagerly teaches us children to dance and to love music.

One, two, step, step, I chant over and over and over as I teach brother Barry the two-step. Our living room is just a-rockin'.

The following Saturday night, our parents go out on the town. They are dressed to a tee, with Mom looking beautiful and Dad handsome. We children exchange excited, knowing glances, *a treat is coming!* We know that there will be a bag of jellybeans or other treat for us to share the following morning.

"We bought each of you a box of Lucky Elephant popcorn, however they are in our car up town." Mom informs us the following morning.

"I will go get the popcorn," Charlie offers eagerly. He walks the quarter mile to town to fetch our treat. He has a trick up his sleeve! He sneakily opens all the boxes to peruse the best prizes! There is a method to his madness! Charlie garners the best prize for himself and allots Barry the second-best prize. I am onto his trick.

I am a little ticked off at Charlie. *Why give Barry the next best prize instead of me?* My annoyance does not stop me from enjoying my treat.

Saturday night is a special night in our household, either to have fun together or to envision a treat the next morning. We bond together as a family.

Rainbow vs Babysitter:

On the occasional weekend our parents have a date night and socialize in the community. Quite often they visit and play cards with Mom's cousin, Marge, and hubby, Dave. Their daughter, Verna, is our regular babysitter.

Verna is a friendly teenager who quite often stops in to have a chat with Mom. Verna is very mature and responsible – she agrees to babysit more because of her close relationship with Mom rather than wanting to care for us unruly children.

On one occasion, Verna receives permission to invite her boyfriend over while babysitting. We children badger them relentlessly.

"Verna has a boyfriend. Verna has a boyfriend. Verna has a boyfriend," we chant in unison. We continue to pester them mercilessly—to the point that they are unable to even talk to one another.

"Go and play," she demands over and over. We do not listen. In desperation, she takes desperate measures. She locks us out of the house! She expects to have some peace and quiet; undeterred, we bang on the doors, peek in the windows, and shout incessantly at them.

Finally, we devise a plan. Our technique to get inside the house will be through the one open window, which is small measuring one foot by two foot and located high on the living-room wall. Barry is the only one tiny enough to fit through the opening. We put our scheme into motion. Chrissy and I bang on the kitchen window to distract Verna and her boyfriend. Meanwhile, Charlie boosts Barry up on his shoulders and positions him at the upper window. Barry climbs through the opening and lands with a thud on the couch. All goes according to our plan as Charlie, Chrissy, and I zoom to the back door. Inside the house, Barry dashes to the back door and unlocks it. In a rush, we noisily stream into the room.

Verna's boyfriend is frustrated and leaves on the spot–he has had enough. Verna is furious with our unruly behaviour and at the end of her rope.

Verna is on the warpath! She comes up with a devious plan. A rainbow has appeared in the sky. I know the rainbow means that God will not flood the earth again. However, Verna tells us a secret about the rainbow.

"There is a pot of gold at the end of the rainbow," she informs us in a conspiratorial tone. She raises her right eyebrow dramatically and concludes in an excited voice. "The rainbow is close. Go get the pot of gold!"

Our feet hit the ground running. King is at our heels. The four of us are excited to reach the wonderful pot of gold! We dash over the field of stubble, enduring jabs of pain to our ankles. We are being poked by the stubble, which is cut stalks of grain remaining and sticking out of the ground after the grain is harvested. Regardless, we keep up our speed; but we do not seem to get any closer to the rainbow. It keeps moving out of reach! We keep running and persevere until the rainbow disappears.

We do not find the pot of gold, but our babysitter, Verna, finds peace and quiet! Verna has outsmarted us. Our lesson learned is that no matter how smart we are, we can always be up-staged.

Two-for-One Babysitter

An emergency has occurred, and our parents must be out of town overnight. Verna will be in charge of us children. However, Dad is worried about her being on her own overnight, so he asks John–who is Dad's right-hand man on the farm and has had prior experience taking care of us–to help with the babysitting and spend the night. Our parents have a high opinion of John and know they can rely on him.

Verna is very responsible with making supper for John and us children. We children behave much better with John present–perhaps because we grew up as neighbours and we view him as a friend and not a babysitter. At bedtime, Chrissy, Barry, and I are tucked into bed in the house; I am envious, however, of Charlie, who gets to sleep in the granary with John. I wish I could sleep in the granary. Dad designated them to sleep out of the house–thankfully, it is a warm night, and they sleep with the doors wide open.

Verna makes porridge for breakfast.

"This doesn't taste right," I grumble, as the horrible taste permeates my taste buds.

"Oh, I forgot the salt," Verna says, upon reading the directions. She continues, "We just need to sprinkle salt on top of the porridge." She grabs the saltshaker and generously scatters salt all over our porridge. I scoop a good spoonful into my mouth and force myself to swallow the contents. It is bland and tasteless. I look around the table to check the reaction of the others. Brother Barry is swiftly spooning the oatmeal into his mouth and in between mouthfuls he is smiling as if he is enjoying the food. John is also digging into the porridge without a complaint. *How can they eat it?* I wonder. *They act as if it is delicious!* I glance at Chrissy and notice that she is eating the contents of her bowl in much the same way as Barry and John–she must like it too. Charlie is frowning and swirling his spoon around in the bowl. He eats a small amount then pushes his porridge away, muttering, "I am full." I am in a dilemma. *Do I force myself to eat it? Do I say I am not hungry? Or do I tell Verna it is disgusting?* I opt to force myself to eat half the contents and, similar to Charlie, I mutter, "I am

Julie Grade four

full." I discern that it would be rude to complain or refuse to eat the porridge.

"Mom," I complain, "the porridge Verna cooked was awful because she forgot to add salt. I struggled to eat half of it anyway."

"You should be grateful that Verna cooked you breakfast," Mom replies, and smiles, adding, "and I am pleased that you did your best to eat the porridge." I learn that I should appreciate the fact that Verna made me breakfast and I also learn that I handled the situation correctly.

Verna was an excellent babysitter, and she knew how to handle us children. She was always kind, caring, and friendly to us children, whether at our house or out in the community. I admired and looked up to Verna and strived to obtain her good qualities.

To this day, when I indulge in a good bowl of porridge I think of Verna and our time together with warm affection.

Chapter 35

Mischief:

I had a wonderful day at school and am now walking home in a tight little group consisting of brother, Charlie, sister Chrissy, and two neighbour boys. Suddenly, the neighbour boys decide to implement some bad words into their conversation. I cannot believe what I am hearing. Charlie appears nonchalant. I, however, am aghast! Bad words or name-calling are not tolerated in our household. We are also taught to think before speaking because spoken words cannot be taken back. Therefore, Chrissy and I are not impressed with their behavior. We arrive home and dash into the house, eager to relay this upsetting situation.

"The neighbour boys used swear words on the way home today," we promptly spill the beans to Mom. She is like a mama bear protecting her children. The next day she trots to the school and reports the unruly incident to the principal.

I am summoned to the principal's office. I shrink in my boots at being ordered out of my class to face the *boss* of the school! I am embarrassed.

The principal indicates a chair, which I slink into and slouch down, trying to make myself invisible.

"Have any boys spoken bad words in front of you?" the principal asks as he towers over me. I shift uncomfortably, avert my eyes to the floor, and do not utter one word. I am speechless.

"You won't get into trouble—just repeat the words that they spoke," the principal encourages me in a soft-spoken voice. Overwhelmed and naturally shy, I remain quiet and silently ask God to get me out of this situation. I wish we had not told Mom. The principal utters, "You may go," and with a sweep of his hand he sends me back to my classroom.

Chrissy is next! She is summoned to the office from her grade-one classroom.

"Have any boys spoken bad words in front of you?" the principal asks.

"Yes, they did use bad words on the way home yesterday," she answers firmly, fixing him with a steady eye.

"Can you remember the words?" he asks gently.

Chrissy, with an expression of confidence, immediately opens her mouth and in a forceful voice blurts out every single bad word.

Chrissy must have felt a sense of freedom to blurt out the words, since it is not allowed at home.

The two neighbour boys did not walk home with us for several weeks. I assume they were reprimanded. I felt bad for getting them in trouble and I missed walking with them. I determined that I should also think before tattling!

Who did it?

We children have our share of troublemaking. Charlie, Chrissy, Barry, and I are lined up in the living room in front or our parents. We are all denying playing in the *seed* grain. Charlie and I are the culprits. I am hesitant to admit my part in the action because I knew better than to climb in the bin of seed grain—I learned this as a young child! I am therefore ashamed that I disobeyed. While I am pondering my next move, knowing I need to admit my guilt, I notice Dad reach into his pocket and pull out a coin.

"I will give a nickel to the one who did it," he announces, as he displays a nickel in front of our eyes. My eyes almost pop out of my head. This is highly unusual, and my mind is in a whirl trying to understand this strange move. Before I can analyze the situation, I feel the swish of air and a sudden brushing of movement on the side of my body.

"It was me!" Chrissy shouts, as she steps forward with her arm outstretched and hand upturned, awaiting the special gift.

Dad and Mom exchange knowing glances–obviously, they know it is not Chrissy. However, with a smile Dad gives her the nickel and we are dismissed. It all happened so quickly that I walk away still processing what just happened. I am guilty but escaped being reprimanded. It didn't seem right. I leave the scene puzzled. *Was Chrissy's admission courageously clever or foolish?*

Dad had a very easygoing manner and accepted that his children made mistakes. He had the mindset that we learn from our mistakes. Offering the nickel was his way of encouraging us to be truthful; however, that day it backfired. Our parents always saw the humorous side of the situation and this event was no exception. It was a future hilarious story to relate.

Admit it:

When an unusual situation presents itself, we siblings stick together.

"Scratch your design, too," Charlie suggests. We are at a picnic site near Hudson Bay, lounging in the log picnic shelter. I know I should not follow suit … however, I scratch my initials as best as I can into the log wall of the shelter. Chrissy follows our example.

"Charlie, come into the house," Mom shouts.

It is the next day and we are lounging under the cherry tree. We glance at one another in bewilderment. *What is the problem? Why does Mom sound upset?* A short time later, Charlie emerges from the house and is returning to our shady spot under the umbrella-like branches.

"Julie, come into the house," Mom calls in a determined voice.

"Just admit you did it and you won't get a spanking," Charlie whispers as we pass by one another. I step shakily into the house.

"Did you scratch letters into the wall at the picnic shelter?" Dad asks in a questioning tone.

"Yes, I did," I mutter meekly.

"You should not have done that, but you will not get a spanking since you were so honest!" Mom informs me. I breathe a sigh of relief and exit the house.

"Chrissy, come into the house," Mom calls in a much softer voice.

"Just admit you did it and you won't get a spanking," I whisper to Chrissy as we pass by one another.

We siblings stand as one and are each other's allies.

Part Five

Latter Childhood Years
Julie 9 - 10 years

Chapter 36

The Lumber Mill:

Lumber is a useful commodity on the farm. Dad builds many structures with regional wood, including our garage, our machine shop, our combine shed, the chicken coop, and our granaries.

The sawmill is situated in the upper right-hand corner of our twenty-acre yard. Large bandsaw blades cut the logs into lumber after the bark is removed. The lumber is then sent to the planer. The planer takes cut-and-seasoned boards and turns them into finished boards that are smooth and have a uniform thickness.

The lumber is layered. The wood is arranged and stacked in neat rows atop one another. The sawdust is shifted over to the side in neat piles. The area is well organized–Dad insists on a ship-shape farmyard. Farmers are bringing their logs to the sawmill to be cut into lumber.

Ever a caring and patient leader, my father directs his team efficiently. "John, please direct the farmers to unload their logs in their designated spot," Dad instructs teenager John.

"You will place your logs in this spot," John informs Farmer J.

"I will not put my logs in that spot," the unhappy farmer indignantly shouts, and storms away in a huff! The farmer marches to where Dad is standing. "That young whipper-snapper thinks he can tell me what to do!" the farmer laments in a loud, complaining voice to Dad.

"John is the yard foreman, so you will need to listen to him," Dad replies in a calm and even tone.

Dad is always fair and respects everyone, regardless of age.

The errant finger:

Dad and Joe Stad partner together to operate a sawmill on our farm. They are a good team, work well together and are very safety conscious. On this typical normal day the circular saw fires up and the air is disrupted with the screaming whine carrying its familiar sound in and around our farm.

Suddenly, an unfamiliar scream shatters the atmosphere. I crane my neck towards the sawmill where all has come to a dead silence. It is evident that a traumatic event has occurred at the sawmill. Dad is racing at a fast pace towards the house.

"Laura, grab a cloth. Joe has cut his finger off on the saw," he bellows into the silent, eerie stillness. Mom is outside hanging clothes on the line and immediately drops her basket of wet items to dash towards the house.

"I will get a towel," she screams in Dad's direction.

"Go to the sawdust pile and look for Joe's finger!" Dad hollers, upon spying us children nearby.

We are horrified by the shocking event but scamper off to do our ghoulish task. Joe is squatting on the ground, looking dazed, his one hand clenched over the other, with blood spurting messily through his fingers. Stupefied at the sight, we begin to scour frantically through the sawdust pile, secretly praying that we are not the one to find the errant finger.

Dad bundles Joe's hand tightly in a towel. The white towel becomes a brilliant red as they begin to move away from the sawmill. Abruptly, Dad bends down and picks up an object.

"I found it," he exclaims. It is Joe's finger!

Our job is done. We breathe a sigh of relief, glad it is the end of looking for that creepy finger. We wait in anticipation to learn if the doctors can reattach Joe's finger. It sounds like a miracle.

It is a no-go. Regrettably, the doctor is unable to reattach Joe's finger. From that day forward, whenever we see Joe minus a finger we are reminded of that frightful day. This is a fearsome First-Aid lesson.

Sawdust pile:

The humungous sawdust pile transforms into our giant playground. It is located in a spot several yards from the sawmill. My siblings and I have very creative minds as we wield our shovels, making mountains, roads, rivers, and houses.

Charlie's friend, Donald G who has a gentle nature often joins us in our adventures whether building sawdust tunnels or swimming in the dugout. Prior to setting up at the sawdust pile we were playing on top of the garage roof. While skittering across the roof Donald slipped and fell landing sprawled onto the hard ground. We scrambled down and rushed to his side – he was motionless and gasping for breath.

"Are you okay, Donald," I anxiously inquired. Donald cannot answer he is struggling to breath. After several minutes he is still gasping-I am genuinely worried and decide to run for help. At that moment Donald grunts and slowly raises his body into a sitting position.

"I am okay," he breathlessly utters, "I just had the wind knocked out of me." This is not the first time Donald took a spill. A couple of weeks ago Charlie and Donald decided to build a tree fort. They struggled valiantly to attach a piece of lumber with twine between two trees on solid branches. As soon as the board was secure, they clambered unto the piece of wood and sat basking in the beginnings of their tree fort. Suddenly the twine broke, their bodies hurtled into space hitting the ground in a resounding thud - instant pain radiated throughout their bodies. They abandoned the idea of a tree fort!

Presently, after Donald recovered from his unexpected tumble from the garage roof, we re-located to the huge sawdust pile.

"Let's make a long tunnel," Charlie proposes. Our shovels move on the double to pitch sawdust on the crest of boards, situated atop parallel rows of sawdust, three feet apart. We become architects, building long, deep tunnels, that lead to a small circular room. The conglomeration resembles a huge caterpillar.

The tunnel looks stable. Dad evaluates the set-up, and we receive the green light. Charlie and Donald enter one after the other and upon exiting exude exciting comments – it is Chrissy's and my turn. I am nervous to go into the burrow. Apprehensively, I enter the passageway and inch forward at a crawl with my insides quivering nonstop. Breathing rapidly, I detect the *thump, thump, thump* of my pounding heart. I am afraid of this deep abyss! I move slowly into the pitch-black until it is dark all around and impossible to see the passageway. My hands flail frantically in and around, discerning the pathway.

Time moves at a snail's pace. Finally, relief floods through me—I have reached the little chamber. There is only room for one person in the lengthy tunnel so I must wait for my sibling to arrive. My mind imagines the worst. *What if the structure falls on top of me?* I am desperate to get out of this black cavern. I pray, *God, help me.*

My prayer is answered. Chrissy arrives, and I scramble to quickly exit the little space. My knees shift swiftly to a steady rhythm. *Go. Go. Go.* I round the dark corner and zip towards the light at the end of the tunnel. Gratefully, I emerge into the bright sunshine to inhale a deep breath of the precious open air. I am thankful that the Lord has kept me safe.

"That was a piece of cake," I utter bravely. My mind, in contrast, muses, *I don't want to go in that deep abyss again!* That summer, however, I fearfully enter the dreaded tunnel many times, along with my siblings.

Today, I am claustrophobic. I wonder why?

Chapter 37

Mountain Climbing:

"Throw the rocks on," shouts Charlie. Mountain climbing is our goal, and we are building our mountain.

Inspired by a movie–*The Mountain*, with Spencer Tracy and Robert Wagner (1956), an exhilarating show–Charlie, Chrissy, Barry, and I are determined to climb our very own mountain.

We are undertaking a daunting project. Our soon-to-be mountain is located on the hill adjacent to the dugout. With blood, sweat, and tears, my siblings and I struggle every day, throwing rocks onto our pile. It is getting higher and higher and higher.

"Here's a big rock," I shout, as I flex my muscles and toss the stone up, up, up to the top of the mountain-in-the-making. Abruptly, a rumbling, jarring noise erupts into the air and the rocks come crashing down in a torrent. We are in the danger zone! "Watch Out!" I yell, and scramble away. There is no time to pray–action is needed. Hastily, my siblings scatter to avoid the volcanic eruption. We are safe; we stand-stock still, stunned,

146

gawking in amazement and disappointment at our precious mountain in disarray.

"Shall we tear it down to the ground and build it back up with a more solid base?" we contemplate. Realizing that we have bit off more than we can chew, we accept the futility of our dream. Even though we have the desire, strength, time, and energy, we cannot complete our goal to climb our own mountain.

We propose finding a new dream. Childhood and imagination go hand in hand. We have big dreams, and a world of fun and adventure awaits us—we know we can always find a new dream.

Kitchen skating:

Charlie, Chrissy, Barry, and I are great playmates. When our parents leave us on our own, we come up with many creative activities. One of our favorite games is to build a skating rink in the kitchen! It is an easy set-up.

"Let's move the kitchen table and chairs into the living room," Chrissy suggests. Charlie grabs a pail, marches to the water barrel to fill it with water and tosses the liquid across the linoleum floor. When the floor is swimming in water, we whip off our shoes and socks and begin water skating. *Voila*, our very own water skating rink.

Whoop, whoop, whoop echoes through the air as we skid across the kitchen floor.

"I can twirl like a figure skater," I shriek. Our feet zoom from one end the kitchen floor to the other. We twirl in the centre of the floor as we demonstrate figure skating tricks. We clutch brooms and mops to play hockey with a dishrag. Water flies upwards in a whirl and splashes everything in sight. The kitchen cupboards that Dad designed and built for Mom is dripping in water.

After our fun is over, we mop up the floor, the walls, the cupboards, and counter. Finally, we replace the table and chairs. It is siblings' secrets once again.

"We scrubbed the kitchen floor for you today," we announce upon Mom's return home. Mom is delighted.

"You are such thoughtful and good children. We are so proud of you." Mom pours on the praise.

To further raise our good character, *we promise to scrub the floor more often*!

Music is in our bones:

Sometimes planning an activity is as much fun as the actual event. One such favorite endeavor for Chrissy and I is our very own talent show. Our inspiration comes from an exciting evening of attending the Country and Western Show performed on the stage in Siery's Theatre. During the performance I am glued to my seat mesmerized at the antics on stage. A Cowgirl is prancing to a lively tune in her flashy outfit: white cowboy boots, red cowboy hat, red and white dress with long white tassels twirling to the beat. Her legs are stepping briskly like a marching toy soldier and her eyes are peeking over her shoulder while singing "I was looking back to see if you were looking back to see if I was looking back to see if you were looking back at me." Strutting close behind her is a Cowboy dressed all in black: boots, cowboy hat, pants, and shirt with whirling black tassels. The cowboy is grinning wildly with a twinkle in his eyes. Suddenly they switch directions, and the cowboy is glancing over his shoulder and singing the same words to the cowgirl. The mood is magical. An event forever embedded in my soul.

Thus, Chrissy, and I spend several hours preparing our very own talent show. We start with choosing our song pieces and choreographing in-sync dance moves. Next, we wind up the gramophone to practice our shuffling steps in coordination with our singing voices. The gramophone is a tall oak cupboard which houses records and the top opens to reveal a phonograph. It has a crank handle that must be wound up to turn the cylinder which plays the 33 rpm records on the turntable device. A small needle fits into the groove on the record and while it is spinning music disperses into the air. We prepare our stage – our double bed – with chairs set in a straight line at the footboard.

"We are almost ready," I exclaim excitedly to Chrissy. "You make the tickets for the show, and I will make the popcorn." She begins her task ripping a sheet of paper into tiny pieces and writing a number on each.

"Pop! Pop! Pop!" resonates from the cast iron frypan as the corn kernels explode in the midst of my shaking the pan vigorously on the hot stove. Removing to add the salt, I moan inwardly spying many burnt kernels; regardless, I fill the cups to brimming with both the good and the bad popcorn.

"Let the show begin," I shout to our expected audience.

"I will sing and dance the first act while you crank the Gramophone," I suggest to Chrissy.

Our clients arrive. Chrissy collects tickets from our parents and siblings, hands out popcorn and then with a swing of her arm she winds up the Gramophone. As the strains of music fill the air I glide in, leap up on the stage and begin my performance dancing and singing to the rendition of Standing on the Corner by The Four Lads. The bed is excellent for increasing the bounce to my whirling frame. Next Chrissy and I perform a duet to Rubber Dolly by Roy Hall – we confidently gyrate our bodies in unison and swing a doll to and fro to the rhythm of the music. Our actions portray professional dancers and singers. After a round of enthusiastic applause from our audience we tidy the room. I am amazed that the popcorn cups are empty, *our audience must have enjoyed the burnt popcorn, too.*

Several years later we include our brothers in our singing group; but we only perform when our parents are absent.

"Let's play our Band," I announce enthusiastically to my siblings.

We have our routine down pat. Charlie grabs the corn broom – his guitar, Chrissy and Barry retrieve a pot and a big spoon – their drums, and I grab two tablespoons – my castanets. I saw our parents' friend play the spoons one evening while visiting and I watched intently to decipher his technique. Thereafter, I practiced and practiced and practiced until I mastered the method.

With our instruments in hand, we zip into our parents' bedroom where I sit on the small bench in front of the bureau - a 1940 waterfall vanity housing a middle small drawer at the bottom of the dip, two drawers on each side and a large round mirror atop which is perfect for our entertainment.

My siblings gather around me. We look in the mirror, strike a pose and lead with a good rendition of Bye Love by The Everly Brothers. Chrissy and Barry bang on the pots – it is so deafening the noise almost drowns out the clinking of my spoons. The guitar makes no sound; however, Charlie makes up for it by belting out the song at the top of his lungs. We represent a rock and roll band singing a country song. In the midst of singing at full volume *Hello emptiness* – a silhouette appears at the bedroom door. We freeze instantly to stare at Charlie's friend, David who is standing with a look of disbelief on his face. The silence is deafening!

"I knocked and no one answered," David utters. "Who are you trying to be – a famous band or what?" he asks grinning wildly.

Charlie and I glance at each other in the mirror and my eyes signal, *He is your friend do something.* Charlie with a silly grin hands his guitar to Chrissy and walks toward his friend, David with Barry close at his heels.

"Oh, we are just goofing around," Charlie explains as he leads David away. My thought, *Thank goodness it is only David.* He is like a brother because he spends a lot of time at our house chumming with Charlie. In later years Dad teaches him to drive the farm machinery. He works diligently and has a caring nature. One time I cooked macaroni and cheese for lunch; however, after I added the cheese sauce, I forgot to turn off the stove. Thus, my entrée became a clumpy mush.

"The pigs won't even eat this," brother Charlie blurts. Of course, Dad reprimands immediately.

"Just be thankful Julie made lunch," Dad declares and then follows with his favorite saying, "If you can't say something nice than don't say anything at all!"

"This is really good, Julie!" David utters. He heroically saves the moment while heartily jabbing a good portion of macaroni on his fork.

Our families are close, David's brother Robert is Barry's friend and his Mom, Phyllis is close friends with our Mom. Phyllis came to Mom's aid when Dad was in the Saskatoon Hospital. Mom was nervous alone in the city and suspected that someone was entering into her rented room, therefore Mom asked Phyllis to come stay with her. Phyllis arrived and suggested that Mom leave, and she would hide in the bathroom to prove that no one was sneaking into the room. After several minutes Phyllis heard someone enter the apartment, her heart rate jumped erratically and, in a panic, she flung open the bathroom door. Standing in the middle of the room was the landlady – caught red-handed. The landlady mumbled something about checking the power and exited in a rush. Phyllis stayed with Mom until Dad was released from the hospital. This is what friends do for one another when the need arises.

Years later, David summed up his relationship with the words, "This was my home away from home."

Chapter 38

Farm animals:

In the earlier days, Mom shipped milk and cream produced on our farm in five-gallon aluminum milk cans. This increased their income at the time; however, with four children, we now use all the milk and cream for our own consumption.

Milking our cow, Blossom, happens in the wee hours of the morning. Mom's hands grasp the cow's udders to expel milk, while she keeps a watchful eye in case a leg rises to kick the bucket.

"Easy girl," Mom murmurs as she gently pats Blossom's backside. Charlie, on the other hand, creates a game while performing his milking chore.

Our cat is in for a treat. We raised her from a baby and call her Kitty.

"Here Kitty," Charlie calls, as he aims the cow's teat at our Kitty-cat and dispenses a flying stream of milk. The cat knows the game. As the milk flies through the atmosphere Kitty opens her mouth wide in anticipation.

If the aim is good, she gets a mouthful of milk; otherwise, she licks her lips to retrieve the milk dripping down her face.

The milk needs to be churned. The milk separator is a centrifugal device that separates milk into cream and skimmed milk. It has conical discs that rotate in a drum at a high speed, forcing the milk to run through the holes of the discs. The skim milk goes to its outer edge because it is heavier, and the fat globules go to the centre of the drum extracting the cream. The job for us children is to whip the handle around and around and around in a flurry, to create the high speed required to separate the cream from the milk. As I turn the crank, my arm aches with the effort. It is a strenuous job.

"Everybody takes a turn," Mom instructs. We are taught teamwork and learn that many hands make quick work.

Blossom Ride:

Could Blossom be ridden like a horse? I ponder this on a hot summer day. I decide to test my theory. Positioning a stump beside Blossom, I step up and fling myself upwards to land on her back.

Blossom bolts! She takes off like a shot and my smallish body is tossed ferociously up and down, jarring my innards. In no time at all I am airborne, flying through the air at tremendous speed. My belly flips crazily, and I land with a harsh thump on the solid ground. Stabbing pain shoots up my back as I lie stunned on the dirt floor. I move slowly, checking for broken bones, and water springs into my eyes. *Why did I do this?* This reminds me of the incident long ago when Charlie and I hitched the little red wagon to the cow's tail. *I should have known better*, I muse. I determine that I will not sit and cry; I pray, *God help me move.* I shift my aching body slowly. Grunting in agony, I struggle to my feet. Hobbling around all day, I suffer in misery and in silence.

Riding Blossom is not a good idea—a cow is more difficult to ride than the pigs.

Pig Rodeo:

Pigs provide food for our family. We fatten them up, and then slaughter the pigs for our own meat; pork is plentiful. Our lard is derived from rendering the fat by cooking the skin and fat in a large vat on the stove. The liquid remaining is our supply of lard. The skin transforms into a crispy, crunchy, tasty morsel. We can only consume a small amount, however, or we will get sick from the richness.

"Let's ride the pigs," suggests Charlie. Our parents are not close by; my siblings and I are all game. Our adventurous spirit is in full gear.

Perched on the fence near the pigs' food trough, we wait for them to approach. Whichever pig comes close—that is the pig we ride.

Mom and Dad with piglets

"This one is mine," I shout, at seeing a pig out of the corner of my eye heading in my direction. I focus on my next step. Leaning way over, I wait for the perfect moment and then quickly pounce onto the slow-moving pig's back.

The pig flees. Emitting a loud squealing sound, the pig charges forward in a mad dash. I clench my teeth, and clutch onto the pig for dear life. The pig is grunting and stampeding; my body is jerking and snapping like a jackhammer. With all the jostling to and fro my body is slowly shifting to the side; my fingers grip desperately to the pig's skin. The next moment, I am flying through the air to land with a tremendous splat straight into the muck.

I am thankful that the squishy sludge makes for a soft landing; looking down, however, I view my body and clothes—full of filth!

"Let's go swimming," I yell to my siblings.

Unbeknownst to us, Charlie, Chrissy, and I have created our very own challenging rodeo!

Chapter 39

Racist:

My sister Chrissy is as dark as I am light; however, when we look at each other we don't notice any differences. She is just my kind, caring, and loving sister. Chrissy has an easygoing personality and just goes along with the flow.

We are heading to the playground at Greenwater Lake.

"Race you to the playground," I shout to Chrissy. Several minutes later she is on the swing, chatting to another little girl.

"I will just run to the restroom and come right back," I told her. On my return, Chrissy is sitting on her own, looking forlorn and puzzled. "What's the matter? What is wrong?" I query.

Apparently, Chrissy and the little girl were playing together when the mother arrived–she grabbed her daughter by the arm and pulled her off the swing.

"You can't play with an Indian," she angrily told her daughter.

"Julie, I looked and looked and looked, but I can't see an Indian," Chrissy blurts out, mystified. I am shaken to my core, and I feel my blood pressure rising. Opening my mouth, no words come forth—I am speechless.

Suddenly, Chrissy's face pales and I realize the light bulb has come on. Comprehension flickers across her face.

"Were they talking about me?" she asks, with her voice quavering. Chrissy is aware of her darker complexion; this, however, is her first experience with bigotry. I am irate.

"I do not know, and I don't care. Let's go play," I answer, in a flash of anger. I wrap my arm around her, she clings to me, and we walk as one.

I am shocked at the display of such outright rudeness. Resentment burns within. Such outrageous behavior is not tolerated in our family. We are taught that we are all equal in God's eyes. I hope this does not leave a lifetime scar on my sister's heart.

Skin color:

"Why is your sister darker than you?" questions a girl who is huddled amongst a group of kids at the multi-town school Sports Day. My mind is in a quandary. *What a strange question. We all know my sister has darker skin than me, so why question the fact? The color of her skin has nothing to do with who she is as a person.* She is my sister, and this is normal in our family.

"Why would you want to know?" I ask in a hesitant voice. The group grins, as if they are really enjoying this encounter.

"It is questionable on how a dark child ends up in your family?" one of the girls replies snidely.

It takes a moment for her words to sink in and I am enraged. I am puzzled at how they can be so cruel. On the other hand, I am on the warpath, and I glare in their direction. No one is allowed to be negative about my family.

Chrissy

"Leave me alone or I will get my big brother to beat you up," I answer in a low but threatening tone. My brother can and will handle them easily. And they know it, too! Immediately, with a look of uncertainty, they button their lips and not another word is spoken. Deliberating on their instant change in attitude I reflect, *I will use that threat again!* Unbeknownst to Charlie, he comes to my rescue again.

Chrissy endured many teasing incidents regarding her skin color throughout the years. She would think, *Why do they pick on me?* Many times, Charlie and I came to her aid, standing up for her and letting her know that she was not alone. Even though I was on the shy side, my bravery came rushing forth when my siblings were in need. Chrissy knew she could count on us to protect her. We encouraged her to speak back by saying, "Sticks and stones may break my bones, but words will never hurt me." Chrissy often pretended that the teasing meant nothing, however, it hurt her deeply.

Today, she looks back and realizes that teasing was commonplace and that it is continues today. She says that all we can do is to teach the young ones to be compassionate and to be more tolerant to the social differences in individuals and groups. I agree!

Chapter 40

Picnic at the lake:

This racial incident does not mar the enjoyment we have at Greenwater lake.

Sunday is a *break* day. Greenwater Lake, an hour away, is on the agenda.

"Go to the garden and gather lettuce, green onions, and radishes," instructs Mom. We children scramble to assemble the salad items. Meanwhile, Mom packs homemade bread, fresh chicken, homemade cookies, and spice cake with peanut butter icing and all the fixins.

"Lunch is ready," shouts Mom. Fried chicken aromas waft through the air. The chicken is cooked in the outdoor kitchen, situated close to the beach, in an open pan on the wood heater. People sniff the air and drool

Dad, Barry, Julie, Chrissy at Greenwater Lake cabin

for our fried chicken. They wish they were us!!! We, of course, take for granted that we are eating a meal fit for a king.

"Are you willing to take my children for a ski in exchange for gas money?" Dad asks a friendly young man. Dad is eager for us children to learn to water ski, but we do not have a boat. This does not deter Dad. His motto is: *Where there is a will there is a way.*

"It was easy," are Charlie's first words upon arriving back from his ski event. He continues, radiant, "What a great feeling. I was flying through the air."

The challenge is on! I am nervous but slip on the skis shakily. My tummy is all a flutter as I grasp the ski handle firmly. I wiggle my toes, and my feet shift inside the boots, which are too big. Nevertheless, I manage to rise out of the water and soon find myself skimming over the lake at great speed. I am jubilant and feel free as a bird with the water swirling all around me. My body sails smoothly through the air–I am weightless; my inner being reflects, *Oh what a glorious feeling.* I will always remember that first ride, flying freely through the air behind the boat. We ski behind many a stranger's boat in the future–with Dad bargaining with gas money.

Julie, Mom, Chrissy, Barry

Most years we spend a week camping at Greenwater Lake. One year we had the pleasure of living in luxury by spending a week in the Greenwater Lake log cabins. The cabins are situated in a row and ours was located in the middle of the row.

On one occasion Chrissy and I were racing back from swimming in the lake to tell Mom that our friends had just arrived at the beach. Chrissy was ahead of me, she swung the door wide and sprinted inside, shouting, "MOM." Suddenly, both of us stumbled to a screeching halt, freezing in position. We gaped in astonishment to see a strange woman standing in our kitchen. The stranger lady looked surprised and frightened, her mouth hung open speechless! Suddenly, the lightbulb came on and I realized that we were in the wrong cabin.

"Chrissy, come on," I screeched, as I grabbed her arm and yanked her back out the door. Once safe inside our own cabin, we broke into peals of laughter. From that moment on, we paid close attention to which cabin we entered.

Our typical accommodation is the tent. Dad is a bit of a tease and will take advantage of a situation to pull a trick or two. One year, Chrissy was helping Dad set up the tent. Once the tent was erected, they entered the tent. Dad could not open the screened window from inside the tent. "Go outside and lift up the window screen cover so we can get some fresh air inside the tent," Dad asked Chrissy. She strolled outside the tent and carefully rolled up and tied the screen cover. Suddenly, Chrissy heard a loud commotion coming from inside the tent.

"Quack. Quack. Quack," pierced the atmosphere.

Embarrassed, Chrissy quickly glanced around; the other campers were staring in her direction. Feeling a hot redness creep up her neck, she whipped around and dashed to the door of the tent. She scrambled through the tent opening and flew through the air, to land with a thud on the canvas floor. Dad chuckled gleefully at his own joke, an expression of delight on his face. Chrissy was not impressed, but later it became her favorite story. A family who laughs together bonds together.

Chapter 41

Bikes:

I wish I could have a bike. I could ride to school, I could ride to town, I could zip everywhere in record speed, if only I could have a bike, I daydream. I know this is an impossible wish because with four children it will be too expensive! My parents will not buy just one bike, it is one for each or none at all! We learn at an early age that fairness is upheld in our family.

"One hundred and one. One hundred and two. One hundred and three," I count, as I skip rapidly on the road. I switch my skipping steps sporadically. The roar of the truck, culminating in a screeching halt with gravel scattering about, interrupts my skipping game. I come to a standstill and jerk my head up to see Dad hop out the driver's door and take a running jump upwards into the truck box. *What is Dad doing?* Suddenly my heart accelerates when I see Dad lift a big bike into the air.

"I was at an auction sale; I bought bikes," Dad shouts enthusiastically.

Goosebumps erupt on my arms. I drop my skipping rope and break into a mad dash, along with my siblings. I feel a flutter in my stomach. *Is this bike for me?*

"Charlie, this bike is for you," Dad says, as he extends the bike in Charlie's direction. Charlie eagerly grasps the bike, hops on, and wheels away. A shiver of apprehension overcomes me as Dad bends over to grasp another item. It is a tricycle. Disheartened, I know this is not for me!

"On this trike, Chrissy, you will drive, and Barry will ride on the back," Dad addresses my younger siblings as he places the tricycle on the ground. Chrissy hops in the driver's seat and Barry stands behind on the runner. They are thrilled; they happily pedal away on the road.

Barry, Chrissy, Julie, Charlie on new second-hand bikes

There are no more bikes. Dad glances at me and my heart plummets into despair. *I do not get a bike.* Obviously, there was not a bike for me at the auction sale. I drop my head and my lips curl into a pout.

"Julie, this bike is for you!" I shriek in delight as Dad's words wash over me. I tilt my head up to see Dad slowly lowering a medium-sized bike. I am ecstatic. My insides swell with excitement, and I am teary-eyed with gratitude. My prayers have been answered. I did not need an expensive bike; a secondhand bike is excellent in my eyes. I have never seen a medium-sized bike before—it is perfectly wonderful and perfect for me.

I am anxious to show off my bike. The following morning, I ride my bike to school. Pedaling up to the front doors, I feel like royalty; with head held high, I gently park my precious prize in the bike rack.

"It is tiny," "It is so cute," "It is adorable," are comments from my peers. They are all agape at such a small bike. They have not seen such a small bike either.

A big boy approaches my bike. Warily, I watch his every move. Suddenly, he pounces on my bike and bounces, up and down, up and down, up and down. I am aghast!

"Please, get off my bike," I ask. He refuses. I am naturally shy and am afraid to demand he stop. He continues his malicious antics and does not budge an inch. I am in despair. *What can I do?* I rush into the school.

"A big kid is sitting and bouncing on my bike," I anxiously blurt to my teacher. She steps outside swiftly; the big boy has disappeared. I am upset and perplexed—he is getting away with ruining my bike.

From that day forward I rode my bike lots—but, never again to school!

A Telling Off:

"Run uptown and purchase a brick of Neapolitan ice cream," Dad instructed.

"Oops, I almost dropped you," I mutter to sister Chrissy. We are peddling towards town, with Chrissy perched precariously on the crossbar of my bike. She sways awkwardly while I pedal madly.

Chrissy is clutching the thirty-six cents, making it a little difficult for her to hold a good position., We continue our mad dash towards town. We are excited; the ice cream will be divided equally into six portions. Unmindful that we are wobbling unsteadily on the sidewalk, we cheerfully discuss the various colors—vanilla, strawberry, and chocolate. We will get a bit of each flavor.

Suddenly, we are engulfed in a cloud of dust. A vehicle pulls to a screeching stop, with gravel spattering on the road beside us. Mr. S hops abruptly out of his driver's door and raises his arm in our direction, with his finger waggling. Puzzled, I halt, jump beside my bike, and look at him with a quizzical expression. *What is wrong?*

"Do not ride double on the bike–it is dangerous," he shouts, and continues to shake his finger rapidly. Stunned, we are silent and motionless. Mr. S returns to his vehicle, leaving us in stupefied silence.

Anger overtakes our shock. *Who is he to tell us anything? He is not our parents and it not his bike!* As far as we are concerned, we can do whatever we want–and we choose to double on my bike. We continue to double-ride on my bike.

"We were scolded for no good reason," we announce to our parents upon arriving home. Angrily, we relate the whole horrible incident.

"You should be thankful. Mr. S stopped because he cares about you and wants to keep you safe," Dad calmly replies after our outburst. The sting of truth in his words cause us to grudgingly agree and wish we had listened to Mr. S.

Everyone takes care of each other. We live in a small town, and it is like a huge family raising children. I realize that everyone in our little village of Weekes watches over, takes care of, and protects each other. This is what our small town does.

Chapter 42

Ailments:

It is trick-or-treat night and I am suffering with an earache.

Mom administers a home remedy. The only time we see a doctor is for emergencies or to get a tooth pulled. Mom is very adept at nursing–especially earaches, since sister Chrissy is prone to them. Mom soaks a cotton ball with camphor oil and places it into the painful ear.

How does my sister handle so much pain? I wonder. The agony of an earache hits home when I develop a piercing throb within my ear on–of all nights–Halloween night. I am too sick to go trick-or-treating. I am sad. The discomfort prevents me from participating in one of the most anticipated fun-filled events of the year. I am not sure what hurts more–my ear, or not being able to partake in the evening's activities. I listen to my siblings clomp out the door while I lie on the living room couch with my head propped up on a pillow, painful ear, housing a camphor-oil-filled cotton ball, aimed at the ceiling.

My mind drifts back to the year prior at Halloween. That night upon arriving home with candy filled pillowcases my siblings and I were amazed to see our mother dressed very strangely. She wore a red and white checked shirt tucked into baggy pants held up by blue and white suspenders and her hair was swept up into a man's grey Tweed flat cap.

"What are you doing, Mom?" I asked.

"Oh, my friends and I are pulling a Halloween prank," she giggled and continued. "We are going into Stinka's Pub for a drink." Her face radiated a mischievous sly grin. I glance around at Mom's friends Kate, Peggy, and Annie and I can hardly recognize them wearing an array of men's clothes with their hair tucked up in caps.

"But women are not allowed in the Pub." I utter with a gasp. I am shocked. Prior to 1960 women were not legally allowed to drink in Public places. By the time women are allowed inside it will be Matvenko's Pub.

"I know," replied Mom grinning from ear to ear. "It will be quite the trick!"

I wave goodbye while silently contemplating, *Will they enter George Cunningham's Pool Hall and Barbershop? It is a gathering place for men, too.*

Mom and her friends enter the Pub giggling like schoolgirls. Ignoring the scrutinizing eyes of the male clients, they march confidently to the middle of the room, occupy a table and order a round of beer. The Bartender, grinning from ear to ear serves the beer to their table. Soon the room is buzzing and amidst chuckles and out-right laughter many patrons offer to buy them a round of beer. Apparently, everyone had a fantastic fun evening. The next day, my Mom and her friends were the talk of the town!

I smile in remembrance quite forgetting for a moment about my painful ear.

Suddenly the door opens and my sibling's troop in, with pillows cases bulging at the seams. They have taken in a good haul of candy. I am jealous.

"You must all share your candy with Julie," Mom announces. It warms my heart as my siblings dump their bags of goodies on the floor in front of my inert form sprawled on the couch.

"Julie, take whatever you want," Chrissy states, while Charlie and Barry nod in agreement. Their sharing demonstrates their caring of me! My heart is full and overflows with love for my siblings.

Ether again:

"The lump needs to be removed," Mom explains, and continues, "You will need to go to the Porcupine Plain Hospital for surgery."

"Why do I have a lump under my arm?" I question.

No one is sure why! I am at the hospital and in record time I am lying on a gurney in the operating room.

"Count out loud," instructs the nurse, as she places a mask over my face.

"One, two, three," I count, as I inhale the vapors and smell the familiar aroma of the ether. I awake in a hospital bed in a room shared with three other ladies. The nurse arrives, and I am bewildered when she begins to pull something out of my wound. *Why is she pulling my insides out? I worriedly wonder.* This was a time when it was sometimes deemed unnecessary to explain procedures to children. I turn my head to take a quick look and notice it is a long, thin piece of cloth she is withdrawing out of my wound. It hurts! *What is she doing? Why is there a strip of cloth in my wound?* Thankfully, she is done, and leaves the room. A short time later, I hear a shout far down the hallway.

"Julie," someone shouts.

"What?" I respond loudly. No one answers. I bellow a little louder, "What?" I am puzzled when no one answers. *Why is someone calling me?* I am in too much pain to crawl out of bed to find out who is calling for me. I strain my ears for an answer; eventually I settle back, in a quandary.

Mom and Dad arrive for a visit, and I blurt out the episode of someone calling me and not responding to my reply. Mom and Dad exchange a knowing look.

"There is a nurse on staff whose name is Julie. They were probably calling for her and not you," Mom informs me with a smile.

I now understand and feel foolish for shouting, "What?"

My parents distract me from my fretting by discussing the happenings at home.

"We just bought a new mattress for you and Chrissy's bed," Mom exclaims. I envision the scene.

"Did the kids jump on the mattress?" I ask excitedly.

My parents exchange a meaningful glance.

"They sure did." Mom replies.

Obviously, they did not want to disappoint me! My imagination outshines reality, however, as I think, *I missed all the fun.*

Tooth mangled:

"Do I need to have my tooth pulled?" I exclaim. It is my bottom molar, and I am terrified. I know all about needles.

We are at the Porcupine Plain doctor's office–with no dentist in town, the doctor pulls teeth. Suddenly, it is my turn! I can feel the blood pumping through my heart as I sink into the chair and clutch the chair arms firmly.

"Open your mouth," the doctor instructs. I open my mouth. He begins to inject the needle into my gum. The sudden puncture elicits a pain so unbearable that I bite down–*hard*! The doctor yelps and rapidly yanks his fingers out of my mouth.

"You've bit into my finger. Keep your mouth open," he demands angrily in a stern, authoritative voice.

Time to pull the tooth. The Doctor inserts the plier-type instrument to engulf my back tooth. I *scream*! My mouth is not frozen. I endure more needles, more yanking. I am in agony and tears begin to flow in a stream down my cheeks. I pray, *Please, God, help me.* Reinserting the plier-type instrument, he initiates a vicious, sharp tug. The doctor stumbles backward, almost losing his balance, and I erupt in a piercing, jarring scream.

"The whole town can hear you," the doctor mutters with a frown. Meanwhile, my mouth is gushing blood. The doctor proceeds to insert a cotton ball and, to his dismay, discovers that the bottom half of my tooth remains in my gum.

It is a trip to the hospital. The doctor will put me to sleep to remove the rest of my tooth. I am experienced with ether. It is administered, and I recollect the strange smell. I count, *One, two, three.* The operation leaves me with a huge gouge cut out of my gum that takes many weeks to heal.

The incident made an impression on my parents because that is the last time any of us had a tooth pulled by a doctor!

Chapter 43

Mom's Exercise Regime:

"It's not a gimmick. It really works," comments Mom. She is constantly taking a shot at the latest diet or the latest dream machine to lose weight. We witness the many "miracle" solutions even though she has the perfect figure.

"Roll off the pounds, is the plan," Mom exclaims enthusiastically. She continues, "This is the perfect solution to get in shape." Quickly, the furniture is pushed against the walls and Mom lies down on the living room floor. She begins with a slow roll from one end of the room to the other. With arms and legs flailing in the air she picks up speed. Whipping up and down the floor, her arms and legs become a blur. This looks like fun, so we children join in and all of us are rolling off the pounds."

A few weeks later we hear Mom saying, "Shake off the pounds is the answer." The Shaking Machine is ordered from the catalogue. Mom eagerly steps on the contraption and wraps the belt snugly around her backside. Tentatively, she turns the key on, and the belt vibrates at a tremendous speed against her form. Mom's body jiggles wildly *up, down, and around*. Apparently, the pounds will rapidly disperse as the extra weight is shaken off the body. The wonder machine does not last very long.

"I have sent it packing–right back to where it came from–it does not work," are Mom's final words.

A month later, we are not surprised to hear of a new way to lose weight. "Sweat off the pounds is the answer," Mom announces. The Plastic Bodysuit is the most entertaining and interesting weight-loss gimmick. It lives up to its name–literally, a plastic one-piece outfit. The ensemble is designed to be worn all day, to sweat the pounds off the body. Mom dons the suit early in the morning before we go to school. The bodysuit squeaks and screeches annoyingly with every step; Mom does not seem to notice. At lunchtime, Mom is still wearing her get-up. Her cheeks are flushed, and she appears sweaty and uncomfortable. However, with a slight regal air, she enthusiastically announces, "I love it. It is definitely working."

Returning after school, the bodysuit is nowhere to be seen! We are puzzled that Mom is not wearing the plastic garment.

"Why aren't you wearing the body suit, Mom?" I ask bewilderedly.

"I have sent it packing–right back to where it came from–it does not work!" Mom replies in a firm voice and raises her eyebrow. It didn't last a full day before reality set in, and it became just another diet gimmick in our household.

Sleep under stars:

"Mom, Dad," I shout into the morning stillness. There is no answer. I wander around the house searching for them. Peering into their bedroom, they are not there. However, I notice that the mattress is missing from their bed.

"Not again," I mutter to myself and roll my eyes. I stride to the back door and poke my head out into the brilliant sunshine. Yup, just as I expected–their mattress is situated on the grass next to the fully bloomed cherry tree. Atop are two bundled bodies, intertwined, and a smaller figure sprawled alongside. Barry is the tiny frame. Mom and Dad love to sleep under the stars.

We children are always welcome to join the outdoor sleepover, so it is not surprising to find younger brother, Barry, snuggled beside them. We have all experienced lying in the dark to stare up at the stars, trying to decipher the Little and Big Dipper. Dad enjoys discussing the possibility of Unidentified Flying Objects which sends us into a magical dreamworld. Outdoor sleepovers always guarantee a good night's sleep. My Dad maintains that fresh air is a good preventative medicine.

Chapter 44

Water:

Hoots of laughter and screaming pierce the quiet, still air. Immediately, we children dash towards the commotion taking place at the dugout. Emerging from the bush onto the dugout we encounter Mom and Dad, tussling beside the water. Suddenly, Dad careens into the air and lands with a tremendous splash into the cool water of the dugout.

Mom is howling with laugher. Dad comes up from the water sputtering.

"My wallet, my papers they will all be wet," he utters. Dad is fully clothed. He crawls out of the dugout, clambering up the steep side, and grabs onto the diving board to haul himself up onto the bank.

Our homemade diving board is held in place by a humungous rock that Dad hauled with the front-load tractor from the field. Dad rigged up the huge rock onto one end of a plank and positioned it so that the other end of the board soared out over the water.

The water gushes in a torrent from Dad's shirt and pants as he emerges from the dugout. Gingerly, Mom and Dad arrange the items–dollar bills, driver's license, wheat pool permit–side by side on the diving board to dry. After the papers are laid out, Dad, with a chuckle, grabs Mom and pushes her towards the water. She is squealing with delight.

Mom learned to swim right after our traumatic incident, when she saved three-year-old me from drowning–she could not swim at the time. Dad taught Mom that very same summer.

Now Dad is playfully pushing Mom toward the dugout and we children join in to pummel her into the water. She comes up from the water laughing hysterically. Dad chucks all us children into the water and then he just jumps in again. We are all in the water fully clothed and having the time of our life.

The clothes will dry! is Mom's motto. It is a well-known fact that anyone standing near the dugout is fair game. Mom and Dad encourage us to have fun and enjoy life to the fullest.

"You need to learn to swim," insisted Dad. We were taught to swim at an early age. At the age of five years, I stood on the

Barry, Charlie, Chrissy, Julie in dugout

shore of the dugout, squinting into the bright sunshine. Dad instructed me to kick my arms and legs like a puppy dog. Mom stood smiling beside me. She had just shown me how she could float on the water and read a book! I was impressed!

Mom gestured for me to try to swim. There was a glare from the sun on the water and the surface shimmered like diamonds. I splashed madly into the water. I do not know if I swam or if I even propelled myself a few feet, but Mom wildly clapped her hands. We had incentive to learn to swim because we were not allowed to enter the dugout on our own until we could swim the entire length of the dugout. We became a water family.

The dugout is our very own private swimming pool. Summer months, we live in the water–swimming, diving, and playing games. First thing in the morning, we don our swimsuit and when we want a break, we hang our swimsuit on the line. Next time, we just jump into the water in our clothes, shorts, and t-shirt. At another break, we hang up the clothes and return to our bathing suit. We just switch all day.

One summer, Gramma Elsie admonished Mom over our attire. "The kids are in the dugout in their clothes," she says. Gramma is horrified.

"Oh, they are just having fun," Mom replies.

On another occasion, I remember that Charlie shook things up with a new innovation.

"I have an idea," Charlie announces. We are all ears! "We should pull the stone boat into the dugout and find out if it will float."

The stone boat was built by Dad to pull behind the tractor to load and remove stones from the field. It is flat-bottomed, made with aluminum

Charlie, Julie, Chrissy, and Barry.
Stoneboat becomes Waterboat

which is wrapped around the curved board sides. It resembles a wide and long deep-sided toboggan. In the winter, it becomes a water trough for the animals. Dad props the ends on big rocks to light a fire underneath to keep the water inside melted for the animals.

We push, tug, and drag the stone boat to the dugout. Chrissy and Barry scooch to the front, Charlie and I clamber into the back. I wield a long piece of lumber to push through the water to the bottom to steer the boat. The boat floats! We discovered our very own makeshift boat. With glee, we hoot and holler–making so much noise that our parents arrive to check on our activities.

Are we in trouble? I wonder. My oar stops in mid-air.

"Wow, it creates a better water boat than stone boat," Dad comments with a smile.

"I will get the Brownie!" Mom shouts. No, it is not cake– it is a Kodak Brownie camera that takes 127-roll film.

The stone boat transformed into a water boat for many summers and gave us hours and hours of amusement in the sun! We siblings bond in our fun together.

Water puddles:

"We are going to run through the mudpuddles," our loud voices echo throughout the house. The storm has ceased and there are water puddles lying all over the huge farmyard.

"Take your shoes off and go in your bare feet," Mom replies casually.

We race towards the mudpuddles. Flying into the air, we land two feet first, smack dab in the middle of the puddle. The black water sprays wickedly upwards and engulfs us in zig-zag patterns, covering our clothes, face, and limbs.

"Who can make the biggest splash?" I shout. This develops into a wild frenzy of dirty water flying in every direction!

We are exhausted, saturated, and dirty. We trudge into the house.

"Either go for a swim or wash up and change your clothes," Mom utters, with a smile on her face. Mom believes in letting kids be kids.

Thunderstorms:

Snap, crackle, boom explodes in the air, with sudden flashes of lightning and the boom of thunder. The sedan vibrates under the exploding rumble and the rain pelts violently on the tin roof. It is raining cats and dogs! Dad is barely visible, as he peers out of the windshield into the pitch-black darkness. He is sitting in our second-hand 1953 four door Bel Air Chevrolet.

Dad is momentarily lit up as the lightening illuminates the sky, pitching an eerie glow into the sedan. He is sitting in the vehicle, enjoying the storm. Dad prefers to be in the midst of the storm, to witness the action in the sky.

It instills in me a desire to observe thunderstorms. Thus, it is a pleasure to sit in the vehicle, watch the storm, and hear the pounding rain on the rooftop. After the storm, the sun peeks through the clouds to emit a glistening bright-ness on all water-soaked items. The air is fresh and clean, with the delightful earthy aroma that comes after a rainstorm. To me, this is God's nature in all its glory!

Charlie, Mom, Julie, Dad and Chrissy in front of '53 Chevy

Chapter 45

Ice skating:

In the winter, we are not allowed on the dugout until it is firmly frozen. We are taught that the ice may appear safe, but that is not necessarily the case. Therefore, we are instructed to wait until Dad drives the tractor on the ice to check if it is thick enough. If it is safe, he will clear off the snow for us to skate.

"I will check the ice," Dad announces, and fires up the tractor. After a few rounds on the tractor the ice appears solid. Dad drives closer to the centre of the ice. *CCRRACCCKKK,* the ice splinters into tiny cracks like a spider web. Dad steers the tractor towards the side of the dugout. Suddenly, the tractor lurches forward and tips at an odd angle, as it plunges headfirst into the black water. Dad utters a piercing cry as his body slants crazily downward towards the icy water. He clings to the tractor seat and calmly contemplates his next move.

The tractor is sinking rapidly. The ice has parted into a huge opening, stretching to the shore. Dad decisively takes a gigantic leap towards the side of the bank and frantically grabs for the land. He plops into the water from the waist down, with his upper half sprawled on the steep side of the bank. He claws his way up the incline and pulls his numb figure out of the water. Dad's clothes are freezing against his frame and his outer body begins to tremble. Dad shakily stumbles towards the house.

"What's wrong? What's happened?" Mom shrieks at the sight of Dad's drenched figure.

"The ice is not thick enough yet–the tractor sank," Dad sighs, visibly upset. After Dad is comfortably taken care of, we all troop down to the accident sight.

It is a frightful scene. I am shocked to see the tractor almost fully submerged in the water. I thank the Lord for keeping Dad safe. *How did my dad escape?* Even more puzzling is, *How will Dad get the tractor out of the water?*

"How will you get the Fordson tractor out, Dad?" I ask.

"It will be easy I will use the big John Deere tractor," he replies. And that is exactly what he did. Miraculously, the Fordson tractor dried out in our machine shop and performed in the same way as prior to the accident.

This instilled in us the importance of always properly checking the thickness and safety of the ice before the winter games begin.

Skating Rink:

"Close the door. Were you born in a barn?" booms a penetrating shout that reverberates within the Weekes Skating Bunkhouse–guaranteeing that next time you will close the door.

"Pump, pump, pull-away," rings out joyous voices into the frigid air while the opposing team weaves in and out across the ice to avoid being caught. This is our entertainment: skating, games, and hockey.

Dad is a volunteer manager. For several years, Dad has taken on the job of managing the skating rink. This entails organizing the water-flooding, preserving the ice rink throughout the winter, supplying a hearty load of wood for the heater, and locking and un-locking the bunkhouse door. This is our hang-out with family and friends after supper during the winter. Our Canadian winter typically involves skating and hockey.

Most Canadian towns own an ice rink and consider skating a basic skill, similar to riding a bike. Many sports entail skating–such as hockey, ringette, speed skating, figure skating, and social skating.

Hockey is Canada's official national winter sport that unites cultural, geographic, and socio-economic lines. We are considered to be the birth-place of ice hockey and regard the sport as our very own.

In our small town, the ice rink is always the hub of winter activity.

Chapter 46

Charlie is a tease:

Charlie and I are great pals, however, in one period of our life he was a big tease.

Charlie has a kind heart and loves to entertain. We interact in a good-natured way, but when he is in the mood, he knows just how to rile me up. His nature delights in teasing—sometimes it gets out of control, especially where I am concerned. I have a carefree nature, however, if pushed to the edge, my temper flies south in a matter of seconds—and then, look out! Charlie gets impish pleasure in riling me up and he knows just how to accomplish the job.

"Hang down your head Tom *Doolie*. Hang down your head and *cry*," sings Charlie. He emphasizes the word, *Doolie* and *cry*! Our parents are out, and Charlie is singing this dreaded song to me again. My dander rises and I react! I fall victim to his premeditated plan. My eyes dart around the room and I spy the teakettle within arm's reach. Charlie is in mid-sentence when I start swinging the teakettle wildly in a circular threatening motion by my side. Charlie flees. The teakettle slips from my grip and flies upwards in a high arc and within seconds it comes crashing down with a resounding *thunk* against the adjoining door. I stare in stunned silence at the gaping hole in the centre of the door. It takes only a moment for the situation to sink in.

"Charlie, come quick, the teakettle slipped and damaged the door!" I scream at the top of my lungs. "What are we going to do? We are in trouble!" I wail. Charlie peruses the damage; he does not come up with any ideas. The door is not fixable. Together we devise a plausible story.

"Mom, I picked up the kettle to fill with water and somehow, I slipped on the floor. My hand let go, causing the kettle to become airborne, and it flew straight into the door," I explain. Story told–story believed. A sibling secret.

A few days later, the teasing resumes. "Hang down your head Tom *Doolie*. Hang down your head and *cry*," Charlie sings softly as he leans against the wall, staring at me. Of course, Mom and Dad are away from the house. The writing is on the wall! My skin prickles and I can feel the blood pump rapidly to the beat of drums. In my peripheral vision I glimpse the broom–it will be my threatening weapon. In a frenzy, I dash after Charlie, shifting the broom to and fro high overhead. I lower the broom towards the kitchen cupboard to indicate to Charlie what is in store for him. The broom connects sharply on the counter and a crashing sound reverberates into the atmosphere. At the same time, my arm whips back, much lighter in weight. I gasp at the sight–I am clutching only the upper half of the broom handle and the lower half is on the kitchen counter.

"Charlie, help me!" I scream. Charlie stops in mid-flight and returns to stare in disbelief at the demolished broom. "What are we going to do? How can we fix the broom?" I screech. Charlie forgets our recent interaction as he observes the broken broom. He contemplates the situation for several seconds.

"I have an idea, just wait here," he reassures me. He appears minutes later with a hammer in hand. Grabbing the two pieces of handle, he clumsily attaches them together with a nail. We devise a plausible story for Mom.

"Mom, while I was sweeping the floor, I pushed down too hard on the broom and it just broke," I explain and add joyfully, "Charlie was able to fix it for you." Story told–story believed. Another sibling secret.

Charlie is at it again several weeks later. "Hang down your head Tom *Doolie*. Hang down your head and *cry*," Charlie begins to sing while we are outside in the yard. Mom and Dad just left the house, and of course my brother gets in my hair. My blood boils. This time I will not threaten with an object and risk breaking something. I will be smarter. I dash into the house, slam the door, and shove a knife into the door jamb to barricade the entry. We do not have locks on the door, which is a typical practice.

"I have locked you out of the house," I shriek with a mischievous laugh. Charlie is mad. He bangs sharply on the door.

"Let me in! Let me in! Let me in," he bellows while continuing to hammer loudly on the door. He reminds me of the wolf in the fairy tale, *The Three Little Pigs*.

"Not by the hair on my chinny-chin-chin," I reply in a sing-song voice, ending with a hearty laugh. Charlie turns abruptly and runs down the three steps to the side of the house. I hear a rustling at the kitchen window and notice Charlie quickly shoving the pane upwards. I dash to the window and frantically grab hold of the top, to push in the opposite direction. I will not let him in! Charlie pushes madly upwards, and I push wildly downwards. We are pushing/pulling, neck in neck! Suddenly I lose my grip–the window zips uncontrollably upwards, exits the grooves, and flies up, up, up, and over my head. A thunderous explosion pierces the quiet behind me, and fragments of glass rise in a torrent into the air. Terrified, I freeze in place as I am battered by tiny splinters of glass attacking my body.

Cold fear wells up within me as, nervously, slowly, I turn to assess the damage. The windowpane is shattered into a million pieces, now lying scattered across the kitchen floor. I am in a state of panic.

"Help, Charlie. Help!" I yell hysterically. "The window is broke. What are we going to do?" Charlie scoots around to the front door of the house. I zip to the same door to fling it open in a wide arc and gesture frantically to the appalling sight. We stand, stock-still, in deafening silence, as we stare in horror at the irreparable damage. The window is totally fragmented–not a single piece remains in the window frame. We are in hot water!

"I have an idea," Charlie says in a calm voice. He always has a good idea, and he does not fail me this time. "Let's clean up the glass and get rid of the evidence." Filled with nervous adrenalin, I viciously attack the disastrous sight. After the clean-up is accomplished, I wonder, *What will be our next step?*

"How are we going to replace the window?" I ask, turning to face Charlie with a worried frown.

"I have an idea," he replies smugly. Following Charlie's instructions, we remove the window from our parents' room and slip it into the kitchen grooves. It fits perfectly. We proceed to put the broken window into their bedroom.

"I can smell the aroma from the cherry tree very strongly through the open-glass window," I announce.

"They won't notice the empty-glassed window or cherry tree fragrance because the bedroom curtains are always closed," Charlie reasons.

We were wrong. However, it did take them a few days to notice their glass-less window in the bedroom. When asked if we knew what had happened to the window, none of us had a clue! Secrets abound between siblings.

My brother is a tease, but he always comes to my rescue.

That was a summer full of teasing fun!

Part Six

Pre-teen Years
Julie 11 – 12 years

Chapter 47

Learning experience:

My Uncle Earl, Aunt Kay and cousins are visiting from BC.

"Your cousin Betty dreams of picking berries and going on a picnic," Mom informs me. "Please take her to fulfil her dream." *This is a strange request. I do not want to fulfil her dream.* I gaze at Mom with pleading eyes. *Please no.*

Betty is the same age as me and I really like her, but her request baffles me. *Who in their right mind would dream of picking berries? And even worse, to actually want to sit on the ground to eat when the kitchen table is nearby?* I cannot fathom such a dream.

I *am* fulfilling my cousin's dream! We cycle to the bush to pick berries.

"This is so much fun," she remarks while we pick berries. I can hardly believe my ears; I pretend to enjoy myself. To me, picking berries is a chore. A feeling of relief overwhelms me when our pails are half full and she is satisfied with her loot. It is time for our picnic. *If I have to sit on the grass to eat, at least we will go to a pleasant spot,* is my thought. We cycle home and I lead us to the perfect location. We approach the cherry tree, ripe with brilliant smallish red berries shining brightly in the sun. We fling our blanket under the shade of the cherry tree where the branches envelop us like arms and provide relief from the hot sun like a huge umbrella. A pleasant breeze drifts in and around us, gently rustling the leaves in the trees. The birds are chirping melodiously to one another. It is quite a pleasant experience even though I feel foolish sitting on the grass to eat. I put a smile on my face and chat amiably as we munch on our peanut butter and jam sandwiches. Surprisingly, I discover that I am enjoying the occasion.

I expected an unpleasant experience, yet I find myself having a wonderful time sitting, chatting, and eating under the cherry tree with my cousin. The moment evolves into a memorable and pleasant event.

Betty is in her glory, and I am pleased that I made her happy. This is my first memory of doing something just to please another. My inner thought is, *Judge not what you have not experienced.* A profound lesson, embedded in my mind forever.

Fudge:

I like to please younger brother Barry who is almost seven years old. Therefore, one day when Mom is away, I decide to make him some fudge.

"Would you like me to make you some candy?" I ask Barry.

"Yes, can I help?" he responds instantly.

I gather the ingredients together into a pan and turn on the stove. My pot needs to be hot enough to boil my Carnation milk and brown sugar mixture. Soon my liquid is bubbling to beat the band.

Barry

"Can I help," Barry asks again.

"Pull up a stool and you can watch the fudge being made," I suggest.

He eagerly shoves the stool close and leans over to watch me stirring the bubbling mixture. Suddenly

I shout, as my hand touches the side of the pot burning my finger. I automatically fling the spoon upwards, causing the hot liquid on the spoon to become airborne. At that precise moment, Barry lets out a blood-curdling scream. I glance at him, horrified to see candy mixture dribbling in a stream down the front of his chest. Barry is shirtless! My burnt finger is forgotten. I shove the pot to one side, yank Barry off the stool and inspect the burn. I am horrified to see that the liquid formed a paste and is sticking to his skin. It is spread in a narrow line, just below his neck and straight down his chest. The candy mixture is still burning his skin. I pull the sticky paste off hoping to stop the pain.

Barry is crying uncontrollably. I put my arm around him and guide him to the kitchen cupboard where I grab a clean washcloth. I liberally wet the cloth, and squeeze water from the washcloth onto his burn. I rationale: *This will wash away any remaining candy liquid.* Barry is howling throughout the process. After several water-filled washcloths dribbled on his burn he calms down and all I can do is hold him until Mom comes home.

I feel miserable for his suffering and guilty for hurting my brother whom I should be protecting. The burn is fiery red and beginning to blister. Woefully, I soothe him, saying, "You are such a brave boy." He is handling the pain like a trooper and his cries subside to a quiet whimper. Thinking he is better, I whisper, "Please don't tell Mom I burnt you."

It is a fruitless request to suggest we keep this a sibling secret because Barry is still whimpering when Mom arrives home. I quickly relate what I did in a sorrowful voice.

"It was an accident," Mom states as she immediately attends to Barry.

Mom reaches for the Watkins salve and gently lays it over the burned area, being careful not to burst the blisters. Next, she grabs a clean sheet, rips it into strips and wraps the strips around Barry's chest. The bandage will keep air off the area, thus reducing the pain and protecting his blistered skin. He has second degree burns.

Barry suffers for days and my heart aches for his discomfort. His skin becomes thicker in the burn area and is a white shade with a few red areas.

After approximately three weeks the burn heals, however scars remain. I feel guilty and sad that I ruined most of his summer vacation.

On our way to school, at the end of summer vacation, I pull Barry aside.

"Don't tell anyone at school what happened," I plead with Barry. I do not want anyone to know about my part in his painful incident.

He did not tell. Sibling secrets again.

Barry is left with a lifetime scar—a reminder of our incident. He doesn't forget and neither do I!

School Bully:

The burning incident becomes the least of my worries. I arrive at school to discover that a new girl has become friends with my friend. And the new girl does not like me! She is a mean girl. I tag along and constantly attempt to fit in. I pray many nights, *Please let them be my friend.* I am too young to realize that bullies are usually suffering from jealousy or insecurity.

I have an idea. In an effort to become chummier I invite the two girls to my house for a playdate and a piece of cake. The girls agree to come over—all because they know my mom is an excellent baker, I am sure! I inform Mom that I need a cake because I have friends coming over after school. Mom is out; earlier in the day she baked a chocolate cake for our snack. The girls immediately dig in and munch the cake eagerly.

"This cake is delicious. Can we have another piece?" they ask. I am pleased. The playdate is going well.

"Yes. You can have as much as you want," I reply. They readily consume many pieces, until the cake is whittled down to half a pan.

We step outside and spy Charlie working in the yard. Suddenly, my friends redirect their attention to my brother. Chagrined, I witness them morph into silly girls vying for Charlie's attention! Charlie continues to help Dad dig a well and totally ignores the girls. Soon the girls leave for home. I surmise, *This was a fruitless effort.* I am right—at school nothing changes. It takes time but, with a little help, I wake up and smell the coffee.

The straw that breaks the camels back is an incident which occurs one day during first recess. While standing in a group of five girls, "Missy" hides candies in her fist and drops one into the hand of each girl in the group–except mine. I am left out; my stomach plummets and I suddenly feel sick.

"What about Julie?" Edith asks.

"I have no candy left," Missy replies. We all know it is a lie.

Why doesn't she like me? I query. I feel the warmth creep up my face, and I feel shame, mingled with anger. Unknown to me she is probably threatened by my presence.

At lunch time, I stay in the classroom. I realize I am not wanted in their group. Resentment burns within, and I sink into my desk thinking, *I don't care*!

"Julie, they don't want you in their group–come and be in our group," Janie calls in a friendly tone.

My head jerks upwards as the kind words wash over me and penetrate my brain. Janie–who is a grade lower but in the same classroom–is smiling warmly in my direction. The cold, hard truth of her words hits the nail on the head, and her invitation to join her group fills me with joy. Chatting with my new friends, I see Missy enter the classroom with her entourage out of the corner of my eye.

"Why are you with them?" Missy begins to provoke me and continues, "Don't you want to be in our group?" I cringe inside and, being naturally shy, I remain silent.

"Leave her alone. She doesn't want to be in your group," pipes up my new friend, Janie.

A feeling of relief overpowers me. I am thankful to Janie for sticking up for me and welcoming me into her group. In the end, I realize that not everyone likes everyone and that I should choose my friends carefully.

The following year, Janie and I are in separate classes. However, God has plans for me–that is the year I meet my best friend, Sandra. Nevertheless, Janie remains a part of my extended group of friends throughout the school years. I will always be thankful for her kindness.

Chapter 48

Television:

In 1959, the world enters our house—via a black and white television set. The elegant piece of furniture with a built-in screen is purchased at Stigen's Hardware store in Weekes. We gather as a family in the living room to watch the first moving pictures appear on the screen. We are enthralled and liken it to going to the movies. News, sports, movies, and family shows expand our knowledge about a world outside our community. We quickly decide that our favorite family program is *Bonanza*, a western show featured on Sunday evening.

The television overtakes our household. Immediately after supper, Chrissy and I work as a team to clean the kitchen. Together we develop our own system for washing and drying the dishes. Working as one we will clear the table, heat the water on the stove to wash dishes, dry items and put away, wipe the table, cupboard, stove and sweep the floor. We complete our chores in double quick time in order to sit and watch television. We do not play cards, checkers, and crokinole as much as we did before the television arrived and I notice that I do not spend as much time reading.

At lunch break at school, we children race home to watch *The Three Stooges*, while munching on toasted homemade bread and tomato soup.

On Saturday nights my parents settle in front of the TV to applaud their favorites teams. In the winter, it is the hockey games, and in the summer, it is baseball. They holler and cheer for their favorite teams–the Canadian Maple Leafs and the Yankees.

Soon, another change is on the horizon. We learn about a new invention that will allow us to watch television in colour.

"We can transform our black and white television into color," Mom excitedly relates while we sit around the kitchen table eating supper. We marvel at the thought of a color television–it sounds too good to be true. "Everyone is buying the item. It is all the rage," Mom explains.

The next day, she purchases this marvelous invention. It is a colored transparent film! The film is divided into three wide strips. The top strip is blue, to represent the sky, the middle strip is orange/red, perhaps representing trees and leaves, and the bottom strip is green, imitating grass. Mom positions the colored transparent film on the front of the television screen.

"Wow, it looks great. We have a color television," exclaims Mom in a high-pitched voice, full of excitement.

"I do not think I like it," Dad remarks. I silently agree. The colored film hinders the visibility of the movement on the screen. The figures on the television appear blurred and are not as sharp to the eye.

However, regardless of our reservations, my mom's exuberance is captivating. She can change anyone's mind about anything! Therefore, we soon agree that it truly looks good. Mom raves about the *color television* for a week and then the colored transparent film disappears–never to be seen again.

"The television is better off without it," she explains.

Our trip to British Columbia:

It is summer break in 1959! With our grandparents celebrating their fiftieth anniversary in Vancouver Island, BC, we are in for a fantastic road trip.

It is an early start at three a.m. We excitedly dress in our new clothes to begin our adventure. We don our white t-shirts depicting various scenes—mine shows a lighthouse, with water in the background. Sporting our much-loved blue and white striped *skorts* Chrissy and I model our matched outfits. A skort is shorts that have a front covering resembling a skirt. We are rockin' the in-style look.

Our trip is breathtaking. Sensational spectacles amaze us as we stop at all the scenic spots. Stretching our legs, we dash across an open meadow or climb a mountain. We picnic on the road, consuming homemade bread with peanut butter, preserved jam, or Prem, obtained from a case tucked in the trunk. We marvel at the changing landscape.

B. C. Trip
Chrissy, Barry, Julie, Charlie
(girls in skorts)

"Why are the people staring at us?" I ask Mom when a group walk by and visibly ogle our small group as we munch our lunch in a pull-over spot.

"They just wish they were having a picnic, too," Mom replies, with a genuine smile. I agree—it makes perfect sense. We continue to eat our delicious lunch. Suddenly, Mom jumps up.

"Oh no. I left my purse in the bathroom at the last service station," she blurts. The station is forty miles back! We are not surprised to discover this problem. Mom is a go-getter, always focused on her next task. This trait results in her forgetting her purse, parcels, or keys anywhere and everywhere.

Dad just takes this all in his stride and promptly makes a U-turn. On the return trip, Mom is in great spirits.

"Look at that beautiful…" tree/hill/stream/or whatever we are passing. "I am so glad we get to see the beauty from this angle," she points out along the way.

"My purse is right where I left it on the back of the throne," Mom states as she clambers back into the car. Her items always seem to turn up somewhere. We did not mind the retracing of our steps because Mom elicited an excitement in us at witnessing the stunning scenery. Her positivity is a wonderful characteristic in her personality. Mom believes that a positive attitude is important.

We pull over to finish our earlier interrupted lunch. Laughter erupts, reminiscing over the incident while consuming our lunch. The event is already a story to be told.

Camping:

Traveling through the mountains, dusk is descending, and we need to find a place to pitch our tent. We scour the surrounding area from our moving vehicle to search for a good location. Suddenly, we spot a flat area with an open expanse amongst the trees. Investigating the space, we are thrilled to note that there is a small brook running close by, runoff from the mountains– instantly we whip off our shoes and wade into the cold water. Playtime is over and we help erect the tent on a level piece of grass. Our tent does not have a floor; we lay blankets inside on top of the grass for sleeping. Dark is descending and we bundle into our tent for a good night's sleep.

"Ouch," bellows Dad in the dead of night. Without a floor in the tent, the bottom perimeter of the tent is exposed to the wild animals.

Peering into the pitch blackness I try to discern the problem. Dad is shifting rapidly to his knees.

"Something bit my toe!" he shouts. Soon we are all scrambling madly to free ourselves from the tightly wound blankets encompassing our bodies.

My heart is beating wildly. I strain my ears to perceive any rustling sound outside the tent. Mom scurries to her feet and flings the tent flap open.

"I am not sleeping in this place," Mom shrieks as she stumbles out of the tent. She disappears into the shadowy darkness in the direction of our vehicle.

Dad's flashlight beams an eerie glow inside the tent. I exchange a frightened look with Chrissy, and we move as one towards the door. We run for safety, holding hands, with our focus on the interior lights of the car. We spend a very uncomfortable night in the car. Somehow, Dad convinces the boys to stay in the tent and they have a wonderful sleep with no more interruptions.

The following night we purchase a motel room. We laugh uproariously over the unfortunate incident and include this event in our road-trip stories.

Tree Swing:

Charlie and I stay at Aunt Marie and Uncle Walter's house. We are thrilled because cousin Kenny is Charlie's age and cousin Melody is my age. We have not seen them since they left Weekes as toddlers, however, there is something special between cousins. We hit it off instantly – melding together and quickly developing a special bond.

"It's a giant swing," Kenny explains excitedly. We are intrigued and eagerly follow Kenny and Melody across the road into the forest. Our eyes stare in amazement at the giant tree stump, approximately five feet high and three feet across. A wooden stick is attached to a long rope hanging from a nearby tree. It is a giant tree swing.

"I want to go first," Charlie shouts, while clambering up the ladder to reach the platform. His hands reach and grasp the handlebar stick to swing off with a huge leap from the giant tree stump. His body surges into the air, high above the ground. Suddenly his hands lose their grip, and his frame is flung into the atmosphere. Emitting a violent shriek, his body plunges to the earth and lands with a tremendous thud. He screams, "My arm, my arm, my arm!" Charlie leads the pack as our small group runs for home. Abruptly, he comes to a skidding halt and his body begins to tremble violently.

"A snake, a snake, a snake!" he shrieks. We come to a standstill. I almost jump out of my skin at the sight of the long, skinny, slimy-looking snake.

"It is only a garter snake," Kenny exclaims matter-of-factly. I am annoyed. *What difference does it make what kind of snake it is—it will kill us!* "It won't hurt you," Kenny adds. With a look of disbelief, Charlie and I skirt a big circle around the snake. I am glad we do not have snakes.

Charlie has a broken arm. At the emergency room he is fitted with a cast and a sling. Our tree swing fun comes to an end. This is a typical incident in our adventurous life.

Auntie Marie settles us down to watch television—mainly to keep us out of trouble. I stare in shock at the TV as I witness liquor being advertised. This is a real eye-opener we do not have these adverts at home. I cannot wrap my young mind around the sight. *How can they advertise liquor? It seems so wrong. I bet God doesn't like it.*

Supper is bountiful and delicious. I determine that Auntie Marie is a good cook, just like Mom.

Vacation over:

"We will travel through the United States," Dad announces in an excited tone. Prior to our vacation, our parents studied the map and marked our route both coming and going. Our return itinerary is through the United States—our first trip through this part of the world. Dad does not just map out our destination route but plans our journey to be informative and stimulating.

"Fresh fruit is not allowed," informs the US border guard. He continues, "Therefore, you cannot take your big bag of oranges into the States."

Dad glances at us children and at the big bag of oranges. Sympathetically, the border guard adds, "If each child held a peeled orange and is in the process of eating it than it would be allowed."

Dad fires up the vehicle and pulls over to the side of the road. He turns to us children and passes over the bag of oranges.

"Peel all the oranges," Dad says with a huge grin. We quickly do his bidding!

Back at the border, the guard peeks in the window. He observes each of us children clutching several peeled oranges in each of our hands.

The border guard straightens up to his full height and, with a secretive smile, says, "You are good to go."

Chapter 49

The special gift:

Christmas is just around the corner. Mom has left for a Ladies Club meeting. Dad oversees us children.

"Do you want a hint for your Christmas present?" Dad asks.

"Yes, yes, yes," we reply in one voice. Dad disappears into his bedroom and soon we hear the melodious song of *Felix the Cat* streaming into the living room via the closed bedroom door. Exchanging looks of surprised pleasure, we breathlessly whisper to one another excitedly. *It is an electric record player!* The song concludes, and Dad emerges from the bedroom.

"Well, do you know what your present is?" asks Dad, with a gleeful grin.

"No," we reply in unison.

"Shall I give you a hint again?" he asks.

"Yes!" is our resounding cry. Dad disappears into his bedroom and shuts the door. Soon the music flows into the living room and we dance around to the harmonious melody of *Felix the Cat*. Dad emerges.

"Can you guess your Christmas present?" Dad asks again, with a huge grin.

"No," is our answer again, in unison. Not surprisingly, we are never able to decipher our present! We spend a wonderful evening listening to *Felix the Cat* over and over and over again. It is the only year that we do not need to snoop for our presents.

Dad is on tenterhooks, waiting for Christmas to arrive so he can give us this wonderful gift of a record player. We keep the incident a secret and upon opening our gift on Christmas eve, we feign surprise. Chrissy cannot contain her excitement.

"Can we listen to Felix the Cat?" she blurts in a loud voice while jumping up and down. Five pairs of eyes flash in her direction. I am horrified at her blunder.

"How do you know you are getting a Felix the Cat record? Mom asks with a puzzled look. We follow Chrissy's eyes as she peeks at Dad. Mom becomes aware of the exchange of glances and the lightbulb comes on-she displays a knowing smile. "Chrissy you can open the next present," Mom murmurs in an amusing tone. I am in a dilemma. When Chrissy opens the gift of a *Felix the Cat* record should I act surprised or not? The gift is opened, but before I can react Mom blurts enthusiastically, "Put the record on the record player." We are soon dancing and singing to the melodious music of Felix the Cat – not surprisingly Dad and us children know every word to the song!

We have the largest Christmas tree for miles around! Our outside Christmas tree is humungous in the front yard. It is strung with hundreds of dazzling, colorful Christmas lights. The twinkling tree towers over our house and can be seen flashing brilliantly–red, yellow, and green–for many, many miles. The lights need to be strung up with the tractor and front-end loader. It is a sure sign of the love Mom and Dad have for Christmas.

"Can we use your record player," Dad asks several months later when our parents are planning a get-together with friends. Of course, we agree.

On Saturday night friends arrive and a record is promptly placed on the record player. A blast of music reverberates into the air - Chubby Checker singing *Let's Twist Again*.

"Let's do the Twist," Mom shouts. I rise from the kitchen table where I am giving myself a manicure and peek into the living room. I hear Mom laugh and give instructions. "Just dry your buttocks with the towel and pretend you are putting a cigarette out with your foot." I see all the woman clutching a towel and swishing it to and fro on their backsides and shifting their feet. I smile at the comical way their hips, arms and legs are gyrating in a strange fashion. It is obvious that the women and the men are having a great time dancing up a storm. With a grin I slink quietly back to the table.

The dancing transitions into playing a game. Whether work or play Dad keeps things under control. Marge is sitting in the middle of the living room with a blanket over her head.

"Take something off that you don't need," is spoken within the crowd. This request is shouted again and again and again after each item is tossed outside the blanket.

The first item is a Ladies watch to be pushed out from under the blanket, then a necklace follows, next a heel is flung into the air, then another heel arises out of the blanket. Suddenly Dad steps forth.

"Marge, it's the blanket. You don't need the blanket!" he exclaims in a loud voice. Laughter erupts around the room. My Dad has ended the game and saved the day.

Sister Teacher:

I chuckle inwardly at the joke while continuing to file my nails. I am using the Manicure Set I received from this year's teacher, Miss Doris Wallace. She is a sister to my favorite teacher, Miss Elsie Wallace. Our whole class received the same Christmas present from our very caring teacher. She has put careful thought into her gift to us students. I treasure my manicure set and keep it with me everywhere I go. Several days later I am in the depths of despair due to an unfortunate incident at school.

"Someone tossed their manicure set down the toilet and we think it is Julie's," twitters a couple of girls to our teacher, Miss Doris Wallace. Just finishing my lunch at my desk, I stare at the girls in astonishment. It could not be mine; I have my manicure set in my back pocket. I reach my hand to my back pocket, stretching my fingers inside. It is empty. My prized manicure set is missing.

I dash frantically to the washroom. I peek down the hole where our waste goes straight down into a holding tank, and gasp in shock at the sight before me—sitting on the top of a pile of muck is a manicure set. Tears well up in my eyes when I realize it either dropped out of my back pocket or the girls found it on the floor and pitched it down the toilet. Either way, my heart hurts at the loss of my prized possession.

I courageously swallow my sorrow in silence. I am without my manicure set, yet I am very appreciative that my teacher cared enough to give me such a thoughtful gift.

I am feeling blue and half-listening to Miss Doris Wallace droning on and on during English class. It is normally my favorite class but today I am sad. Suddenly, my ears perk up when I hear her begin to explain our English assignment.

"You will write an autobiography. This will be your life story and you will be the author," she explains. My attention is piqued, and my heart skips a beat. I am thrilled with this assignment. Miss Wallace has unknowingly flipped my unhappiness into a feeling of joyfulness. She has just made my day—what a great teacher!

Writing stories is my forte. I can write a great story because I have been involved in many thrilling, dangerous adventures. I quickly delve into my life's events. Trying to keep up with my racing mind, my pen frantically writes words onto the scribbler. The writing makes me think about my life—to remember incidents, to appreciate my parents, and to realize that I learned many lessons from my past. I write page upon page upon page, and at completion I eagerly hand in my paper.

As soon as I receive my manuscript back, I promptly open the pages to view my teachers big red sentences. She writes, "This is an exciting autobiography. It is well-written. How did you ever survive?" I smile with pleasure. I am an author! That night I dream of becoming a famous author.

My teacher, Miss Doris Wallace, opened up a whole new world for me and from that moment on I knew this was something I wanted to pursue. I revelled in writing mini stories of exciting incidents in my life. It is amazing to think back on how all those past events shaped my life, my thoughts, and my personality.

Tall Tale:

One such occasion gave me the opportunity to write a very short story. The Prince Albert radio station announced a tall tale contest, whereby they encouraged individuals to send in an unbelievable whopping story.

The idea for my tall tale derives from my bother teasing me, saying, "If you cried hard enough your tears could put out a fire." My mind quickly zipped to the tall tale contest, and I had my idea. I wrote the story and Mom mailed it into the radio station. I was excited to hear my tall tale announced on the radio:

Our house caught on fire and huge flames rose into the sky. I bawled my eyes out! I cried, and I cried, and I cried. My eyes shed buckets and buckets and buckets of water. Suddenly, the flames diminished. I was amazed to discover that my tears put out the fire!

"I heard your story on the radio and it was very amusing," exclaims the girls at the Apostolic Girls Club.

"Thank you, I am glad you heard and liked my tall tale," I reply.

I do not win, but I receive a lot of accolades amongst my peers. I am popular for several days. The praise I receive is more important than winning.

Chapter 50

Faith:

My faith begins from a small child. In our home, our parents do not preach at us–they teach their belief with action not word. Prayer is important to Mom. While travelling, we share a bed. After the lights are out and it is dark, I can hear murmurings and I know Mom is praying. I also pray every night – I know it is important and I believe in God.

We attend the Apostolic Sunday School from a young

Grampa Nelson in rear. Back: David, Charlie, Sam, Leonard. Front: Julie, Janie

age, as well as the Apostolic Boys and Girls Club, Vacation Bible School, and Bible Camp.

The Apostolic Vacation Bible School is a week-long event that takes place in the summer months during school break, to classes of different age groups. The purpose of the program is for the leaders to entertain us children and teach Christian education.

Our excellent leaders are Pastor Wes MacNaughton, his wife, Mrs. Lucille MacNaughton, Mr. Andy McDonald, the elevator agent–and one year my Grampa Nelson was visiting from BC, and he taught a class. Charlie and I were in Grampa's class, so we had to be on our best behavior and be very studious.

My friends and I look forward to this week-long get-together. We enjoy the Bible stories, arts and crafts, and recreational games. Life lessons are learned in a fun environment. We act out Bible stories–I enjoy pretending to be a person from the olden days–we learn new songs and I love singing. Also, we play games such as Kick the Can, Hide and Seek, and Tag. This is a time of bonding with one another and deepening our faith in God

The Apostolic Church Boys and Girls Club promotes character building to the children in our community. The club helps develop relationships and instills a sense of belonging. We learn new skills to build competence and confidence in a safe place with a responsible leader. Mrs. MacNaughton leads the Girls Club and Mr. Andy MacDonald, who years ago drove Charlie and me to school one cold winter day, leads the Boys Club.

We girls are taught to knit slippers, hand sew simple projects, paint a picture, and other items at the Church manse. I am very proud of my completed projects and feel a great sense of accomplishment. And I enjoy bonding with my friends. The boys gather at the Pool grain elevator and learn skills with a handsaw. They build bird houses, bird feeders, and animal cut-outs. The boys do not take snacks because their leader always brings them something to eat. We girls, however, prefer to take turns bringing snacks, knowing we will have a variety of home-baked goodies. We enjoy our snack as much as learning a new skill.

It is my turn to bring a snack to the Apostolic Girls Club.

"This is so good," erupts around the room. We are munching on my mom's famous spice cake with peanut butter icing. Our belief is that good food and good friends is a great combination.

We attend Sunday school regularly on Sunday morning and occasionally on a Sunday evening for a special service such as Christmas, Easter, or a visiting pastor.

On one such evening, during the Apostolic church service, we are invited to accept Jesus into our hearts." I notice Charlie rise from his seat and shift into the aisle. My mind flips into overdrive, *I do not want to be left behind. If Charlie is going then I am going!* I jump up quickly and follow behind him like his shadow.

I answer questions: 1. Do you believe that you are a sinner and want forgiveness? 2. Do you believe Jesus died on the cross for your sins and rose from the grave? 3. Do you accept Jesus into your heart, and will you trust and follow Jesus as your Lord and Savior?

"Yes," I answer emphatically to all questions, and we pray.

The Apostolic Bible Camp provides an adventurous Christian camping experience where we are encouraged to respond to the gospel of the Lord Jesus and grow in our Christian life. Our camp is two hours away located at a lake.

Our cabin has four sets of bunkbeds. Chrissy and I grab one bunkbed; she sleeps on bottom, and I sleep on top. Every morning we scramble to make our bed, sweep, and dust because there will be a cabin inspection later in the morning and a prize is given for the best cabin.

Our meals are all homemade and delicious. I know some of the meat comes from our farm because our parents bartered with our fresh pork to pay for our camping fees. Each cabin takes a turn at peeling potatoes; if a person misbehaves, they are relegated to KP duty–peeling potatoes. We have "tuck" every day: chocolate bars, candy, and other goodies, from the Canteen snack bar. Recreation is a daily softball game where two captains are named, who take turns choosing players. I was thrilled when the captain called my name–we had been eyeing each other for days. I never did get up the nerve to talk to him or vice versa. Swimming is my favorite part of the day along with the nightly campfires, where we sit around singing songs and listen to our leader tell a Bible story. We have a designated time for arts and crafts and Bible study. Our final evening is a church service with a guest speaker.

During the church service we are invited to be "saved by accepting Jesus into your heart." My mind is filled with anxious questions. *Am I saved? Maybe it did not work because I just followed my brother? What if I do not get to go to Heaven?* These thoughts weigh heavy on my mind, and I reflect, *I better go again—for myself.* I rise and proceed down the aisle. Perceiving footsteps right behind me I jerk my head around—my sister, Chrissy is following me like my shadow.

I am guided through a familiar process. Chrissy is still in conversation when I return to our bunkhouse. She takes forever to return. I wait and wait and wait—minutes seem like hours. I am getting worried and debate inwardly as I pace the room, *Should I go check on her?* Moments later, Chrissy walks into our bunkhouse.

"What kept you so long?" I demand.

"They wanted to make sure I didn't just follow you to the front!" she replies. I nod my head—I completely understand.

I have the innocent faith of a child. I rely on God completely; in dicey situations I always ask for help. As a teenager I waver in my faith, yet I still call upon God for help in dire situations. God answers my prayers, even if not always in the way I expect. I am thankful for the teachings and the wonderful leaders of the Apostolic Church in guiding my way from an early age. Most grateful of all is the many blessings I receive from the Lord throughout my life.

Chapter 51

Farm Incidents:

Joe Stad arrives for work at our sawmill. He is driving his brand-new vehicle.

"It is the latest model," exclaims Joe with a huge grin. He is pointing to his ruby red vehicle, glowing brilliantly under the sun's bright light. I do not notice his vehicle, rather I notice his hand minus one finger—a reminder of the sawmill accident. My parents' attention, however, is directed at Joe's gleaming new vehicle—it elicits genuine *ooohs* and *ahhhs*. The prized possession glitters like diamonds parked on the farm driveway. Dad and Joe amble off to work at the sawmill, located approximately a hundred yards from the house.

"Move the Fordson tractor over to the mill," Dad shouts in the direction of Charlie and me. We sprint to the tractor, racing each other. Unfortunately, Charlie arrives first and quickly ascends to plop down on the tractor seat.

"Please let me drive," I implore, while shoving and pushing his frame on the tractor seat.

"What is going on?" Mom asks, noticing our loud ruckus.

"I want to drive; Charlie always gets to drive." I beg Mom with pleading eyes.

"Charlie, let Julie have a turn at driving," Mom instructs. I am pleasantly surprised and happy.

"How do I put it in gear?" I shout, as I position my figure behind the steering wheel and step on the clutch. I look in bewilderment at the gear shift. Mom instructs Charlie to show me how to put it into gear. Charlie swiftly marches over and shifts it into third gear, points to the lever to rev it up to the appropriate speed and he leaps out of the way. I rev it up to the highest point and release the clutch.

The tractor jolts forward like a shot out of a cannon. My body jerks sharply backwards as the tractor charges forward in a mad dash. My hands clutch desperately to the steering wheel, clinging on for dear life. The tractor careens like a bull into the side of Joe's brilliant, gleaming brand-new car!

I gape in horror as the tractor violently continues to crash against the vehicle, again and again and again. The Fordson charges relentlessly at the vehicle like a ram.

"Charlie, help me," I scream, horrified and in a state of panic. With a look of terror, Charlie surges forward to come to my rescue. As his feet touch the running board, I leap and hit the ground running. Zipping away as quickly as possible, I aim to escape this catastrophic situation.

Dad on combine dispersing grain

I whip my body behind the house. Spying the huge trunk of the cherry tree, I crawl behind it and scrunch into a tiny ball. I am invisible. I am filled with fear. Cocking my ear in the direction of the yard, I cannot decipher the reaction. *Am I in deep trouble? What will my punishment be? I am scared!*

No one calls for me, no one looks for me. *What is going on?* I pray, *God help me!* My thoughts take me to the edge of despair.

"Julie, come in for supper." What a dilemma! *Should I remain hidden, go in for supper or run away?* I rise slowly and trudge in trepidation towards the house.

The luscious aroma hits me as I enter the kitchen. Mom is grilling pork chops and flipping sliced potatoes in the cast-iron fry pan. Dad emerges from the living room. Apprehensively, I stop and stand stock-still. We exchange glances. My eyes are fearful, but Dad's amber-brown eyes appear warm.

"Charlie should have stayed on the tractor with you," he declares. I realize that Dad expects Charlie to be the responsible one—being the oldest.

"It's okay," Mom announces in a soothing voice. "We are thankful that no one got hurt and Joe's car is insured. It can be easily fixed." It takes a moment to comprehend, but as the words wash over me, I feel the tension leave my shoulders and my insides well up with joy. I exhale a deep breath and my mind whirls. *This is a miracle!*

We eat. We chat. Our family of six gather around the supper table as if it is a normal day. Well, in our household maybe it is a normal day! Our parents believe that we learn from our experiences.

Picking stones.

It is the first day of school break and I am thinking of the glorious summer days ahead. Upon stepping outside, I pause on the front step to listen to the silence. I can hear the wind whistling through the trees.

Squinting my eyes in the brilliant sunlight, I glimpse a robust figure coming into view. A slight smile appears above Dad's firm jawbone.

"Julie, what a great day for stone-picking," he announces as he sweeps a lock of black hair back from his face. I press my lips tight, envisioning picking rocks under a blazing hot sun.

"Do I have to?" I utter, while rolling my eyes upwards.

Picking stones is a laborious job. A tractor is used to pull the stone boat, which is filled with rocks from the field and then taken to be dumped on the rock pile, situated at the side of the field.

"You can drive the Fordson tractor while Charlie and John pick the rocks," replies Dad. The first thought that pops into my head is, *I didn't fare very well in my last episode of driving the Fordson tractor.* However, I am experienced now because Dad insisted on giving me lessons. Picking stones will be much more fun having the task of driving the tractor. John will be in charge of this project. He is our neighbor, an older teenager hired to help on the farm. Mom and Dad have a high respect for John and trust him to oversee Charlie and me.

I have a pleasurable job! Sitting on the tractor, I gaze up at the luminous blue sky and large woolly clouds. My duty is to move the tractor a couple of feet and stop for Charlie and John to pick the rocks, and then move another couple of feet. Since I am stopping so often, I opt to keep my foot pressed on the clutch rather than constantly shift gears to neutral while stationary.

Out of the corner of my eye I see a shadow. Charlie is approaching the tractor. I assume he has something important to relay to me. As he comes up in front of the large tractor wheel, I lean over to hear him.

Charlie makes a sudden move. His hand rears up and flies in my direction—his fist opens, and I see a handful of dirt hurtling towards my face. As the dust hits its mark, I squeeze my eyes shut and fling my body backwards. Instantly my leg jerks upwards, releasing the clutch causing the tractor to lunge wildly forward. At the sudden movement Charlie hurtles his body in reverse. He is too slow. The huge tractor wheel plunges over his legs.

The still air is broken by his ear-splitting shriek. Blindly, I jam my left foot on the clutch, stomp my right foot on the brake, and fling the gearshift into neutral. I madly swipe the dirt from my eyes and, with tears spilling down my face, I crane my neck towards the racket. I gasp in shock, horrified as I comprehend that I have just driven over Charlie.

"You broke my legs, you broke my legs, you broke my legs!" Charlie is jumping wildly about and screeching at the top of his lungs, shattering the atmosphere. Time stands still. I am terrified and fear fills my soul as I hear Charlie continue to scream, "I am telling Dad you broke my legs." I can feel the blood pumping through my heart. I pray. *Please God make Charlie better.* I know I am in a pretty pickle.

I am distraught! In a dazed state, I glimpse John approaching in my peripheral vision. He reaches over and grabs the key to turn the tractor off. He leans over in my direction.

"If Charlie broke his legs, he would not be running, jumping, and kicking his feet," he whispers in a sympathetic voice.

His words penetrate my frenzied mind. I scrutinize Charlie stomping, jumping, and kicking up dirt, while ranting, "You broke my legs, I'm telling Dad." It slowly dawns on me that John is right—Charlie is not displaying broken legs! I am thankful to John for drawing this fact to my attention.

The soft dirt saved Charlie from any injury. The field had been cultivated and harrowed earlier in the week; the tractor wheel just pushed Charlie's legs into the soft dirt causing no harm.

Dad arrives. Charlie runs to him, displaying a wicked smile aimed at me. I am puzzled—in the past we always stood beside each other, we do not tattle! Dad and Charlie stroll towards us and I am wary as to what will happen next. I give Charlie a questioning look. *Did you tell?* Charlie grins and slinks away. I am bewildered, yet quiet—in case I stir up trouble.

"How is everything going?" Dad asks John.

"All is going good," John replies.

There is no mention of the incident or broken legs. Dad leaves, and we return to work. John saved the day and protected both Charlie and me! Without further incident, John and Charlie continue to pick stones and I happily drive the Fordson tractor. Charlie and I are friends once again; we are life-long buddies.

Combine vs Hopper Box:

"We will be up late tonight," Dad informs the family. It is harvest time!

"Make hay while the sun shines," Dad exclaims. Thus, we need to reap the ripe grain while the weather is agreeable. Combining continues into the wee hours of the morning, until the grain is too tough to garner. A combine is used to separate the kernels of grain, which are retained in the machine, then emptied into the wagon and trucked from the field to the granaries.

"Julie, you drive the Fordson tractor with the Hopper Box," Dad instructs.

Dad designed and built the hopper box–it has tall sides that narrow towards the bottom, where the grain exits through a small door. We transport the grain from the combine to the granaries, where the threshed grain is stored until the grain is sold and delivered to the elevator.

Dad with Fordson tractor and Hopper Box. Charlie on Combine

I drive the hopper box alongside the combine downspout, to collect the grain and then transport the seeds to the granary.

This is fun. With each trip, I'm faster at maneuvering the Fordson tractor into position. Zipping up beside the combine, I suddenly feel a sharp, jarring movement and hear a terrible clamor. Slamming on the brakes, I crane my neck in the direction of the crunching noise. I have driven the tractor and hopper box too close to the combine; the corner of the hopper box is wedged into the combine spout!

This is a disaster. A huge dent appears in the spout. This incident may delay the progress of harvesting. I feel a chill whip up my spine. This is not a good scenario. *What will be the repercussions of my accident?* Dad observes the damage. A shiver of apprehension rushes over me and I mutter a quick prayer while awaiting his reaction.

"Are you okay?" Dad asks, looking in my direction.

"Yes," I answer nervously.

"It is a small dent; I will hammer it out," Dad says, with a small sigh. Dad pounds out the dent. The grain exits okay.

"Just keep an eye on the corner of the box as you enter under the combine spout," instructs Dad. Teary-eyed, I wonder why I was so worried. The combine is fired up and harvest continues.

I encounter many vehicles travelling on the highway, and I smile and wave. We live in a small community, so everyone waves. It can vary from a full-on hand wave to just the raising of a finger from the steering wheel. I smile and acknowledge the greetings by raising my hand high into the air with an aura of self-confidence.

I grew up thinking this outward act of friendliness occurred everywhere. The realization that this was not the case occurred while we were on our trip to B.C. While driving through Vancouver a vehicle honked its horn.

"Stop, someone knows us," Mom shrieked to Dad. Thankfully, Dad did not slam on the brakes, but it was a rude awakening to learn that the city was not as friendly as our small town!

Combine vs Fence:

Harvesting the home quarter enables the combine to be driven right up to the granary to disperse the grain. The combine spout drops the grain towards the ground onto the blades of the grain auger. The grain auger is basically a long tube that houses a rotating screw blade to move the grain from the ground to an opening in the roof of the granary.

Front Combine: Mom and Charlie.
Back Combine: Dad

"Okay, push the lever," Dad shouts to Charlie and I sitting on the combine. Dad has finished adjusting the grain auger to the correct position for the grain to plunge directly to the perfect spot.

"Can I push the lever?" I inquire.

"Sure," Dad answers.

"Which lever do I push?" I ask Charlie. He points with an extended finger in the direction of several levers; I am unsure which lever he indicated. Perplexed, I glance around to get clarification, but Charlie has vanished into thin air. Contemplating the various levers, I hesitantly choose the closer knob. I push the lever.

The combine lurches abruptly and unexpectedly backwards. My body jerks sharply; I topple erratically and struggle to remain upright. In the meantime, the combine is moving at a steady pace to the rear. I cringe at the deafening sound of crunching wood. Desperately, I scan the front area for the brake; it only takes a second to realize that I do not know how to stop the combine.

I catch a sudden movement out of the corner of my eye. Dad is springing alongside the combine. He flings himself up on the steps and moves quickly up the short ladder. I jump out of the way, as he thrusts himself into the driver's seat to bring the combine quickly to a stop. With a heavy heart, I pray as I clatter down the steps to assess the damage. Wood is strewn everywhere in a haphazard manner. Our fence has been demolished by the runaway combine.

"I was not sure which lever Charlie meant to push," I blurt in a low, quivering voice. Feeling Dad's eyes on me, my insides turn to jelly, and I clasp my trembling hands together tightly.

"The combine is not damaged, and we don't need the fence," Dad replies, after assessing the damage. My shoulders relax and with relief I gaze up to the clear blue sky and whisper a thankful prayer. Dad wiggles his finger in the wind to indicate for me to follow him. We clamber up the combine and Dad proceeds to point out all the mechanisms of the machine.

"You should have stayed on the combine to instruct Julie," Dad admonishes Charlie. Being the oldest boy, he is responsible for helping and protecting his siblings. Charlie learns. Throughout our life, Charlie always steps up to the plate to comfort, support, and assist.

After the incident, I am taught to drive the combine. Dad believes that teaching is a part of our life lessons. I learn to listen to the sound of the motor and watch the rows of grain being gobbled up by the spinning augers at the front of the combine. If the stalks of grain pile up and the engine chugs, I slow down or halt until the sound of *Kerchunk, Kerchunk, Kerchunk* ceases, and the grain stalks are clear. I then move ahead, always listening for any irregularity in the motor and keeping an eye on the front auger for pileups. In addition, I periodically check the seeds in the grain tank to determine if it needs to be emptied.

My harvest duties vary on the farm–from delivering meals, to hauling grain with the Fordson tractor, to combining. I enjoy it all; I especially love driving.

Lost in Grain:

The grain-filled wagon is at the building, ready to be unloaded.

It is our duty to scramble inside the granary, where the threshed grain is housed, and to shovel the grain to the walls as it plummets in a downward stream and heaps upwards, like a teepee, in the middle of the room. As the building fills with seeds, a piece of lumber is added across the door entrance; the opening gets smaller and smaller.

"Chrissy, you can hop into the granary," Dad instructs. Chrissy is the smallest–she is last inside the granary. I am in the wagon, shoveling grain towards the opening. Mom and Dad are shifting any over-spill plunging from the wagon onto the grain auger. Charlie is in the field, cultivating.

Suddenly, a weird sound arises from the granary. A piercing *screeching* noise makes us glance quickly in the direction of the commotion. Astonished, we observe the granary walls swell and sway illogically outwards. We witness the building come apart abruptly, bursting at the seams and the walls plummet outwards. The grain plunges crazily in all directions.

Either the granary walls were weak from age and/or the building was just getting too full, and the pressure exceeded the holding power of the walls.

Instantly, Mom and Dad jump into action. Shovel in hand, they dash frantically to the top of the pile of grain. The still air is broken by the frenzied sound of *swish, swish, swish* as each shovel slices madly into the grain. The seeds scatter in every direction like falling rain. The agonized and distraught expression on their faces fill me with dread. Chrissy is buried in the grain.

Scrambling onto the grain, my smallish hands fly rapidly as I desperately dig into the mound of seeds. Time goes at a snail's pace. I feel a flutter of fear deep in my tummy as I speedily shift the grain; I pray, *Please God, help us find my sister*. We desperately shift the grain in dead silence. Focusing on our vital task, we are determined to find Chrissy. My hands are red and sore from thrusting the seeds into mid-air.

"What are you doing?" a smallish voice asks from our rear. Shovels and hands halt in mid-air. We turn and remain stock-still in stunned shock. Standing before us, displaying a puzzled expression, is Chrissy!

It takes a moment for our brains to comprehend our vision. Chrissy is not buried in the grain! Breathing a sigh of relief, I feel joy well up inside. She is safe!

"Chrissy, where were you?" Dad asks in a trembling voice.

"It got dusty in the granary, so I went to the house for a drink of water," she replies.

The Lord's timing is always perfect.

Farm duties change... it is the last day any of us work inside the granary. A lesson is learned from this frightful experience.

Chapter 52

Vulnerable:

I am alone. My parents and siblings have left in the car, to check on the crops. I remain behind to complete my homework.

The light has turned to dark. I draw the curtain aside and peer out the window. The kitchen light casts a vivid glow through the window-pane for about six feet and then it is

Charlie, Chrissy, Julie, Barry
in back yard

pitch black. The dark is a little daunting–I am glad my family will be home soon. Uneasily, I return to my math homework.

Suddenly, a noise disrupts the tranquil silence. The strident sound of furious barking explodes from the darkness nearby. Our dog, King, is warning me of danger. I am startled, wondering, *What is he barking at?* King is a smallish black and white Lassie-type of dog. King is a part of our family–a very friendly dog but also a great guard dog. He warns of any strangers coming into the yard.

King is in *warning* mode. I hear it in his harsh barking tone as he races down the driveway. Something is wrong. I am filled with fear. Someone is coming. There is no beam of car lights streaming down the driveway–the person is walking. This is odd because we live a quarter of mile out of town. I do not expect anyone. Something is out of sync–my trembling fingers clutch my pencil tightly as my eyes dart about the room, contemplating my next move. My sixth sense shifts into gear and I fling my body out of my chair and sprint out of the kitchen, through the living room, and into my parents' bedroom. I hide in the clothes closet.

We do not have locks on the door. I have a growing sense of alarm. *Do I have time to slide a knife in the door jamb to prevent it opening?* I reflect on the familiar saying, *Trust God but lock the door.* It is too late. I hear a rustle at the front door. King is still barking.

He does not knock: a resounding *click* as the knob turns, followed by the familiar *screech* as the door opens. My heart accelerates, thumping loudly within my chest, and my breath turns rapid and shallow. There is complete silence. I wait with bated breath. *Who is in our house?* As soon as the person enters the house and shuts the door, King ceases barking.

His shoes emit a dull tap on the linoleum floor, indicating that he's entering the kitchen. I listen to his faint footfalls as he steps farther into the house. Suddenly, the advance of footsteps halt. In my mind's eye, I position him near the table, towering over my homework open on the table! I am shaking in my boots! *Is he questioning the presence of someone in the house? Does he touch the chair to feel if it is warm? Does he now realize that someone is in the house? Does he comprehend it is not an adult?*

The house is too quiet. I am a bundle of nerves. After several minutes, his steps resume. Abruptly, the sound changes to a muffled scuffle–he is walking on the carpet. The prowler has entered the living room. Every cell in my body is on high alert. Adjacent to the living room is the bedroom–my hiding spot!

Frantically, I stare out the open curtained window. From my hidey-hole I have a straight line of vision through the bedroom window down the driveway. I search for headlights to appear on the highway that hopefully will turn into our driveway.

Shuffling footsteps. I hear the distinct movement advancing nearer and nearer and nearer. He creeps forward and I can feel his aura filtering into my room. My body trembles. *Please, God, send Mom and Dad home.* I am helpless. I feel rather than see the trespasser at the bedroom door! My breath catches in my throat. *Who is it? What if he finds me? What will he do?* The doorknob rattles.

I am frozen in time. I dare not move a muscle. I dare not breathe. I am a statue. Suddenly, I see a set of tiny headlights moving along the highway. With trepidation I pray, *Please turn into our driveway.* At the same instant, the movement next door comes to an abrupt halt. He spies the headlights. We are both watching the same vehicle and awaiting the next act.

The car appears to be traveling too fast to take the approach. With pounding heart, I reconcile myself to the idea that it isn't my parents. Suddenly, at the last minute, the vehicle turns. I feel a joy so painful it overwhelms me. The car headlights shine their wonderful rays into the house and all around.

Instantly, I hear the *shoosh, clunk* that signifies the quick release of the doorknob. The intruder moves. I detect the scrunch of rapid steps racing across the carpet, transferring to a forceful stomp on the kitchen floor. Relief floods over me. The piercing *screech* reverberates throughout the house as the door opens and closes sharply. The stranger has left the house.

Instantly, King resumes his ferocious barking; he is barking up a storm. His constant, deafening yapping shifts to the side of the house opposite the driveway. The ruckus travels into the distance as King engages with the intruder until he leaves our property. I am traumatized; I peer into the dim room and slowly exit my secret hidey-hole.

I relate the story to my parents. They are shocked and commend King for warning me of the danger. King is my rescuer. My parent's debate whether to inform the authorities. This has happened before, and they have an idea who the culprit is—they are certain it is a *woman* and not a *man*!

My parents did not inform the authorities and they did not confront the lady. Instead, my mom sat me down to explain who she was and why this incident occurred. This was my introduction into learning that the elderly can get a disease called dementia. Mom explained that this lady was probably confused and suffering from a lack of common sense. I understood that this lady did not know what she was doing and had no intention of hurting me. After hearing the story, my heart went out to the lady, and I actually felt very sorry for her condition. Mom suggested that when I was at home on my own, I should slip a knife in between the doorjamb which would wedge the door shut. However, I made a point of never staying home alone ever again.

Young–vulnerable:

We are going for an ice-cream cone. Charlie, Chris, and I are in a vehicle with an older male visiting our parents—he is buying us a treat.

"Julie, do you want to drive the car?" he asks. Sitting in the front seat near the side window, I am thrilled to hear his words.

"Yes," I excitedly reply. I love driving.

"Scootch over beside me and take the steering wheel," he says with a smile. I quickly shift over close to the driver and clutch the steering wheel eagerly, craning my neck to see over the car hood.

I feel a hand slip under my shirt. *What is happening?* The hand rubs my rib cage and then shifts upwards to my smallish breasts-I have just begun puberty. I assume he accidently touched me. Puzzled, I wonder why he does not move his hand out of my shirt. *I feel uncomfortable.* Confused, I do not know what to do. I keep driving and remain silent.

"How come Julie gets to drive? I want to drive," Charlie says in a pleading voice. At that moment I wish it were Charlie driving!

"Julie is driving," the male firmly answers. He does not relocate his hand. I feel uneasy. The ride is over–I am relieved!

The next day, he takes us children to pick berries. We are strolling along the bush trail, enjoying the nature all around us and carrying our little pails of berries.

"Julie, come walk beside me," the male asks. I ignore his request. Suddenly, he moves over to my side of the trail and pulls me close. I am fearful. His hand slowly extends under my shirt again! I really do not like this at all. I decide that I will not give him the opportunity to touch me again.

I avoid him like the plague. For the remainder of his visit, I do not go on any of his offered excursions. However, my young mind is bewildered. *Is this normal? Why does he do this? Does he do this to other girls? Is it just me? Does he think I am from the country and naive?* I feel shame mingled with anger. I do not tell anyone.

I bury the incident deep in my soul, never to tell anyone. My mind tries to forget but my body doesn't. In time I learn that *if it doesn't feel right than it isn't!*

Bedroom Angel:

Someone or something is in my room, grasps my drowsy mind. Waking suddenly from a deep sleep, I feel rather than see a presence in my bedroom. Alarmed, my ears perk up; I listen intently and peer into the dim light. Oddly, my eyes are magnetically drawn to the foot of the bed. Observing a ghostly figure, my body instantly transforms–my heart accelerates, and my breathing becomes shallow and rapid. Instantly, I am wide awake and shiver in the dark.

A female apparition! Peering into the vague light I see her, wearing a transparent gown billowing outwards in waves. A bright light shimmers around her frame, filling the room in a warm glow. She hovers above the footboard in midair and emits an aura of grace and peace. Her long blond hair frames an angelic face and I get the impression that she is a teenager, a couple of years older than me at age twelve. *Is this a figment of my imagination?*

Under the blankets, I shift my body downwards. At the bottom of the bed, I shift my foot to kick gently up towards the inert figure. The blankets tug at my flailing foot, bringing it to a standstill. I am unable to touch this phantom image.

I am not afraid. The spirit is looking down on me lovingly, with gentle and compassionate eyes. I feel a sense of calm and peace descend upon me. This is not a ghost–this is an angel!

I recognize her! Strangely, I know who this angel is even though I have never met her. This angelic figure passed away at the age of six months from crib death. She is my older sister, Judith! God has sent me my very own angel.

"Quick, look," I whisper to my sister, Chrissy, as I tug on her pajamas. However, upon glancing back to the foot of the bed, I see that my beautiful angel has disappeared.

I am in a state of wonder. Slipping into a comfortable sleep I grasp that my sister, Judith, is watching over me. She is my precious angel and I feel safe and secure. I know that angels live among us.

I keep this incident to myself, worried that others might accuse me of seeing things or dreaming. However, throughout my life, I feel and know that I have a guardian angel watching over me.

Part
Seven

Early Teens
Julie 13 – 14 years

Chapter 53

Ghosts of the Mind:

Terror runs through my veins whenever I walk in the dead of night past our neighbourhood's ghoulish, ghostly cemetery. The field of bones is snugly tucked between town and home, skirting the highway and bordering our farm. My only means of travel to and from Weekes is to bypass this cemetery harboring the spirits of dead people. At nightfall, the graveyard summons the ghosts to roam in the inky darkness.

Several years ago, our Uncle Raymond played a trick on us. He asked us how many people there were dead in the cemetery. We children ran to the cemetery and counted every single grave and returned with the exact number.

"No," Uncle said, "that it not the correct answer." We were stunned and insisted that we had counted every single grave. Uncle jokingly responded, "That is not correct–they are all dead." Uncle belted out a hearty laugh. We caught the joke and burst out laughing, too.

The cemetery looks innocent during the day. It seems a peaceful and quiet last resting spot for the dead. However, after sunset it transforms–the graveyard comes alive in the black of night! Walking home via this route, I am prey to frightening images.

On one occasion, I am enjoying a pleasant evening visiting with friends seated in a booth in Mark's Café. My mind briefly thinks of my inevitable walk past the graveyard in the dark, to meet my curfew of eleven o'clock. Ignoring my lingering thoughts, I sip my pop, chat, and giggle like a typical teenager. Time passes quickly and soon the clock displays a quarter to eleven–it is time for me to go. I wave goodbye and begin my quarter-mile walk home via the dreaded cemetery.

The full moon lights up the atmosphere. Looking heavenward I notice that the clouds have dispersed to reveal the brilliance of many twinkling stars. Their light guides me towards the cemetery; it is clear enough to illuminate any dancing spirits or terrifying visions from the spooky graves. The graveyard is illuminated by the heavens, but the graves cast long shadows. The scene elicits terror in me.

I am afraid. Despite my fear and foreboding, I step gingerly forward with my heart pulsating, and my body trembling in fright. Nervously glancing toward the headstones, I tread slowly, step by step by step, closer to the haunted graveyard. Scanning the area, I shudder, and keep my sight focused on each individual headstone to decipher any unexpected flickers.

My breath catches in my throat. I hear a queer, shrill whine, hissing over the tombstones. I shift my attention to the spine-chilling sound. I cannot identify the whine that is coming in waves through the night air. I stop, stock-still, rigid in fear. *Is it time for fight or flight?* I am alone, vulnerable, isolated, and terrified. Cold fear wells up within me. I concentrate on the peculiar noise as it whirls, howling, from the darkness nearby.

A tremor runs through my body. My legs tremble as I force my feet to creep forward, inch by inch by inch, to slink past the gateway to the ghosts. My eyes ogle the graves and I feel rather than see the spirits moving amongst the headstones. I am afraid. With jarring gasps my heart accelerates, and I unsuccessfully attempt to calm my inner terrors. My eyes are riveted to the graves—I am afraid to avert them.

Normal sounds become haunting sounds. My shoes crunch on the coarse gravel, echoing eerily into the still night. A sudden movement. Out of the corner of my eye, at the edge of the yard—a commotion atop the corner gravestone. There is a sudden whir and flash of a flying ghost as it flits into the air. Clutching my purse to my body, I feel my knees buckle, and out of the blue I collapse, to sprawl in a heap on the ground. I freeze in time—rigid, like a statue. Every little noise is magnified. I attempt to control my shaking body. Finally, in the recess of my mind, a little voice is whispering, *A bird, a bird, a bird.* Relief floods throughout my frame as reality sinks in—it is just a bird.

I stagger to my feet and stride hurriedly onward. My eyes stare fixedly into the boneyard, on the lookout for any spectacle or ghostly image. The eerie whining sends another chill up my spine! Courageously I dash forward envisioning the devils right behind me, eager to scoop me up. The crunch of my shoes on the gravel is deafening. I glance behind and sense rather than see the *unknown thing* nip at my heels.

I feel the horror of snatching bony fingers! A wisp of movement glides across my upper back. Disbelief radiates inside my being! I hit high gear! Instantly the moaning whine increases, the hiss comes in surges, and I am more terrified than ever. I pray, *God, please get me home safely.* Fear grips my heart; I muster all my energy to charge swiftly ahead, to travel on the double to home. Turning sharply into our lengthy driveway, I am elated to see bright lights shining. I thank the Lord; I am within screaming distance of our farmhouse.

Safety is straight ahead! Hurtling down the driveway, the wind whips harshly at my face, and my heart is throbbing as I careen towards the house. Feeling a flutter caress my neck, I shake uncontrollably, and silently scream, *Help me. Help me. Help me.* I pick up my pace to gallop around the corner and leap onto the cement sidewalk. Trembling, I dash recklessly, rushing up the front walkway and at the steps skip every second stair in my haste. Frantically, my quivering fingers stretch for the front doorknob to grasp it tightly; I rapidly twist the door handle.

The *unidentified creature* is right behind me. I am petrified and in desperation. I forcefully shove against the door. My momentum is excessive, and as I thrust open the door, I burst through the opening and my body flies with great speed into the room. I land with a thud flat on my face and collapse in disarray on the kitchen floor. I am stunned and motionless. I am emotionally exhausted.

Am I safe? Dead silence surrounds me, but I sense I am not alone. A shiver of apprehension runs through my body! Shifting from my chaotic position, I look upward and am shocked at what I see. Five pairs of bewildered eyes gawk in my direction. Time stands still; the silence is deafening.

"What in the world has happened to you?" Mom asks, with a confused look.

For a long moment I lie immobile, with my breath coming in shuddering gasps. Shaking my head slightly, my hair brushes my shoulder, and in a flash, I recognize the slight flutter of bony fingers.

"I wanted to get some exercise, so decided to run home from town," I desperately blurt. It is at that precise moment that I identify the hissing whine, surging through the night air. Mystery is solved! My imagination has run away with my mind. Boldly and calmly, I continue: "It sure is a powerful wind whining and whistling through the trees tonight, isn't it?"

Ump:

Walking past the graveyard on my way to school the next day, I wonder why I was so scared—the boneyard appears peaceful and tranquil.

After school we have a softball game. In order to obtain an *ump*, we enter Mark's Café.

"Will anyone ump our softball game?" the team captain questions in a loud voice.

My mom volunteers.

The game begins. I am up to bat. The ball flies towards me and I swing the bat–it connects with a wallop and zips far into centre field. I am safe on first base. Legs ready to dash, I keep an eye on our batter. She whacks a good one. I scramble to second base and quickly crank my neck to see if she made it to first base. She is sprinting and almost there.

"Go! Go! Go!" I yell. In the meantime, the ball is in the air, moving towards the first baseman. She catches the softball several moments before my teammate slides into first base.

She is out! It is obvious my teammate slid into first base after the ball arrived. There is an audible sigh from my team and my heart sinks as I realize that she is just seconds too late. But wait, the ump, my mom, is jumping up and down and waving her arms wildly.

"Safe! Safe! Safe!" she is yelling. I am about to die of embarrassment as I realize that Mom is cheering not umping! I cringe a little inside and there are stunned expressions all around. *What will happen*? Well, there is no question. The ump has the final say–she is safe!

Did my mom ever ump again? No, but it is a known fact that she is always willing to pitch in anywhere and anytime. Her character is impulsive, caring, and fun-loving. She is my mom and always willing to lend a hand.

Chapter 54

Regatta:

The Kelowna Regatta is coming to town! Fortunately, Mom and I are visiting Aunt Evelyn and Uncle Raymond in Kelowna, BC. Unfortunately, we do not have the extra money to attend. Uncle Raymond suggests getting a job at the nearby Okanagan Fruit and Vegetable Farm to earn a few extra dollars. The next day Mom and I apply, and soon find ourselves on the edge of a never-ending row of pole beans. Our fingers nimbly pluck the beans and deftly chuck them into sacks slung around our necks. At the end of each row, we empty the bounty into our own specific bucket. It is hard, tedious work, bending up and down under the blazing hot sun. We focus on the famous Kelowna Regatta.

Finally, the big day arrives. We arrive at the Regatta where the sights, sounds, and aromas fill us with exuberance. Several hours later, the adults stop to study the map to decide our next move. Out of my peripheral vision, I notice a young boy my age approaching me.

"Would you like to go on the Ferris Wheel with me?" the young lad asks. This sounds exciting so I agree and, without asking permission, I disappear around the corner onto the ride. Unfortunately, the adults do not see me go.

"Where did my family go?" I exclaim, upon alighting from the ride. I am shocked that Mom and my relatives are nowhere in sight! *Why would they leave me?*

"I have a free pass to all the rides and boat races so let's just enjoy ourselves," my new friend suggests. *What else can I do?* Therefore, we run from ride to ride, having a glorious time all afternoon. Towards the end of the day, we watch and cheer from the stands at the exhilarating boat races.

"I need to find my mom," I announce, noting that it is late afternoon. We begin to scour the grounds for my entourage. Unknown to me, they spent the whole day searching for me. Eventually, I see them huddled in a small group. They notice me. A chill travels through my body as all eyes stare angrily in my direction. I turn to my friend with a worried expression.

"They look angry. Thanks for the fun day–I need to go," I utter hurriedly to my friend. Without another word, I dash away from my friend and scurry to face the music.

"Where have you been?" Mom demands. I am silent. "Were you with that boy all day?"

"Yes," I blubber timidly. Mom frowns and without another word we depart the Regatta. The silence is deafening! We exit the car park.

"You should know better than to just disappear," Uncle angrily states. I am lectured all the way home. My exciting event has turned into an unfortunate incident. Relieved to arrive at Uncle's house, I slink in disgrace to the playhouse in the backyard to lick my wounds. *How will I face anyone ever again?* I am too embarrassed to pray.

The playhouse door swings open. Suddenly, my cousin Fern, the same age as me, bounces inside.

"Julie, are you in here?" she shouts. I groan inwardly. *Oh no, another lecture!* However, I am taken by surprise by the look of admiration written all over her face.

"I hear you experienced an exciting day. Tell me all about it. I hear you were with a boy!" she exclaims animatedly.

Soon I am relating every detail of my adventure. Fern pumps me for details; I fulfill her wish about my friend.

"He is handsome, friendly, and nice. He had passes to all rides and events. He must be rich!" I regale her with every single action—even embellishing some of the points. I have a captive audience—my cousin sits entranced by my thrilling tale. She gobbles up every word, and her eyes are full of admiration. In a matter of minutes, I journey from the depths of despair to the glory of fame.

Mom has a happy-go-lucky nature that prefers harmony; it is impossible for her to stay mad! The next day we go shopping. I purchase my first purse and moderate-high heels. All is well in my world again.

In retrospect, it was a foolish stunt on my behalf, and life experience once again taught me a lesson. I am thankful that the Lord watched over me, once again!

Chapter 55

Best friend:

Upon arriving home from Kelowna, I am excited to show my best friend my new purse.

Best friends are priceless! I met my best friend at the beginning of grade seven. Charlie, Chris, Barry, and I are taking a shortcut through the schoolyard on the first day of school. Suddenly, bursting around the side of the school I see two girls running at great speed in our direction.

"Julie, will you sit by me in the classroom?" Sandra-R gasps breathlessly as she stops in front of me. This is music to my ears; I have several casual friends, but not a best friend.

Mrs. MacNaughton in rear. Back: Sandra C., Janie, Della, Faye, Julie, Sandra R.. Front: Charlie, Leonard, Danny at Vacation Bible School

Do I believe in friendship love at first sight? Yes, that day we are destined to become best pals. Sandra is good-natured, has a kind heart, is always smiling and has a friendly personality. Throughout our school years we do everything together - Girls Club, Sunday school, Vacation Bible School, school events, evening typing, and French classes etc. etc.

In our teens, we practice jiving until we move in unison, as one. We rock the floor at school dances and at many a weekend wedding dance. We have sleepovers on the weekend and double date. We laugh outrageously over silly things, confide our innermost thoughts, discuss crushes, our loves, our break-ups—all things that belong to teenage friends. We have other friends, but we are best friends. We rely on each other and are joined at the hip. My adolescent years are full of the many memories created with my best friend, Sandra. We are like two peas in a pod!

One day at Greenwater Lake we are double dating. Before heading home my boyfriend leans down to put the fire out and unintentionally let *gas go*. Simultaneously Sandra and I burst into laughter. We are soon out of control in a fit of giggles. In an attempt to restrain our chortling, we leave the scene and go to the restroom. Our rolling raucous laughter reverberates throughout the whole campground. Eventually we quiet ourselves, return and are soon on our way home. My boyfriend obviously uncomfortable leans into me and whispers quietly, "It wasn't that funny!" I titter, and a chuckle erupts from the front seat. Soon Sandra and I are hysterically laughing again. My boyfriend is embarrassed, and it is a little mean, however we are totally out of control again. We laugh fitfully all the way home. Sandra and I are definitely two peas in a pod.

Best Friends
Julie and Sandra

Therefore, upon Mom and I returning from B.C. I am eager to see my best friend; however, since we do not have a phone, I will need to walk into town.

Sandra is strolling down my driveway. I am excited to view her figure approaching and my body overflows with joy as I run out to greet her. I realize at that moment how much I missed my best friend.

"Look what I bought in the city," Sandra utters excitedly, as she gyrates to reveal a purse slung over her shoulder.

"Come see what I got from the city," I reply. Laughter erupts at the discovery that we both purchased a purse. Clutching our prized possessions tightly, we grin gleefully as our eyes beam the message, *We are so grown-up!*

"Let's go up to the café for a pop," Sandra suggests. I agree, discerning that we can show off our up-to-date image. What a sight we make—two young teens frolicking down the driveway, swinging our purses wildly by our sides. We are happy, chatting joyfully—clearly enthralled to be together again. Our hands clasp, symbolizing our friendship. Together we formed a special friendship that brought joy and caring into each other's lives throughout our school years.

Chapter 56

Driving:

Vehicles have always been a part of my life. I have become a very capable driver of tractors and combines through my many learning incidents. I am now ready for the next step, and that is to drive the truck.

Dad is teaching me to drive the Chevy half-ton truck; the shift is "three-on-a-tree." In other words, it has the lever mounted on the steering column with three gears in the transmission. Shifting into first gear, I release the clutch. The truck jerks sporadically a few inches while my body lurches in unison; the vehicle stalls and stops.

"What is happening?" I shout and gasp for breath. Dad calmly gives me step-by-step instructions. My dad is patient, and we are soon travelling along the highway. Suddenly, the truck swerves towards the deep ditch.

"The road is too narrow, and the truck is too wide," I announce, perplexed. Unperturbed, Dad casually guides me. Dad emanates the motto, *Patience is a virtue.*

It is Mom's turn to teach. I proudly begin to show off my excellent driving skills.

"Woap! Woap! Woap!" Mom bellows. Startled, I slam on the brakes and Mom almost careens out the front window. She is still screaming.

"What is wrong?" I ask, worriedly.

"You almost hit the ditch!" she shouts anxiously. Mom's flustered bellow combined two modes of halt: telling the horse (the prior mode of transportation) "Whoa," and an order of "Stop." "Whoa" and "Stop" became "Woap!"

Mom never offered her driving services again! Thus, Dad taught us to drive, and Mom bragged of our great driving skills.

Our parents insist that we practice, practice, practice to become good drivers. Keeping in mind our past driving incidents, they suggest we practice driving on our own driveway. We drive to the end of our extremely long driveway, then reverse and back up. Back and forth. Back and forth. Back and forth. We become excellent *back-up* drivers! Our parents believe that learning to drive will bring us a sense of freedom throughout our lives, and they are correct.

Cars, Trains, Teens:

We are teenagers who are constantly seeking opportunities to branch out and exert our independence. Sometimes, pursuing new experiences can get us exposed to situations that are dangerous or harmful to ourselves and others.

On one occasion, Charlie, Chris, and I are packed in a vehicle with several friends, motoring around town. It is a glorious hot weekend, and we are cruising aimlessly with the windows wound down, allowing the breeze to whip briskly through the sedan.

"This vehicle can motor along the railway tracks without me driving," announces our friend.

In disbelief, we all argue that this is impossible. We laugh sardonically at the idea that he can step on the gas and not touch the steering wheel.

"I will prove my theory," he announces. We are soon sailing down the tracks. Astoundingly, no one is touching the steering wheel and we are zipping along, with the trees flying by in a blur. It only takes a short time for the wonder to subside and reality to sink in.

"What if a train comes?" Chris whispers with a quavering voice.

Fear grips my heart at our perilous situation. I clutch the door handle, prepared to jump out at the first sign of a train engine

"Maybe we should go back," I mutter, hesitantly and nervously. I send up a quick prayer. *God, please keep us safe.* Our driver slams on the brakes, shifts into reverse, and suddenly our machine is flying backwards. We are not sure if we are able to just veer off the tracks; regardless, with the deep ditches running alongside the tracks, we need to go back to the railway crossing where we entered. Once we are on solid ground, I breathe a huge sigh of relief. We are fortunate that our vehicle tires did not pop, leaving us stranded on the railway tracks, and also very blessed that a train did not come flying around the corner.

I vow to never to do that again. I will *think before acting.*

Joyride:

Another opportunity arises to exercise our ingenuity when we hear that Mom and Dad are driving to Tisdale to get parts for the combine. Charlie, Chris, and I furtively glance at one another with gleeful grins—we will be on our own babysitting Barry. Mischief prevails! With great excitement, we peek out from behind the curtains to watch until our parents exit the driveway. Instantly, we race to the station wagon, which was purchased for Mom's school bus run. It has a school bus sign installed on the roof.

Of course, Charlie gets to the driver's seat first. I settle Barry in the back seat with Chris and clamber into the front passenger seat. In eagerness, Charlie promptly steps on the gas and with a shudder the vehicle moves swiftly on the road. We turn left to drive through town. Whizzing around town, we are thrilled to discover that the station wagon has power. Like a skyrocket, it zooms around town and creates an aftershock—a huge dust cloud that billows out rapidly and lingers, to float in the air. We have a jolly good time, laughing and waving to everyone.

Problems arise the following day. The townspeople snitch on us.

"I was told that you children were tearing up and down the town streets in the station wagon," Mom states matter-of-factly. We are dead silent. Cold fear engulfs us as we contemplate our punishment. Mom appears quite indignant and very upset. We know we are in trouble. Before we can defend ourselves, she continues, "It must be someone from out of town, with a similar vehicle. I know my children would not do that."

We are astounded and cannot believe what we have just heard. Mom expects us to be better behaved. We live up to Mom's expectations and never take the vehicle again! Is she naïve or is she smart?

Chapter 57

The Secret Pact:

Teen life is carefree. I dance, hang out with friends and siblings, and just live life to the fullest. My siblings and I are close; we run around together. Thus, they are with me on that dreadful day. Our parents are oblivious to almost losing three of their four children in this tragic incident. It is on this earth-shattering day that our small group upholds a promise of silence, ultimately pledging a *secret pact*!

It is a secret between me and four other teenagers that is preserved for over 57 years. A catastrophic event occurs in the late summer of 1963, so dangerous and deadly that we almost perish. A frightening image roots itself in my mind for many decades, and for a long time I am powerless to tell a soul. I am ready to tell my story.

We are unaware that storm clouds are on the horizon. The sun is blazing hot and the heat oppressive even in the shade, as I, along with my siblings and friends, hang out together. At fourteen years old, I am second oldest in the family. My passions are dancing and driving. My brother Charlie is a year older and always looking for fun and excitement. Sister Chris, being a year younger, enjoys hanging out with her older siblings. She is even-tempered and just goes with the flow. Floyd is a couple of years older: he is carefree, kind, and the sort to give the shirt off his back to anyone in need. Billy is Floyd's friend, and he is always game for anything. These very personal qualities contribute to our ill-fated escapade: Floyd (giving of himself), Billy (along for the ride), brother Charlie (eager for excitement), me (wanting to drive), sister Chris (just delighted to tag along).

Enjoying the happy-go-lucky life of teenagers, we do not foresee the upcoming trauma. Chattering cheerfully, we are cruising in Floyd's vehicle on the graveled road of Highway 23 in northeastern Saskatchewan. We zip along merrily with a massive dust cloud billowing from the rear of the vehicle.

A discussion is in full swing. We are determining the benefits of partaking in an extraordinary mission. At the heart of the controversy is an old '36 Chevy four-door sedan, sporting a faded quail-gray coat and worn gunmetal interior. It belongs to our friend Floyd's family and is parked on their vacant farm, situated in the bush, with no license plates.

The old jalopy has piqued our curiosity. Floyd's portrayal points out its unique bi-fold hood, that opens on each side, and the large front grille, bathed in chrome, rounded at the top to descend, narrowing, towards the bottom. He talks about the peculiar doors that open in the middle with the hinges located at front and back. In later years they will be referred to as *suicide doors*. Visions come alive with such an intriguing illustration, and we are all beaming, eager to take it for a spin!

This incredible vehicle is off limits to Floyd. We hammer out the possibilities, deliberating the pros and cons of our quest.

Suddenly, I jump with a start as a blast of thunder explodes and rain begins thumping down harshly, pummeling the roof. The windshield wipers fly madly through the air, swiping at the ribbons of water. Glancing at one another uneasily, I wonder, *Is this an ominous sign? Is God giving us a warning?* Silence cuts through the atmosphere. I ignore my lingering thoughts and proceed to encourage our venture.

"I am game!" I announce with a smile. "Can I drive?"

"It will be exhilarating to ride in an ancient coupe," Charlie states, his eyes ablaze with excitement.

"Yes," Chris quietly murmurs and nods her head.

"Yes," Floyd, eager to please, answers with a grin, and Billy readily approves. Mission accomplished!

We arrive at the farm. There is a momentary lull in the storm, and the sun shoots its warm rays into our midst. Thrashing through the thick, wet brush, the twigs slap us in the face while the moist grass saturates our shoes. We stop abruptly, as one, to stare in amazement at the unbelievable coupe. Outlined against the towering fir trees, the sun's shadowy rays enshroud the sedan like a blanket. Its bucket headlights protrude visibly from each side of the grille, beckoning to us like bright eyes. It is out of this world! Frantic with excitement, there is no hesitation—at the sight of the sedan our adventurous spirit is in full gear.

We move together as one, striding swiftly forward. The tall grass, heavy with moisture, soaks us from the waist down. We appear like drowned rats, with our wet clothes clinging snugly to our skin. The up-turned roots poke sharply into our shoes, and the mud from puddles coats the undersides. Hurriedly, ten scrambling shoes race to the car and five pair of hands stretch out to grope the side-by-side door handles. We scramble inside the grimy and musty sedan. Shimmying into our seats, we are engulfed in a dusty film that settles into our hair, noses, mouths, and clothes.

Immediately I plunk my body behind the steering wheel. Scanning the front dashboard, I note only two dials. One dial registers the speed, and the other dial shows the oil pressure, voltage meter, and the fuel. My heart skips a beat to discover that the shift is four-on-the-floor. In other words, the shift lever is in the middle of the car with four gears in the transmission. The gear shift is not the same but is similar to the Fordson tractor. My confidence is surging ahead!

Miraculously, the key is in the ignition! Without hesitation, I turn the key and push the start button; to my dismay I only detect the *sput, sput, sput* noise from the motor.

"Here's what we will do," Floyd, who is sitting next to me, calmly explains. "I will pull the throttle to choke the gas, while you push the start button and simultaneously pump the foot pedal." We apply this technique, and, with a groan, the motor roars to life.

The needle points to a quarter tank of gas. We are astonished and pleased to discover the gas gauge works. Enthusiastically, I place one hand on the three-spoke steering wheel, and hastily grasp the gear shift knob. I attempt to shift into first gear. The apparatus is very stiff, so I wiggle and jiggle the gear stick until, with a grind, it pops into first gear.

The Chevy launches forward. Slowly moving towards the bush road, the vehicle shimmies and shakes over the rough terrain, and we are instantly covered by a flurry of dust from inside the vehicle. Finally the sedan surfaces safely onto the bush road and with a loud grinding noise I shift into second gear. Sailing smoothly down the lane, with the trees flying by in a blur, we emerge into an open area. The grassy road is spongy and slick from the rain; I rapidly shift into third gear and step on the gas pedal.

We progress at a reckless tempo. Without warning, the sedan skids erratically across the road. Frightened, my arms react automatically to twirl the steering wheel fiercely to the left and then just as swiftly to the right. Cold fear overwhelms me as I fling the steering wheel back and forth in an attempt to correct the sporadic movement of the out-of-control vehicle.

"Help me! Help me! Help me!" I screech in a panicked voice.

"Stop turning the steering wheel," I hear Floyd yell in the far distance. However, before I can comprehend his words and respond, the vehicle flips and flings over and over and over. Bodies fly everywhere and I find myself bouncing off the ceiling amidst a swirl of dust. The sedan comes to a stop. The vehicle lands next to the side of the bush road, positioned on its roof.

Time is at a stand-still! Surprised to be sprawled on the road, too weak to move, I strain my ears to detect any voices. All is eerily silent. I am filled with dread at the sight of the overturned sedan. A dust cloud hovers above the auto and its wheels are still spinning. *Is anyone alive?* I silently pray.

There is movement in the meadow. Relief floods through my body as several figures stagger to their feet and slowly stumble towards the road. We assemble, taking stock of each other to determine if all are present. In a flash, we are horrified to realize one person is missing! In a panic, we frantically holler for Billy and cast our eyes in search of him. A shout shatters the silence; we glance towards the inverted sedan, where we spot a figure crouching near the window. Billy crawls slowly out of the window opening to escape the wreckage. He is alive!

The Chevy is demolished. Standing as one, we congregate in shock and in pain as we gawk at the wrecked sedan. We conclude that the sedan has rolled over three times. Relief overpowers us …

We all survived! Considering the scene, we should have perished in the wreck, but Fate had a different plan. The vehicle is demolished. The roof is crushed into a deep *Vee*, the doors scrunched like an accordion, the hood hanging on by a thread, the grille crumpled, and all the windows smashed to bits.

God has given us a second chance at life. The enormity of God's intervention in the outcome of this accident is realized years later. Of course, we did not realize it at this time, as we stand huddled together on this damp, cloudy, muggy afternoon. Covered in dirt and visibly shaking, we are in a state of shock. Trembling and cowering together on the road, we examine our injuries. My arm is in pain, bent and immobile. Billy's shoulder is throbbing. All others suffer agonizing aches and pains. We are in quite a dilemma.

"We cannot report this accident—no vehicle registration, no license plate, and Julie with no driver's license," Floyd groans. My heart sinks. Unsaid is the fact that Floyd does not have permission to drive this '36 Chevy! The air feels thick and heavy as we crowd together, nestled in a close circle on that lonely road. Fear grips me at the vision of the wrecked sedan as we strive to solve our complicated problem. Genuinely worried, our unanimous conclusion is decided:

'36 Chevy

no one can ever know the truth, and we need a cover-up story. Our group of five teenagers formulates a secret pact!

Floyd solves one problem. He volunteers to take the blame and confess to his parents that he wrecked the sedan. Our injuries need to be addressed; thus, we must devise our cover-up story before departing to the hospital. Shivering, half-frozen in shock, we struggle to create a story on the spur of the moment. Suddenly, Chris remembers that a few days ago at Shady Lane someone broke a huge branch from a well-known gigantic tree.

A plan begins to formulate. Shady Lane is a scenic spot where many families go to take pleasure in a picnic under the shade of this magnificent tree, which towers over Shand Creek. This creek is teeming with crabs, crawling along the bottom; we are mindful to keep our feet up and moving when we venture in for a swim.

A perfect plan materializes. Our story will be that all five of us climbed the infamous tree at Shady Lane to sit precariously on the huge branch, when it broke abruptly to propel us all tumbling to the ground.

We agree. It is a good cover-up story—so unbelievable and unique that it has to be true. Without another word, we hurriedly take off to the hospital.

"Were you in car accident?" the nurse asks. Although embarrassed to relate the tree story, we hesitantly blunder through the plausible tale. "It sure is a lot of dirt for just falling out of a tree," she replies suspiciously. We stick to our story. We lie on the white gurneys, our bodies spreading dirt all over the white sheets.

We are assessed. My arm is not broken; it is severely sprained, and I am destined to wear a sling for several weeks. Billy has a wrenched shoulder and receives a tight dressing. We are informed that the pain from all the other minor sprains and bruises will eventually subside. We are thankful that our injuries are not life threatening.

Our story has passed the test. Fortunately, our parents are more concerned about our injuries than the broken tree branch. Climbing a tree is innocent fun in their books. Brother Barry, age ten years, listens in awe to our story and bombards us with questions.

"Were you scared? How high was the branch? Did it break right off?" We hesitantly murmur answers to his numerous queries.

We visit the scene of our car accident a few days later and reminisce on how fortunate we were to survive. We are pleased that our story has past the test – we are unaware that trouble brews over the supposed tree incident.

Much to our chagrin, the owners of Shady Lane confront our parents over the "tree" incident. Apparently, the owners, along with the towns-people, are furious with us for breaking the tree branch from such a monu-mental landmark. It is a tree that towers over a wide expanse and provides abundant shade for many picnicking families. The big question they pon-dered was how all five of us could have fit on the tree branch. We take the blame, feel the wrath, and endure the darts thrown our way for many, many days. We wonder who the real culprits are who broke the tree branch–obvi-ously someone else with a secret!

Charlie, Floyd, and Julie

Our cover-up story serves its purpose; however, it has its downside. Floyd suffers the consequences for wrecking the sedan. His parents are upset, as they planned to gift the '36 Chevy to his younger sibling, Wilmer. Nobly, Floyd takes the harsh criticism in silence.

Wilmer is the same age as Chris, and we all chum together – fortu-nately Wilmer was not with us that day. Mom and their Mom Ina are good friends so I wonder if Mom will hear about Floyd's incident of wrecking the vehicle. However, we hear nothing, so I assume that Mom was not told, or she was just thankful that her children were not involved. Wilmer must have been upset that Floyd wrecked his car, but with a pleas-ant personality and being very easy going - he does not tell a soul. Also, Billy's sister, Sharon is my friend who fortunately was not with us on this dreadful day. I spend many weeks wondering if she will question me – she does not. We as a group abide by our secret pact!

The tall tale causes me uncomfortable moments.

"I can't believe you are still climbing trees at your age," a teacher at school leans into me and softly whispers. I feel shame mingled with annoyance, but silently cringe inside. The following evening at a hall dance, a young man picks me up for a whirl.

"What happened to your arm?" he politely asks. Of course, after the teacher's comment I am not going to say I fell out of a tree.

"I tripped over a block in the yard," I glibly reply.

"How did you manage that?" he asks. I am pondering the question when, at that very moment, another couple swings by us in a whirl.

"Hey, Julie, I hear you fell out of a tree!" the guy shouts in a loud voice. Shuddering, I feel hot blood creep up my neck; I want to sink through the floor and disappear. Strangely, the young fella does not ask me to dance again—I wonder why not?

The toughest predicament occurs the following day.

"Julie, you can drive us home for dinner," Dad announces. We were working together in the field several miles from home. My knees tremble, my armpits drip profusely, and my mind is anguished. *No. No. No.* In my normal world, this would be an exciting offer; I cannot, therefore, admit that I am too nervous to drive. Consequently, I hesitate, yet I slide cautiously behind the steering wheel. Gritting my teeth, I shift into gear and propel us in a comfortable but dawdling pace along the road.

"Why are you driving so slow?" Dad exclaims, several minutes into our ride. He continues with his familiar chuckle. "Step on it a bit! At this speed, by the time we get home it will be suppertime instead of dinner!" I force a little laugh and, with a heavy heart, thrust my vibrating leg downwards to press my quivering foot firmly against the gas pedal. My hands are clammy, and I pray as I grip the steering wheel and begin to move at a faster pace. The aftereffects of the accident linger in my bodily movements and in my frantic mind.

This will be a quick, but slow ride home, I conclude. Gradually relaxing, I get back into the groove and feel my bravado rebuilding. Entering our extended driveway, I am engulfed in a blanket of calmness. I have restored my self-assurance and am driving with confidence once again—thanks to my dad.

Our traumatic experience produces safety-conscious drivers. As the years pass, we grow up to leave our little hometown of Weekes, to prepare our own way in the world. Many times, my siblings and I gather under the cherry tree and whisper together, reminiscing over the haunting event, thankful that God stepped in and took care of us that day. The Lord watches over us and is our protective shield even when we are unaware.

We believe that it was an act of God to permit each of us to walk away from the accident unscathed. The Lord is our Saviour!

Chapter 58

Siblings' accident:

The Chevy incident continued to haunt me, and I felt its echoes into the future when Charlie, Chris, and I traveled to Greenwater Lake for a day of fun.

Upon arriving at the lake, I met up with friends, and waved goodbye to Charlie and Chris after setting a time to meet in a couple of hours.

However, within an hour, I see Charlie and Chris waving frantically to me from the parking lot. They look distraught.

"What is wrong?" I gush immediately.

"We were in a roll-over accident," Chris replies. My heart skips a beat and I am stunned.

"Oh no, not again!" I shout, "Who? What? Where?"

"We were invited to take a spin in a fancy car by a friend. We didn't know the driver because he was a friend of our friend," Charlie answers shakily. My heart accelerates and pounds to the beat of drums. This feels strangely familiar, and I am having flashbacks of our recent accident.

"Are you both okay?" I inquire. Upon receiving an affirmative answer, I hastily comment, "Let's go home; we need to inform Mom and Dad before they get wind of it." We are from a small town and news travels quickly on the grapevine.

We hurriedly exit the park. Travelling home, we delve deep into our own meditations—the silence is deafening.

The terrible news is delivered. Our parents are thankful everyone is safe; however, they are angry from fear.

"Why would you get into a vehicle driven by a stranger?" Dad quizzes Charlie and Chris. "Why, at the moment of erratic driving, did you not get out?" Finally, Dad turns to me, bends down to meet me face to face.

"Where were you? Why were you not taking care of your sister?" he demands in a loud voice. My Dad does not normally shout—I know I am in deep trouble! I know that I am expected to take care of my younger sister! Hanging out with friends will not be a good excuse! My mind is in a whirl.

"I was with John. In a boat. Fishing." The words spring forth in short bursts from my mouth. I am under pressure and am reacting and thinking on the spot. Our parents have a high opinion of John, thus my explanation calms Dad. Unknowingly John has come to my rescue.

"You must always look out for your younger sister," Dad replies in a lower, composed voice as he rises slowly to his full height. We receive a lecture on the importance of safe driving. He ends the discussion with firm words. "The vehicle is a powerful machine. Treat it that way."

Dad's words penetrate my being and I have a sick feeling in my stomach. I know only too well that the vehicle is a powerful machine—I have experienced this firsthand with the Chevy incident. I hope my siblings are taking note of Dad's advice, too. I send up a quick prayer, thanking God for keeping my siblings safe.

Chapter 59

Friends:

Friends are always welcome in our house, day or night, and we often end up with several in the double bed that sister Chris and I share. We sleep head to foot to take up less room.

One summer, we moved our bedroom into the abandoned summer kitchen. The summer kitchen was used when our house had a wood cookstove. In order to keep the house cool, Dad built the summer kitchen and installed a wood cookstove; all the cooking duties were performed in this building so the house could stay cool in the summer. Our house now has an electric stove, so the summer kitchen is no longer required. This building is nestled under the trees; it is cool under the shade of the trees.

On weekends, we offer our friends to stay overnight—we can invite our friends over at any time, without asking our parents. It's a good thing that Mom cooks plenty of food at mealtimes. My girlfriends spend nights at our house, and I spend nights at their houses.

At Jean's house, we wake to the pleasant sounds of her mother singing. Jean enjoys singing as much as I, so we lie on her top bunk bed and belt out our voices. She teaches me a new song, "Pick me up on your way down." We discuss the important things in our lives. At the moment we are excited with the prospect that in just over a year we will turn sixteen, and eligible to obtain our driver's license.

At Sandra's, we get to sleep past ten in the morning. This is a real treat because at my house we must be up by that time. After breakfast we tackle the bed sheets – it is her Saturday chore. Our time together is always special because we are best friends thus, we spend most of our free time together. Sandra's sister Brenda is good friends with my sister, Chris, which means the four of us quite often end up snug as a bug in a double bed at our house – a sleepover. And we spend many hours in our swimming pool – the dugout.

Back: Sandra, Julie. Middle: Jean, Janie, Charlie, Leigh. Front: Brenda, Chris. Leonard leaning on fence

At Jenny's house, we wake to breakfast on the table. A treat for me, because my parents drive school bus and are gone by the time I get up. Therefore, we children are quite adept at preparing our own breakfast. On Saturday evenings, Jenny comes to my house early and we laugh together over the antics of *The Beverly Hillbillies* on television. After the show, we chat amiably while applying mascara and putting the final touches on our hairdos before we are on our way uptown to the café to hang-out with our friends

At Nellie's home, she lives with her dad and brother. It is very different at her house, where we make our own meals and take care of ourselves. Nellie is not only my good friend, but she is also my brother's girlfriend.

She spends many nights at our house, and I enjoy having her–she is like another sister!

At Shirley's, we are tricky. I am allowed out this evening - she is not. In her upstairs bedroom I peer out the open window at the ladder. descending way, way, way down to the ground.

"You go first," Shirley utters in a low voice. I shift my body backwards and shimmy out the window, my legs flail in the dark searching for the top rung of the ladder. With a sigh of relief my foot connects, and I slowly but shakily descend downward. At the bottom rung I jump quickly – thankful to be on solid ground. "Duck down," Shirley shouts in a loud whisper. I duck down. Together we scrunch our bodies downwards and slink past the downstairs living room window where we can hear the television blasting out a show. We clasp hands and run to meet Shirley's best friend Sharon who is waiting for us in the school yard. Sharon has an easy-going personality and is also a part of my group of friends. Dashing away I quickly glance backwards to see if we are being pursued - I only see the ladder extending up to the second story window. Shirley's parents are unaware and amazingly not suspicious of the ladder propped under Shirley's upstairs window. Perhaps they consider this an escape route in case of fire

Prior to our escapade we painted our nails, practiced jiving, and sang the latest songs. Shirley has a wonderful melodious voice and I enjoy singing. Shirley is the oldest and her younger sisters look up to her with admiration and enjoy being around her friends, so I get to interact with them as well. They refer to my brother Charlie as *Elvis Presley with blond hair*. When their baby sister is born, it is a heartfelt honor when I and sister Chris learn that she will be our namesake and bear both our names, Christine Julie. It is an extra special moment when we learn that the children had the honor of choosing their baby sisters name and because they liked us, they chose our names. Our parents are chuffed at the news and relay that her parents said, "We hope our baby Christine Julie grows up to be as nice as your girls." In retrospect, I wonder, *Their words or Mom's words?* In either case this is a proud and treasured moment in our lives.

In addition to viewing various family dynamics, I also experience different types of food and cooking methods. For example, at Janie's house I learn a quick way to make hot chocolate. At home, we milk a cow; we therefore use whole milk, warm it up in a pot on the cookstove, and add Quik chocolate mix. At Janie's house, at breakfast, her mom has water boiling in the teakettle. She fills our cup with hot water, we add the Quik mix and pour in evaporated milk. This is a lot quicker than our old-fashioned way of preparing hot chocolate. I am impressed. Janie and I are tired since we chatted the night away reminiscing about our recent trip to B.C. together. We travelled in her brother's vehicle with her Mom Mary, my Mom, and Dolly Tyacke. It was an eventful adventure where we encountered a flat tire, froze while tenting in the mountains and were thrilled when we caught the attention of a group of boys in a car. We laughed until the wee hours of the morning. That is considered a good sleepover!

I prefer the overnight stays at my house. I am a homebody. Our parents are very welcoming and there is always plenty to eat. One evening, we are served our typical huge bowl of chocolate pudding.

"Do you get this much all the time?" my friend whispers to me in astonishment.

"Yes," I answer. This is the norm in our family.

Our home is an open house. Our parents never know how many people will turn up at the breakfast table. Laughter rings throughout the house – a good indication that our parents and our friends blend well together. Our parents believe, *If our children entertain at home, then we can keep a watchful eye and get to know their friends.*

Chapter 60

Stealing:

"Let's go uptown for a pop," my friend suggests. I am in a quandary. I do not have any money. I have an idea, but my mind wonders. *Should I, or shouldn't I?*

In the spur of the moment, I decide—I will. I eye Mom's coat hanging by the front door and thrust my hand into the pocket. *Bingo,* I feel a coin. I glance in my open palm to discover a dime. I grin—it is the exact amount I need for a pop.

Clutching my dime, I happily prance uptown with my friend. However, as we get close to Mark's Café, I begin to feel uneasy. The dime feels like a weight in my hand. We enter the café, and my heart comes to a standstill. *What am I going to do?* The word from the Bible reverberates through my mind. *Thou shalt not steal.* My friend orders a pop and then it is my turn.

"Oh, I don't feel like a pop right now," I say in a composed voice.

I realize my faith does not allow stealing. Arriving home, I fling open the door, step in and glance around. No one is in sight. I swiftly drop the dime back into mom's pocket. With a sigh of relief, I feel better.

I am determined never to do that again.

Privacy Store:

I seem to learn my life skills by experience. On one occasion, my encounter begins innocently enough when Mr. Wallace, owner of the Co-op Store hands Dad his monthly invoice. Mr. Wallace generously allows the townspeople to charge items in the store and pay monthly. The statement is open in plain sight, so I peek over Dad's shoulder to analyze the amount. Suddenly, I am sure that I notice an error on the invoice.

"I think there is an error on …" I blurt out to Dad.

"We will talk about this at home," Dad interrupts, before I can finish my sentence.

"We do not discuss private matters in public," remarks Dad upon leaving the store. In our family, money, farming, and personal business is private business. In addition, we are not allowed to gossip about anyone or anything.

Our parents have a unique way to discuss private matters. Many times, Mom and Dad will go to look at the crops on their own–it is a sure sign they need to discuss personal matters about the farm that do not need *little ears* tuning into the conversation.

Thus, I determine that money matters are private matters, gossiping is not allowed, and discussions are between interested parties only.

We witness the respect, love, and unity between our parents. They never make negative remarks to or about each other and we see their love expressed openly–they are often found snuggling together on the couch.

Do not gossip:

The following week, I learn a life lesson while visiting with Dad at the neighbours. It is a beautiful spring day, and the dust is rising around our sedan as we depart from our neighbours' dirt road.

"Her matrimonial cake is not as good as Mom's," I mutter to my dad. Earlier, we were served cake for a snack.

"Julie, that might be true; however, you should be thankful that she is kind enough to offer us something to eat," Dad replies in a soft voice. He is teaching me to look for the positive rather than the negative. Immediately, I think of Dad's favourite saying, *If you can't say something nice, then don't say anything at all.*

I am reminded of this saying a few days later when Mom and I arrive in town to pick up the mail. Spying a friend's new boyfriend strolling along the sidewalk, I turn to Mom with an indignant look.

"I don't know why my friend is going with him, he is ..." I begin; I am abruptly interrupted.

"That person has a mom and dad who love him like I love you. Just remember–they think he is special, too," declares Mom. She adds, unnecessarily, "What would Dad say?"

"If you can't say anything nice, then don't say anything at all," I answer in a jovial voice. We burst out laughing. I get the message! Mom relates to us teens; she laughs, talks, listens, joins in our joy, and yet guides us in proper behavior.

Our parents expect us to have good characters. We should be thoughtful, considerate, and respectful to everyone, including siblings. If we argue amongst ourselves, we are immediately reprimanded. Mom often makes her favorite statement, *Appreciate and love one another: your brother/sister will be with you throughout your entire life!*

Smoking:

My friends and I are sitting in the booth at Mark's Café sipping on pop, discussing our plans for the weekend and joking about smoking "O.P." cigarettes ... *other people's*! We have a single cigarette going round the table and we take turns to puff the shared cigarette. It is my turn. Raising the cigarette to my mouth, I suck in swiftly and exhale a stream of smoke into the air. Suddenly, the door to the café opens and six pair of eyes dart in that direction. Horrified, our faces flash with fear to discover my mom.

Immediately upon seeing her step inside, I plunge the cigarette atop the ashtray perched in the middle of the table. The end of the cigarette burns a bright red and a huge cloud of smoke hovers above our table. We all put on an innocent face.

Mom hesitates, then raises a hand to gesture a *Hi*. We wave back, praying that she does not notice the burning cigarette or smoke drifting hazily around our booth. No one raises a finger to retrieve the cigarette, which is ironic, considering how earlier we all scrambled to clutch the cigarette! A smoky haze billows above us like a cloud, but with a look of innocence, we chat amiably while waiting for mom to leave the café. Our discussion takes a different turn. *Who will take the blame?* No one volunteers! Eventually, all the parents discover the smoking incident; however, no one can pinpoint the culprit. We just blame each other.

Several days later, on an idyllic warm afternoon, I slip outside under the luminous blue sky and large woolly clouds. Around me, clumps of flowers are sprouting everywhere. Spring is in the air! I lower myself onto the grass in the shade of our humongous cherry tree. Gazing up, I perceive the millions of tiny white flowers crowded and densely layered in the branches like a cloud. A slight breeze is in the air, causing a few of the delicate petals to gently drift around me and I inhale their sweet scent. My heart is full, and I am awed by the stillness. In a state of contentment, I gingerly slip from my pocket ... a cigarette. Lighting it up, I breathe in the hearty aroma, lean back, and take in the beauty of nature.

I am in la-la land. Deep in my *teen girl* thoughts, I take another long drag of my cigarette and wave to Dad who has just poked his head out the back door.

"Julie, what are you doing? What do you have in your hand?" Dad's words bring me back to earth with a thud. I am panic-stricken. I look at Dad then glance back at my raised hand, holding the cigarette in the air like a baton.

"A cigarette," I stutter nervously, unable to deny the obvious.

"I didn't know you were smoking," Dad sadly replies. Without another word, he turns and walks back into the house. The stillness reverberates within my soul. I am genuinely worried. I sway between guilt and sadness at disappointing Dad. I am annoyed with myself. *How could I get so relaxed that I forgot I was smoking!*

Mom will lay the law down, I predict. Shortly thereafter, Mom comes to sit by me under the cherry tree.

"Dad and I have discussed your smoking, we prefer that you don't smoke," she softly explains. I shuffle

Back: Cousin, Cousin, Grampa Nelson, Gramma Nelson, Dad. Middle: Cousin, Mom, Chris, Julie. Front: Barry, cousin

uncomfortably and shift my eyes downward. "But if you choose to do so, then smoke in front of us and not behind our back," she concludes. From that moment on, I smoked in front of my parents; however, ironically, I did not smoke as much anymore. I was a casual smoker until age twenty-five, when I gave up smoking cold turkey, knowing that the cigarettes were not good for my health.

Chapter 61

Teenage Social Life:

Like all teenagers, I had my share of youthful romances. And while they brought me lots of joy and excitement, they also some-times ended in heartbreak. On one particular occasion, a spat with my high school boyfriend sent me into a world of misery!

It all began when we had a date for New Year's Eve. I waited and waited and waited. The clock is quickly ticking the minutes down. It is later than I expected for him to show up. He has not arrived; I leave for the dance with a neighbor boy. Eventually, my date appears at the dance hall and confronts me.

"Where were you?" he demands.

"I did not think you were coming," I mutter in a faint voice.

My new
outfit

"We had a date, why weren't you home?" he stresses. Obviously, his feathers are ruffled. I squirm at the sting of truth in his words. My mouth opens to speak, yet no words come forth. I cringe and am tongue-tied as his words hang in the air. He turns and walks away.

My whole world is in a shambles and I am in the depths of despair! For days, I sulkily mope, am teary-eyed, and drag my feet. Daydreaming becomes my refuge; I stare out at the Cherry tree laden in snow - my mind imagining it in the summer where I could sit under its wings and wallow in my self-pity. My parents are worried about my well-being.

Mom devises a plan to cheer me up. From the Sears catalogue she orders a pair of stretchy pants and a colorful sweater. A week later, a parcel is placed into my hands.

"What is this?" I ask, with a puzzled look. Mom smiles secretively and gestures for me to open the package.

My spirit soars at the vision! Brand-new garments spill out of the package. Walking on air, I don my new outfit and cavort about the room modeling my new look. My face glows with delight. The next day, smiling and confident, I am eager to attend school and show off my ensemble. My number one priority is prancing about in my marvelous up-to-date attire. I am on top of the world.

Mom's vision is that a stylish outfit will mend my teen girl's broken heart. My vision, dressed to the nines, is that a great boyfriend is on the horizon. She is right and so am I!

Teasing remarks:

A short time later, I begin dating a boy who has a happy-go-lucky attitude. We get along like a house on fire. Our relationship is easygoing; we have fun and laugh a lot. Gray enjoys teasing just to get a reaction out of me and create gaiety in our lives. He reminds me of my brother when he used to tease just to get me riled up! Normally my boyfriend's teasing causes us to laugh uproariously; however, one of his schemes goes awry. He fabricates a disparaging story about my brother. It is a bad move.

"That is not true," I bluster angrily to Gray. Furiously, I shoot darts at him with enraged eyes. Suddenly, I note his expression—the glint in his eyes, and the crease around his smiling lips. The light bulb comes on and I realize that he is teasing.

"I criticized your brother on purpose. I enjoy watching how you always passionately protect him," he replies with a chuckle.

I realize too late that his aim is to tease me—predicting my reaction and relishing the drama. I am furious but I hold my tongue.

"I dream of Julie," he whispers in my ear, grinning. He is referring to a popular television show *I Dream of Jeannie.* He is trying to butter me up. I am not sure who I am more annoyed with—him for teasing or myself for being fooled. I see the humor and burst out laughing.

"Just don't make snide remarks about my family," I playfully reply. He makes a good point — it is true — I stand up for my family. Our relationship eventually comes to an end; however, we remain good friends and he continues to tease me about my *family loyalty.*

This loyalty is instilled in us early on: *Your siblings will always be the ones that are there for you throughout your life, so stand together at all times.* This is the unconditional love of our family. We siblings stand together.

The Jiving:

My biggest passion as a teenager is dancing! Charlie and I spend entire evenings polishing our jiving skills in our living room. We take in all the dances in the surrounding community. If I need a ride, I often hitch a ride with Charlie and his girlfriend, Nellie.

"Next up is the Jive contest. Take the dance floor," is announced at a Prairie River dance. I scan the room and discover Charlie, standing near the back. We exchange a knowing glance and at once we stride towards each other, to meet on the dance floor.

Joyfully, we dance up a storm. At dance end we remain motionless awaiting the winning announcement.

"The winner is the young couple standing to the left front!" We win!

Winning is fun, but our love of dancing is more important than a prize. We constantly search for opportunities to kick up our heels. On one such occasion, we made a plan to attempt to appear on *The Hop*.

The Hop is a popular television show. The Prince Albert television station holds a dance show on Saturday afternoons, for teens from around the area. Therefore, Charlie, Chris, I, and a couple of friends decide to travel to Prince Albert and gamble on the idea that we be allowed to take part in the television show.

We are thrilled to be welcomed to join *The Hop*. Charlie and I once again dance up a storm. Upon returning home, we are informed by many observers that, "The camera was on you and Charlie most of the time!" We are celebrities in our little town of Weekes. Charlie and I are dance partners, united by the beat of the music in stepping through a period of our life.

Part
Eight

Mid-Teens
Julie 15 - 16 years

Chapter 62

The Edgy Ride:

Mom and I are taking the train to Vancouver, BC; Gramma Nelson is very sick and not expected to live. Dad and Chris take us to the train station in Saskatoon.

We wave goodbye. Dad and thirteen-year-old Chris depart for the three-hour drive home. Chris is disappointed that she is not travelling to BC and is looking down-trodden while heading home. Dad straightens away from the steering wheel, leans against the seat, and glances at Chris's forlorn figure.

"Do you want to drive the car halfway home?" Dad gently offers. Excitedly, Chris jumps at the chance to drive.

"Yes," she hurriedly replies. She is shaking like a leaf as she maneuvers her tiny body behind the steering wheel. She is scared! Dad is patient and calm.

"Chris don't hit the hole," Dad remarks, noticing a huge divot in the road. She promptly hits the cavity! Dad quietly murmurs, "You would not have hit it if I had not mentioned it." Surprisingly, Dad falls asleep an hour from home. Shocked, Chris's mind worriedly races. *What do I do?* She continues to drive in an anxious state, wondering how Dad can sleep. They arrive home safe and sound.

"I don't know how you managed to sleep–even I was nervous," Chris comments to Dad.

Meanwhile, our trip is not a vacation for Mom, who is tending to her mom, Gramma Nelson. For me, on the other hand, it is a great vacation. I spend all my time having fun with my cousin, Earl. He is staying with his grandparents, Aunt Helen, and Uncle George. We become instant friends.

While we're there, the famous Pacific National Exhibition is on in Vancouver! "It has the world's largest roller coaster," Earl shouts excitedly. I am fifteen years old, from a small town, and this sounds like a terrific amount of fun. I am going to the exciting PNE Exhibition.

When we arrive at the exhibition site, I stand in awe. The roller coaster's wooden structure soars steeply upwards. It is outlined against the luminous blue sky, appearing to dominate it. My tummy flip-flops and I begin to have second thoughts about this exhilarating ride. Earl runs up the entry ramp, and I shakily follow his retreating figure. Climbing into the car, my knees tremble and I grasp the handle for dear life. Plunging–a ninety-degree drop–my mouth opens and emits a blood-curdling scream, piercing the air. I continue to bellow as we fly straight up into the sky. I cannot stop shrieking and I am scared to death.

Laughing beside me is Earl. I cannot fathom his excitement. He laughs, I scream. Relieved to come to a stop, I stagger to my feet, and unsteadily exit the roller coaster, thankful to be on solid ground. I swear to never go on a ride like that ever again. Smugly, I look at Earl, with a gaze that says, *I did it.*

"Let's go again," he unexpectedly and eagerly blurts out. Stunned, I am silent; I *do not* want to go on that ride again.

"Okay," I murmur, hesitantly and nervously. I do not want to *act like a sissy girl*. Unfortunately, Earl wants to ride the roller coaster again and again and again. I am exhilarated and joyful each time after the ride; however, walking up the ramp, my tummy flipflops and my legs tremble.

Darkness cloaks the daylight as we depart the fair. Hopping on a bus, we exit at the local park entrance. There are no streetlights visible as we step apprehensively into the pitch-black park. Illuminating our sidewalk is a small beam of light from Earl's tiny flashlight.

"Just last week, in this very park, a gang of five raped a young girl," Earl reveals, with a voice that echoes eerily in the dark. Instantly grasping his arm, a cold fear fills my soul as my eyes dart into the blackness all around. The sound of our footfalls scraping loudly on the cement echoes spookily through the stillness. As the darkness engulfs us, I feel rather than see a gang waiting to pounce on me! My thoughts run wild. I cling tighter, fear grips my heart, and a shudder runs through my body. I have faith in God, so I silently pray.

Frantic with fear, I tentatively stride swiftly forward on our creepy walk through the park. My breath comes in shuddering gasps as I try to inhale deeply and regularly. I cling tightly to my cousin as my imagination takes flight. *Is this for real? Are we in danger?*

Upon rounding the corner, the house is in sight and my mind silently shouts, *we are within screaming distance!* Eager to get home I break into a run. Earl joins me, and soon we are racing down the sidewalk. Fleeing up the walkway, we push at each other and simultaneously grapple for the doorhandle. We fly through the door, melded together, and burst through the door as one. We erupt into peals of laughter. It is the most memorable and fun day ever.

I consider the roller coaster to be a very scary ride. I am unaware that a more terrifying ride is lurking just around the corner.

Chapter 63

Night of Terror:

Our terrible escapade began at the end of our time in Vancouver.

It was touch and go for Gramma. However, she pulled through and was feeling better. Probably healed with Mom's love and compassion. Mom is a young parent; at thirty-five years she is easygoing, caring, and full of love. I am a teenager of fifteen years and enjoy life to the fullest. I am not ready to leave Vancouver–it has been a fun time with Cousin Earl and a great holiday, in my books! Mom and I have a great mother-daughter relationship and enjoy being together. We do not realize what is in store for us and that we will soon encounter the most terrifying time of our lives.

Julie, Mom, Gramma Nelson

We prepare plans to return home. Unfortunately, a railway strike has hit!

This is a tumultuous labour-relations period for the railway. In the 1960s, unionized workers are trying to protect and build on gains made in the postwar years of prosperity, growth, and accommodation. As a result, strike upon strike, *wildcat* or *legal*, occur, reaching an historic peak. (*The Book of Samuel: The Railway Run-Through Commission*)

The railway line is our mode of travel, and it is now unattainable; this spells many hours via the bus. Mom claims it will be a great trip for, in her view, we will see plenty of scenery. Upon examination of the bus schedule, we discover our bus departs tonight. Considering it will be a four-hour drive for Dad to pick us up in Saskatoon, we phone to relay the time of our arrival tomorrow.

I don my new outfit and feel quite grown up. My spiffy outfit is stylish capris with matching waist-length top. The material sports a white back-ground and rusty geometric pattern in the foreground. Mom looks svelte in her casual brown pants and light multi-colored top. We are all packed, all set, all ready—time to go!

It is a bleak, rainy evening. Grampa Nelson and Uncle George drive us to the Vancouver station. Crowds are everywhere and the bus depot is teeming with people in a scramble to get to wherever they are going. Sold out! Sold Out! Sold Out! The bus tickets to Saskatoon are completely sold out. We are in quite the dilemma.

"We can't get a bus ticket. Bill will be in Saskatoon waiting to pick us up. What are we going to do? We need to get on the bus," Mom shouts and carries on and on and on, non-stop, in a frenzy. Panic-stricken she frantically waves her arms in the air; her words come out in a steady stream, fast and garbled. Grandpa and Uncle are bewildered as to how they can remedy this state of affairs. Worry floods my soul with the vision of Mom going to pieces.

In the midst of our chaos, a young man of average stature, with short brown hair, sporting casual khaki pants and a tan windbreaker, approaches our small group.

"I am Axel," he politely introduces himself. "I am travelling on my own to Calgary and stopped here to offer a ride to anyone going my way."

"Saskatoon is our destination," Mom immediately replies, sounding disappointed.

"Since it would be easier for you to catch a bus in Calgary, why don't you ride along with me?" Axel says with a croaky cough. "We can take turns driving, and travel without stopping," he explains. Reaching into his pants' pocket, he produces a driver's license and presents it to Grampa to verify his good intentions. The outcome of a short discussion between Grampa, Uncle, and Mom, is a unanimous decision. We will take the ride.

We exit the station. Clouds have momentarily departed, and only a slight drizzle trickles down on the three of us. Darting to Axel's vehicle, I observe that it is relatively new, medium sized, dark in color, and displays a strange, small light atop the roof.

"We can all sit in the front seat," suggests Axel, as he enters on the driver's door. Much to my dismay, I am positioned next to Axel. I feel a twinge of discomfort–sitting next to him is too close for comfort.

Travelling along the highway, Axel flips a switch. Suddenly the dark is lit up by a flashing yellow light, similar to a tow truck.

"The police will *not* stop me if I have this light flashing," Axel's explanation is followed by a spat of coughing. Puzzled, I contemplate his words. *Why would he not want the police to stop us? How odd.* I glance at Mom and see her face momentarily aglow, lit up by the yellow beam of light as it flashes in her direction. Her face exhibits an alarmed expression and cold fear wells up inside my body. I shiver with apprehension. Our first hint of trouble is that yellow light, flashing, flashing, flashing into the pitch-black darkness.

The setting is perfect for a scary movie. Traversing the dark highway, the rain pours down in a torrent, with the wipers flashing madly in a futile effort to disperse the steady stream of water. The headlight's beam casts a blurry glow for about five feet amidst the rain causing the road to appear disjointed. Blackness extends beyond the hazy light.

"What career plans do you have when you leave school?" Axel inquires, while he expertly maneuvers the car through the blinding rain. This feels like a normal conversation. My suspicions, I realize, are just my imagination working overtime.

"I will take a course to become an airline stewardess," I proudly reply.

"All stewardesses are hookers," Axel retorts in a scornful voice and with a sneer he laughs sardonically, triggering a coughing fit. Shocked, I glance at Mom, a worried expression crosses my face.

"Please don't talk to her like that. She is only fifteen years old," stresses Mom in a firm tone. A flash of foreboding hits me full force. He is weird! Time passes in dead silence.

"I know of a fruit farm just off the beaten path where we can pick up fresh fruit for a reasonable price," Axel says tentatively to Mom, in a sociable manner. He hesitates, and adds, "Do you want to pick up some of this fruit?" The offer and the phrase "off the beaten path" sound ominous to me! My insides tremble. *Are we in danger? What scheme is he planning to perform by deviating onto a dark, isolated side road?*

"No, thank you, we need to catch the bus in Calgary because my husband is waiting to pick us up in Saskatoon," Mom replies in a strained, yet friendly style. Realizing that Mom is attempting to control the fear in her voice generates terror deep in my soul. I start to pray to God to keep us safe. *What is on Axel's mind?*

Darkness enshrouds the town of Hope. Our headlights shoot a spooky beam of light into the slashing rain. A sinister scene emerges, with explosions of thunder alongside luminous flashes of lightning. I flinch at the sudden touch of Axel's hand on my leg. I unsuccessfully struggle to shift my leg out of his reach. His hand moves to caress slowly upwards. With a jolt, I shove my body into Mom's frame, jab her, and nod my head downwards to indicate the problem.

"Stop it! Get your hand off her leg," Mom shouts sternly. With a smirk in my direction, Axel removes his hand. Revulsion rises up within me. Several miles further, Axel slows down and pulls the car to the side of the road. My nerves are on high alert. We are in a lonely and isolated spot! *What is happening now?* I wonder, as I hold my breath.

"Your turn to drive. I will ride in the back seat." Axel speaks firmly to Mom. Axel is in the backseat, and Mom is driving. I am not sure if I should be relieved or scared. Swiftly shifting gears, Mom pulls out on the road to drive carefully, yet hastily, through the rain. The road is barely visible as the wipers swipe in a useless endeavor against the streams of rain battering the windshield.

Out of the corner of my eye, I notice a sudden movement in the rear. Without warning, Axel leans his body far over the front seat. He extends his frame around me to reach into the glove box. Innocently, I expect he is getting cough medicine since he cannot seem to stop his coughing fits.

Axel seizes an object and whips it swiftly under his overcoat. He wrongly assumes that I did not witness him retrieve the gadget and conceal it under his coat. I cannot believe what I am seeing. It is a wrench! A large wrench! Cold fear wells up inside me. Every cell in my body is on high alert. *We are in deep trouble.* I wonder if Mom is suspicious or if she assumes, as I did, that he is obtaining cough medicine. How can I warn her of the danger?

Our situation is deadly. I am aware that Axel has positioned himself right behind me. I shiver in apprehension. Perhaps his plan is to use the wrench to whack my skull. My stomach is tied in knots. I need to find a weapon. Cautiously, I draw my purse close to my side. I open quietly the clasp and sneakily slip my hand into the interior. Fumbling around I finger my perfume bottle and clutch the item firmly in my fist. My young mind is in a turmoil. *Will I hit him? Will I spray him? How will I employ my weapon? Spray his eyes! That is what I will do. Just one small, threatening action, and I will spray his eyes!* I shift my body slightly to sit sideways on the seat. My plan has materialized, and the perfume bottle gives me courage.

Sixth sense tells Mom that something is out of sync. Perhaps my furtive actions and angst have raised her maternal antenna. Mom glances at me and our eyes silently communicate our growing sense of concern.

271

"We need to go to the bathroom," Mom informs Axel, forcing a normal, friendly voice. "We will stop at the next filling station."

A sleepy little town soon materializes; however, it is after midnight, and all is in darkness.

"Pull over to that filling station. It is closed but I will check out back to see if the bathrooms are open," Axel states firmly. He exits the vehicle. I whisk around to face Mom.

"Axel took a large wrench from the glove box, it's under his overcoat right now," I blurt in an edgy voice. Desperation and fright instantly fill Mom's eyes. Fear erupts into my inner being and I grip Mom's hands tightly. "Does he plan to kill us?" I mutter. Before she can answer, the back door is brusquely opened.

"It's all good. You can go behind the garage," Axel informs us in a casual tone.

"No, we want to go where there is light. We will return to the town a short stint back," Mom stammers, sounding genuinely worried. Mom shifts the vehicle into gear and Axel has no choice but to hop and jump in as we begin to move slowly ahead. As the car door slams, Mom stomps on the gas pedal and makes a sharp U-turn in the middle of the road. Axel is mad.

"I checked it out. You can go behind the garage. Turn around and go back," he demands angrily. Despite her fear, Mom steps on the gas.

"We want to go where there is light. We will return to the prior town where there is a motel," insists Mom in a calm, but stressed, voice. Obviously, Mom has had a back-up plan. I had not noticed any motel in the last town! My heart is pounding as I doggedly clutch my perfume bottle. Safety is not far away, yet not near enough. I pray, *I do not want to die. Please Lord, help us be safe.*

A blast of thunder explodes and shatters the atmosphere. I flinch, almost dropping my perfume bottle. It is followed by lightening that illuminates the sky, pitching an eerie glow into our midst as it discharges in a zig-zag pattern across the pitch-black night. Speeding through the storm on the dark, deserted, dangerous road, the sedan plunges into deep puddles; water sprays wickedly upwards, and splatters our windows. Axel skulks in the back seat and I am a bundle of nerves. This is like a scary movie and we are the main stars in it!

Safety is imminent. Appearing like tiny specks in the far distance, I glimpse the neon lights shining vividly. I silently thank the Lord. Relief fills our souls upon entering the parking lot with the expectation of safety. However, it is a sad and desolate sight. The motel is all in darkness.

"We will attempt to enter the office because I see a faint light inside, and they will have a washroom," Mom declares, breathlessly. She whips the vehicle right up to the front of the motel and parks. Mom and I hastily exit the car and stomp up the front steps. Mom apprehensively tries the doorknob; it turns, and the door opens. We enter our safety net. Eyeing the little bell on the counter, I aggressively set it a-banging, signaling for help.

Shuffling from a back room, a sleepy-eyed couple emerges. The man wears faded blue pajamas and his wife is adorned in a bright, flowery nightgown. They display an appearance of annoyance to be wakened at such an ungodly hour. Their expressions radiate disbelief during our stammering account of affairs–perhaps an honest reaction, given such strange and bizarre happenings.

We book a room and request their help. There is a momentary lull in the storm; they agree to stand on the hotel steps while we retrieve our luggage. Axel frowns upon viewing four figures emerge from the motel door and his eyes shoot vicious daggers in our direction. We are on edge.

Mom rushes down the steps. Axel leans against the open passenger door. He is scowling, obviously disappointed at his plans going awry. Mom strides to the trunk.

"We have decided to stay at the motel, we will need our luggage," she announces. Axel is outraged, this is an unexpected turn of events, and has disrupted his plans.

"Why, are you doing that?" he demands in a cruel voice. The challenging question is overheard by Mr. and Mrs. Motel-owner; fear flickers over their faces as they stand stiffly and warily on the top step.

"It is late. We want to get a good night's sleep. We will catch a bus on our own from here tomorrow," Mom stresses, feeling relatively safe. Axel's eyes blaze and his mouth is set in a snarl.

Still in possession of the car keys, Mom hastily nips around to unlock the trunk. Axel, with *eyes to kill*, glares at me; hatred radiates from his soul. I am afraid to avert my eyesight, fearful of his intention. His eyes burn into my core. Yearning to look away, I force myself to stay focused on his every action. Walking past him with a suitcase, I shudder uncontrollably as he glowers at me, enraged. I am frantic to escape this madman.

Clutching our suitcases, we dash up the steps. We join our rescuers on the top steps and move together as one to enter the safety of the motel.

"Can you please assist us to our room?" Mom asks. With room key in hand, Mr. Motel-owner nods. He accompanies us through an entryway, up the staircase, and unlocks the room located next to the stairs. Extending his hand to the light switch, Mom whispers in a panic, "Don't turn the light on, please. We will go inside in the dark." Quickly withdrawing his hand, Mr. Motel-owner gazes at Mom in an odd manner, puzzled by this strange set of circumstances. With nerves on high alert, we shut and lock the door. An armchair is positioned against the door, with our suitcases piled atop. This gives us a sense of security.

We orient ourselves by the faint light filtering inside from the streetlamp.

"Why can't we put the light on?" I ask Mom in bafflement.

"He is watching from the parking lot; the light will indicate which room we are occupying," she replies. I am amazed that my mom is so smart. We drop on the bed and burst into tears, hugging and crying in silence. We are drained.

Abruptly, we are startled to detect a faint commotion. The sound reaches us from far away–down the hallway by the fire escape door. We hear the door open and shut, followed by a small hoarse cough. Gasping in shock, we freeze–we recognize the cough! It could only belong to Axel! Every little noise is magnified through the thin walls. We remain wrapped together as one on the bed and monitor his every move. He creeps down the central hallway that leads from the fire exit. We can distinguish the split-second his steps stop their scuffling on the carpet as he pauses to listen quietly at every door of every room. Paying attention to his stealthily shifting footsteps, we remain immobile in order to be quiet. We cling together, shaking uncontrollably and crying soundlessly. We are scared stiff.

Our bodies are trembling. We hunch blankets snugly around our frames to still the shuddering—we are glued to our bed. In fearful apprehension we wait. Our turn is coming. Our breathing is rapid but shallow as we endure the slow transition of his pace coming nearer and nearer and nearer. Ours is the last room in the hallway. We pray silently. Axel halts by the adjacent room. He is on the verge of our door—we are next! We are in grave danger!

Axel is here! We stare at the shadow of his feet under the door as they come to a stand-still. His presence emanates through the door with his heavy and labored breathing. We hold our breath, we are rigid, we do not budge. I am petrified. *Please God help us,* I pray, again and again and again. I am so afraid! We hear the doorknob jiggle; the lock is doing its job. My mind is in panic mode. *Suppose he picks the lock? Suppose he breaks the door down? Why is he standing at our door for such a long time? Why does he not move?* Time moves at a snail's pace; minutes seem like hours. We are more terrified than ever. The shadow under the door is shifting.

Axel moves! He scuffles away to the staircase adjacent to our room. We listen to his footfalls recede as he tiptoes down the stairs. He is on his way to check the ground floor. Elated that Axel has not detected us, we squeeze each other with a sigh of relief—a noiseless sigh. We are still not safe. Axel will return!

Time stands still. We are all-ears when we hear the signal, a small hoarse, cough by the stairway. He is back. We cling to each other tightly. With bated breath, we wait cowered together fearfully. We hear his shoes scraping lightly on each step as he creeps up the stairway. He shuffles slowly along the carpeted hallway, slinks up close to our door and stops. The menacing shadow of his shoes come into view under the door. His presence is strong; again, his raspy breathing penetrates the room. We are motionless. He lurks, listens, and lingers for a prolonged period. We do not move an inch. His shoe shadows shift slightly to the left, and with a guttural cough he plods along. We listen to the retreating footsteps. With a sigh of relief, our rigid bodies crumple. Axel skulks along the hallway, stopping for several minutes at each door. Finally, the fire escape door opens noisily and shuts. He is gone! For the moment we are safe.

Aches and pains attack our tense bodies. We stretch and twist to alter the effects of static muscles. Suspicion sets in—we are wary that he may still be in the hallway, waiting for an indication of our room location. We become still once again, and we do not make any noise for a long time. Hesitantly, after hearing no sound, Mom slowly slides off the bed, and tiptoes to the window. She gently cracks the curtain slightly to the side.

"He is sitting in his car in the parking lot," Mom whispers. In the dim light she can see the outline of a figure crouching down in his car. He is waiting for us, and I realize, *We are still not safe.*

"I have to go to the bathroom," I whisper to Mom. The bathroom is not in our room; unfortunately, it is at the end of the hallway! What if he comes back and we are trapped in the bathroom? We dare not leave our room! Mom glances uneasily around the room.

"I have an idea. Wait for a big truck to go by and zip to the sink then wait for another truck to pass to zip back to the bed," Mom suggests, upon spying a sink in the corner of the room. Our safeguard is to pair all actions to the rumble of the trucks. We are very thankful for our unknown protectors on the highway. Several times Mom slips from our static spot to peer into the parking lot. Axel's car does not move–he continues to lurk inside his vehicle.

Sleep is unthinkable. We are overwhelmed: tears flowing, hearts pulsating, bodies trembling, and souls terrified. It is a long night and we do not get much rest. Nestled together, we only reposition to peep out the window or to use the sink. The night gradually passes; finally, sundrenched rays fill the room with brilliant light, a sign of a new day. Tiptoeing to the window, Mom peers out through a tiny slit in the curtain.

"He is gone. The car is gone," she joyfully exclaims. We are jubilant that we are safe.

On cloud nine, we depart our haven. It is time to catch a bus for home. Arriving at the front desk, we are met with a curious, candid gaze. Mr. Motel-owner is apparently mystified by last night's episode.

"May I help you?" he asks, in a curious fashion.

"Yes, where is the bus depot in town?" Mom questions.

"There is no bus depot in our small town. You will need to go back to Hope."

"Where is the taxi company in town?" Mom probes.

"There are no taxicabs in this small town," he replies in an apologetic tone.

"Do you have, or do you know anyone who may have, a car for hire?" Mom asks in exasperation.

"I do not. However, the garage next door may have a car for hire," he replies in a helpful manner.

With thanks extended, we readily make our exit. Axel's car is not in the parking lot! It is answered prayer. The garage next door becomes our immediate goal. Proceeding at a steady pace, we glance around tentatively, scanning the area for any sign of Axel. We walk into the garage workshop, using the car entrance, where a group of men stare, gaping at our appearance. We resemble a couple of party animals with our wrinkled clothes, red eyes, and puffy faces.

"Is there any chance that we could hire a car to drive us to Hope?" Mom inquires hesitantly. Curious eyes question, *Why would these females, with luggage, in the middle of nowhere, need to ask for a ride to Hope?* The men's glares show the conclusion they're jumping to: *Stranded hookers.* A car is offered for hire at an inflated price—we promptly agree. Driving to Hope, conversation is sparse, with neither party in a communicative mood. The atmosphere is edgy.

We pray that we can get a bus ticket. Arriving an hour later at the Hope bus station, we cautiously roam through the crowd—our eyes darting to and fro, on the lookout for Axel. Thankfully, we do not spy him! We manage to purchase tickets and are excited to depart in an hour.

Mom needs to make a phone call – she digs into her purse for a dime. We need to communicate our situation and location to the BC family. A collect call is placed to Grampa in Vancouver. Shocked at our traumatic experience, Grampa admits that upon their return home Gramma angrily queried, "Why would you allow them to go with a stranger?" Grampa apologizes profusely to Mom and insists that she call him upon arriving home. Sadly, we are unable to call Dad; he will be on the road, travelling to Saskatoon to meet us, and there is no means of communication. Dad will meet our original scheduled bus. We will not be there.

There are a couple of policemen seated in the café. I look at Mom, questioningly. "If we report the incident, we will be delayed, and we do not have concrete evidence," she whispers. I understand and pick up the menu. Mom, who is a bundle of nerves, can only handle a cup of coffee; I feel safe with police nearby, so I eat hungrily and heartily.

Still, we are suspicious. Upon boarding the bus, we choose seats in the back to have a clear view of everyone. Relaxing for the first time in a long while, we settle back, feeling safe, and enjoy the peaceful ride. At the next bus depot our driver departs, and we remain in our seat to gaze calmly out the bus window.

Axel is here! Gasping in shock and stunned to the core, we are horrified to view him ambling about the bus depot. My heart sinks: Axel is waiting for us to arrive. We shrink back and peer out the corner of our window. Our eyes are glued on him; we watch his every move. I am in fear of this terrible man. He strolls amongst the buses and casually saunters around each one, peering into every single window. Axel is searching for us. His cold, hard, menacing eyes penetrate the interior of each bus. *What is his plan? What can he do?* Deep in my soul I know his intentions are evil!

We spy him approaching our bus. Immediately, we duck down and become a small mound on our seat. I am petrified, my body is vibrating, my heart is pulsating, and once again we are like statues. We are motionless, unspeaking, shifting only to peek furtively to monitor his position. Axel circles the opposite side of our bus; as he wanders to our side of the bus we hunker down lower, as low as we can go. Fear grips my heart. We wait and wait and wait; we need to be sure he has finished looking into all the side windows.

Our fellow passengers gawk at us in bewilderment. I am more terrified than ever. We have a deep fear of this predator. We inch upwards, with our eyes peering cautiously out the window. Axel is stomping to the next bus; we are not discovered! *Will he come back?*

We remain crouched in the seat until our bus departs. Astonishment and curiosity are clearly portrayed on the countenances of our fellow passengers, seated nearby. They have scrutinized our actions and witnessed our spectacle of strange antics. We do not explain. We are silent. We pray. We are thankful God keeps us safe.

Will he be at the next bus stop? Shattered, we do not get much rest on the long bus ride. At every stop, our eyes anxiously peruse the area. Axel is not in sight! Aside from our anxieties, we have a peaceful journey.

When Saskatoon finally looms in the distance it is a welcome sight! We are ecstatic to almost be home. Relief overwhelms us as we alight into the bus station in Saskatoon. Strolling over to the staircase, we glance down to see Dad beaming with a huge smile on his face. We descend the steps swiftly and dash into his outstretched arms. Dad spells safety.

Why are they missing? Dad worried yesterday when we did not arrive on our scheduled bus. He had spent all his time at the bus depot anxiously monitoring every bus that arrived from Vancouver.

Arriving at the bus station today, Dad was uncertain if we would be on the bus; he therefore retained his hotel room. We will be staying the night in Saskatoon.

"Bill, shall we go downstairs for a quick drink before supper," asks Mom, once we are settled in our hotel room.

"Julie, will you be okay to stay in the room for a short while?" Mom questions me. I understand that she wants to fill Dad in on our dreadful experience.

"Yes, I will not leave this room," I reply, and I mean it. I will not leave this room under any circumstances.

I read my book quietly. The door is locked, and I keep my ears tuned to any noise or movement outside the door. Twenty quiet minutes pass and I am engrossed in my book when I realize I need to go to the bathroom.

The bathroom is down the hallway and there is no sink in this room. The mere thought of entering the hallway is terrifying. However, I desperately need to go.

It is a necessity. Cautiously, I slowly open the door a crack and peek down the hallway. It is unoccupied, so I gingerly step out of the room. Following the toilet signs, I stride at a hasty pace down the hallway and around the corner. Arriving at the restroom I see no one and am relieved in more ways than one! Leaving the room, I cautiously open the door a crack to peer down the hallway–no one is in sight, so I sneak quickly and quietly down the hallway.

It is clear sailing down the first hallway. Rounding the corner, I am startled to see two men walking towards me. Shocked, I stop. I am immobile. *What do I do? Do I run back to the bathroom? Do I try to outrun them? Do I carry on past them?* Tentatively, I keep walking, staring guardedly in their direction. Their eyes bore into mine! *Are they about to grab me?* I am frightened. I tremble but continue to creep suspiciously towards them. Our eyes lock, and I feel a shiver of apprehension zip down my spine. My mind races and I determinedly clench my hands into tight fists. My strength is a weapon, and I will fight them.

I focus on my weapon. I move nervously ahead until I am abreast of them, and I glare at them intently. Our eyes lock! I tightly clamp my fists, prepared to put up a hard-hitting fight. Gradually, we bypass each other. I am in the clear!

With a sudden burst of energy, I break into a run. Unable to hear chasing footsteps, I glance back to see if I am being pursued. I see the two men just standing and staring at my retreating form with a puzzled look on their faces. Still not reassured, I zoom down the hallway, fling myself into our room, lock the door with fumbling fingers, and jump onto the bed in a flying leap. I am motionless like a statue; I will not be discovered!

"I was almost accosted," I relate to my parents on their return. Conveying my chilling story, my body is vibrating, my voice is quaking, and I am in a state of fear! My parents exchange a worried glance and look at me with a caring and understanding expression.

"We should not have left her alone," Mom utters softly. Dad agrees. They are correct! I am traumatized!

We arrive home and life returns to a new normal. Attempting to push our harrowing event into the background, life carries on. However, Mom appears more wary, and I am suspicious of everyone and everything.

This event forever alters my personality. My nerves are on high-alert, and I keep an eye out for any unusual actions around me. Every uncomfortable act sends me into panic mode. For example: upon arriving home from Greenwater Lake with a group of teens in a vehicle I was put in an insecure situation. A couple boys grabbed me to prevent me from exiting the vehicle. Immediately my heart jumps into high gear, and I fight viciously – pulling and kicking to breakout of their grasp. I am terrified!

"Let me go. Let me go. Let me go," I growl while struggling to free myself.

Fortunately, John, our former neighbour, friend, and Dad's prior right-hand man is the driver. He turns around from the front seat and quickly comes to my aid.

"Let her go and let her out!" he demands in a calm but firm voice.

They comply. I thank John with a grateful glance. My parents were right – John could be depended upon to keep me safe. I scurry like a scared rabbit into the house and into my room where I struggle to regain my senses. The feelings of defenselessness I had during the B.C. trip had come to raise its ugly head. I needed to feel in control at all times! In addition, my trust of people is altered. Prior to our trip to B.C. I believed and trusted everyone; now I am skeptical and cautious of most persons and situations.

Chapter 64

Snowdrifts:

Our house is located next to the Weekes highway–a popular spot for vehicles to skid on the ice and hit the ditch as they come and go from town.

Dad is the go-to person. He is constantly in demand, jarred many times from his sleep, and yet he willingly goes to the rescue. Even our boyfriends are comfortable asking for help. Our doors are always unlocked–open for anyone in need. This generosity instills in us the importance of always lending a helping hand.

Bang, bang, bang, reverberates throughout the house. I am disturbed from a deep sleep and upon peering into the blackness I determine it must be after midnight. Straining to listen to the commotion, I detect the shuffling of Dad's footsteps approaching the front door.

Whispers! I cannot distinguish the words. Curious about the murmurs drifting through the quiet house, I slowly slip out of bed and creep silently across the floor. Cracking the door open a slit, I squint into the dim light.

"Bill, can you please pull us out of the ditch with your tractor?"

"Sure, I will need to warm the tractor up first," Dad replies. It is minus forty on a freezing cold winter night. I feel chilly in my drafty room, so I quickly crawl back into bed, deep in my thoughts. *Oh boy, here we go again!*

The house comes alive. Mom and Dad prepare to come to the rescue of yet another stranded person. The stillness in the dark night air is broken with the rumble of the tractor as it springs into life. It drones deafeningly, causing the house to shudder as it thunders past on the driveway. Our parents are known to be very generous–willing to give a helping hand to anyone in need, to the point of giving the shirt off their backs.

A week later, on a glacial Saturday winter evening at forty degrees below zero, my friends and I encounter a blizzard after a dance. The snow-flakes are falling frenetically, and the wind is whipping wildly. The road is a sheet of ice with flurries of snow flitting swiftly across the road and the line between road and ditch are obliterated by the snow drifts. In addition, the windshield is fogging up and the heater is barely producing any heat. We carefully glide down the road, wary of the treacherous road conditions

We strike a patch of ice. Spinning wildly out of control, our vehicle swings in a circular motion to suddenly veer off the road into a huge snowbank. The guys jump out to peruse the situation. I can hear their boots crunching through the top layer of snow as they attempt to shift the vehicle from the snowbank. They stamp their boots on the frozen ground to keep their feet warm.

My girlfriend and I are freezing. Inside the car, the cold steals my breath from my mouth, my face is numb, and my nose feels frostbitten. My boots are like blocks of glacial ice; I slip them off and tuck my feet under my butt. The polar temperature pierces deep into my bones and my body begins to shiver. *How are we going to escape out of the snow mound?*

I keep an eye on the time–I am way past my curfew. I silently pray that we can get out of the snowdrift. Suddenly, two tiny circles of light appear through the blinding snow on the highway. I am excited to see the brilliant beam of car headlights come closer and closer and closer. The vehicle stops and someone gets out and approaches us.

"Do you need help?" echoes in the still air. With a sigh of relief, I see chains being attached to both vehicles. Our vehicle is yanked out of the snow embankment with the help of the passersby. I now understand and appreciate the importance of my dad rescuing those persons whose vehicles hit the ditch.

I arrive home past my curfew. I am in trouble. I notice the porch light on, which signifies that Mom is up, waiting for me to arrive.

"Where have you been?" asks Mom in a worried voice.

"We hit the ditch and I am frozen," I blurt out apprehensively, squirming in my boots. Mom holds my cold hands in her warm ones.

"I am glad you are okay," she whispers in an anxious tone. Her words wash over me, and I exhale slowly, annoyed with myself for being nervous. It is obvious that Mom has been very worried; she cares, and I know I am loved.

Instantly, I am hustled in and comforted. Mom props my feet up in front of the propane heater, wraps me in a blanket, and rustles up some hot chocolate. Sipping on my luscious drink, with feet extended to the heater and blankets tucked about me, I feel like I am floating on a cloud. I lean back, warm and contented. *This is the best part of hitting the ditch.*

Stranded bus kids:

Winter creates all kinds of fun activities from skating at the rink or tobogganing on the hill at the railroad tracks. On one occasion an exciting winter event begins while attending school.

Glancing out the window, I shiver and scrunch over my desk in the warm, sturdy building. What a sight outside! The earth is frozen, rooftops covered in a cloud of fluffy snow, chimneys shoot jets of smoke into the atmosphere, and snowflakes fly forcefully in a torrent. The forecast– a blizzard.

"All buses are cancelled due to the weather. All bus children will make arrangements to stay with families in town," is announced over the intercom at day-end.

Our group of friends huddle together to decide who will go where; I ask Jenny to spend the night with our family. Instantly, plans emerge. Everyone will gather uptown this evening in Kipling's Café. Clarence Kipling purchased the café from Tony Mark in 1964.

Excitedly, we get ready to head uptown. Living a quarter of mile from town, Mom always insists that we dress for the weather. Thus, Jenny and I prepare for the bitter cold weather. We slip on our parkas (winter jackets) and pull up our seldom-used hoods to cover our heads. We plan to flip off our jacket hoods before entering the café. We don warm boots, woolen mittens, and wrap scarves snugly around our faces and necks.

Julie and Charlie

The café is overcrowded and a-rockin'. We are soon sipping pop, chitchatting, laughing, joking around, and jiving madly in front of the jukebox. It resembles a huge party. It is a fantastic night.

Eleven o'clock strikes—it is time to go home. Jenny and I step outside into the frigid air. The highway is lit up by the moonlight and bathes the snow drifts with shimmering and glistening white diamonds.

We are bundled warmly. Parka hoods wrapped snuggly about our heads, wearing warm mitts and scarves pulled up over our noses. Charlie and his friend have joined us for the trek home. Charlie is dressed quite warm, but his friend is acting cool, so he does not pull a scarf over his face.

"I am in pain," groans Charlie's friend the next morning and continues, "Last night I froze my nose."

My thought is, *A good defense for the cold weather would have been a warm scarf!*

285

Chapter 65

Party:

"We need to spend this Saturday night out of town," Mom announces. Charlie, Chris, and I exchange knowing glances in silent communication. A party is on the horizon. Frantic with excitement, we secretly plot the upcoming event. Our plans evolve quickly, regardless of not having a telephone—*we use word of mouth.*

We go hog-wild planning the party. We will push the furniture against the walls—room for dancing. Everyone must bring their own drink. And the most important rule: at party-end, all must clean up to remove any evidence of the event.

A few days later, our party is in full swing. The music blares deafeningly; dust rises from the floor from dancing feet and liquor is flowing freely. We are having a blast.

Abruptly, our fun is interrupted by a loud hysterical voice shattering the atmosphere.

"It's your parents' car," bellows David above the din of the music. Instantly we come to a stand-still and all eyes glance towards the window to see the brilliant beam of headlights traversing the driveway. In the space of a minute, the situation changes. Immediately, stumbling bodies fly in every direction–out of doors and out of windows.

What are we going to do? Charlie, Chris, and I stand stock-still, huddled in a small, distressed group, stunned into silence at our dilemma. The house is in upheaval and there is no time to hide the evidence. My siblings remain frozen, but I move swiftly away. I have devised a slick plan. Hopping into my pajamas, I jump into bed and close my eyes!

In the meantime, our parents cannot believe their eyes. Bodies are streaming from all areas of the house. However, upon entering the house, they comprehend the situation. The scene is a topsy-turvy living room with bottles strewn everywhere. There is no denying a party has been in full progress.

Angry words erupt! I listen to my parents scold Charlie and Chris.

"Where is Julie?" Mom finally asks.

"She is in bed sleeping," Charlie answers, in a doubtful voice. Mom pushes open my bedroom door and a stream of light falls across my bed.

"Julie, Julie, Julie," she calls. I remain silent, breathe heavy as if deep in sleep, and keep my eyes tightly closed. With a sigh of relief, I detect the door closing quietly.

"She is fast asleep, why can't you be more like Julie?" I hear Mom's words distinctly. *Was this a ploy to get my siblings to confess that I was in on the party or for me to fess-up?* I hold my breath: *Will I be exposed?* All remains silent. I feel a twinge of guilt for my siblings taking all the blame. It is another sibling secret and a testament to our loyalty to one another.

Party on the grapevine:

A month later we hear about an upcoming party on the grapevine! Streaming on the unseeable news line is a Saturday night party at a house in town. Eagerly, Charlie and I discuss the prospects of a night of hanging out with friends and dancing. Unfortunately, Mom discovers the planned party and informs us that we are *not* allowed to attend.

Saturday night arrives. A friend and I take in a movie at the Porcupine Plain Theater, twenty miles away. After the movie, our discussion turns to the party in town. We are in a dilemma. Should we or shouldn't we go? I know am not allowed to go; however, I decide there is no harm in popping in for a few minutes. I will be home in time for my curfew. We arrive at the party, and I scan the smoky room. I am surprised to view a familiar figure leaning against the curved wall. He turns and grins; it is Charlie.

The music is blaring, and many of my friends are present. I dance up a storm! I am having so much fun that I lose all track of time. Suddenly, I realize it is way past my curfew. I am in hot water! My friend and I depart immediately, without saying goodbye to anyone. Upon my arrival home, I notice the porch light is on—a sign that signifies, *You are late. Get home, now!* Mom awaits me in the foyer of the kitchen. Her face flashes a look of annoyance.

Billy, Julie, John, Sharon

"Where have you been?" she demands. My mind is in a whirl, and I devise a plan on the spot.

"I went to the show with John and then we drove around a bit." John has been in our family since I was little – he was our neighbour, he babysat us, and he was Dad's right-hand man on the farm from his early teens. Mom and Dad have a high regard for him, thus they trust John and know we are safe with him. I am well aware of this so John is my instant *go-to-person*!

"You must have been driving around a long time," Mom comments with a hint of skepticism.

"Yes, we did," I murmur quietly.

"Did you see Charlie?" Mom asks.

"No," I reply. A shiver runs through my body—I am skating on thin ice! I quickly bid her goodnight and swiftly turn to escape.

The front door opens—Charlie steps inside.

"Where have you been?" Mom demands.

"I was with John!" Charlie's mutters with a faint rasp. Obviously, Charlie also knows his *go-to-person*!

I swiftly turn around, my mouth drops open, my eyes grow wide, and I shake my head vigorously. The thin ice has cracked.

"You both could not have been with John," Mom stresses sternly with a frown. Charlie and I exchange guilty glances; he views my stricken face.

"Julie was with John," he hastily blurts out. Mom is suspicious of us both; however, we stick to our story. Charlie saves the day and so does John although he is unaware of the situation! I am thankful that John comes to my rescue both knowingly and unknowingly many times!

Barry and Julie

The next morning, my younger brother catches the drift of the story. Barry is too young to partake in our activities; however, he observes and overhears everything.

"I will tell Mom," he threatens me. Mom overhears his comment.

"What did you say Barry?" she questions.

Barry is loving, kind, caring, and adores his older siblings. However, he is in a bind since Mom has overheard his comment. My heart is racing as I await his answer.

"It was nothing, I was just talking to Julie," Barry mumbles quietly.

I breathe a sigh of relief. He is not a stool pigeon. Mom does not insist on an answer—she discourages tattletales. Siblings protect one another.

Not drinking:

My Grandparents arrive from B.C. for an extended vacation - the whole summer! Our parents create a bedroom for them in the summer kitchen to allow them some quiet and privacy.

Grampa and Gramma are very comfy. Due to having an electric stove in the house, the summer kitchen has been transformed into a summer guest room.

Grampa likes to whip the boys into shape. He has Charlie and friend David digging a new hole for the outhouse and when completed they construct the outhouse building. The building will consist of a wooden bench seat with a round hole in the middle, used for the toilet seat. The waste is collected in a huge cavity dug into the ground under the building. Upon completion Grampa aims to keep the boys busy and sets them about getting the yard shipshape. Gramma helps Mom in the house with preserving fruit and tackling the time-consuming job of making a couple of homemade quilts out of scraps of material. After the square pieces are sewn together, they are attached at the outside edges to batting and a flannel sheet. The quilt is thrown on the living room floor where Mom and Gramma kneel while inserting a piece of yarn through all three layers in the middle of each square and knotting it at the top. The quilt looks very decorative with the ends of the yarn flittering about atop the various different colorful squares. My Grandparents are a big help on the farm. However, an unfortunate incident occurs unexpectedly.

On this particular day, my aunt and uncle arrived and are also visiting our family. There are lots of people around.

This disastrous incident occurs on Saturday evening. Charlie and I plan to join our friends for a fun evening at a wedding dance in the Weekes Hall. This is our weekend entertainment–locating a wedding dance that is open to the public. Feeling quite *spiffy* in my blue dress, nylons, and make-up, I exit the house.

"You are too young to wear make-up and go to a dance," Grampa utters as I walk past them sitting outside on lawn chairs. I smile pleasantly but think, *Thank goodness Mom and Dad have a different view.*

The dance is in full swing. My body is whirling around to a polka when I glimpse Dad and Uncle step into the hall. Puzzled, I wonder why they are at the dance. Uncle and Aunt are staying for the weekend and the adults had planned to spend the evening visiting at home.

The music winds up for the next dance. Dad walks over and extends his hand, requesting a dance. Dad is a good dancer, and we bop rhythmically to a two-step.

"Julie, have you been drinking?" Dad asks in a low voice as he leans towards me. I am bewildered.

"No," I reply. We continue to dance as I ponder the question, thinking, *That was a bit strange.*

"Can I smell your breath?" Dad inquiries quietly. Now I am really mystified.

"Sure," I reply. I have not been drinking. Dancing is my passion! Drinking age is twenty-one and our parents expect us to abide by the law. I do, on occasion, have a drink; however, just drinking for drinking's sake is not my forte! And if there is dancing then I am dancing, not drinking! Dad leans towards me, and I blow my breath, aiming at his nose. Dad straightens up with a smile. After our dance, Dad and Uncle depart. I am baffled. *What was that all about?* Pushing my perplexed thoughts aside, I continue to dance and have a wonderful evening.

The next morning, I discover the problem. Apparently, Grampa and Gramma went to visit friends in town. They just *happened* to drive by the Weekes Hall to stop and view the people milling about outside the dance hall. They told my parents that I was drinking outside the hall, that I shouted vile words in their direction, and that I threw a beer bottle at them. I am shocked.

"You know I would never do that, and besides, I spend my time dancing not drinking," I cry out emphatically. Mom and Dad suggest that I go and talk to Grampa and Gramma. I agree. I love my grandparents and respect them. I do not understand how they could even perceive me treating them so rudely.

I must clear the air. Willingly I step out the door and stride quickly to their makeshift bedroom. At the sharp rap on the door, Grampa opens it in a wide arc and motions me to a chair. I sink into the chair, feeling a bit uncomfortable.

"It could not have been me. I was in the hall, dancing, all night," I blurt.

"It was you; I clearly saw you," Grampa insists.

"I would not do that," I murmur, as my bottom lip trembles. "It wasn't me," I utter more forcefully, as tears well up in my eyes.

"You can lie to me, but God knows it was you," Grampa bellows. As his words wash over me, I leap up and I bolt out of the room. Tears begin to stream down my face. He is wrong! *God knows it was not me!*

"Grampa called me a liar," I blubber to my parents. My body quivers and I am bawling uncontrollably. In a state of despair, I repeat our conversation, word for word. I am broken inside. Mom wraps me in her arms.

"We believe you and that is the important issue," she croons softly.

I am relieved. Mom and Dad step into to the next room to whisper quietly. Shortly thereafter, Dad exits the house to have a meeting with Grampa and Gramma.

I do not know what transpired. However, the next day Grampa and Gramma avoid eye contact and do not speak to me. In addition, they decide to cut their vacation short. What I do know is that I have a support system in my parents, who shelter and protect their family in every situation.

My relationship with my grandparents was on shaky ground for a bit; however, I am like my mom and prefer harmony over conflict. By the time we visited with them a year later, all was forgiven. I did not mention the incident and neither did they! We hugged, smiled, and chatted like there was never a problem.

Chapter 66

Swim near-misses:

"The water is warm, dive in," I shout. We are enjoying our summer break. The cool, refreshing spray hits me like a rushing waterfall. I frantically churn my feet until my head breaks the surface and I shout, "Come on in, the water is really warm." We are frolicking in our swimming pool, the twelve-foot-deep dugout.

A saltshaker is a must at the dugout. The leeches are usually on the weedy side of the dugout; the odd time, we find one on our body. Therefore, we always have a saltshaker on the shore. If a leech attaches itself to our body, we sprinkle it with salt, which causes them to wrinkle up and fall off. It is interesting to watch. Regardless of the leeches, we are the envy of the *town kids.*

My friends often ask if they could go swimming. On such occasions, I implement a clever plan. "Come and weed a couple of rows in the garden and afterwards we can all go for a swim," I reply. This is one of my chores.

The dreaded weeding is accomplished quickly, and I am able to go for a dip with my friends.

Sometimes, intruders sneak into the dugout. The dugout is out of view from the house separated by a small forest of trees. Therefore, on several occasions we are unaware of children sneaking in for a quick swim.

Swimmer Beware:

It is a beautiful blazing hot summer day. We are comfortably eating our lunch of bologna sandwiches in our relatively cool kitchen. Mom has drawn the drapes to keep the previous evening's cool air inside the house. Our lunch is interrupted with a frantic yelling that pierces the stillness.

"Help! Help! Help!"

Instantly we scramble, jumping to our feet and sending our chairs flying in every direction. We dash out of the house to encounter a panicked young lad emerging from the bush.

"My friend Jim fell in the water. He doesn't know how to swim," the young lad blubbers in a trembling voice.

We race down the bush lane. Scurrying along the path, we emerge out of the forest of trees. We see Jim staggering and stumbling from the dugout. Grasping his reeling body, Mom gently lays him on his stomach. She proceeds to move his arms back and forth, back and forth, back and forth, just as she was taught in her First Aid training. Spewing out water, Jim coughs, rolls over, and dazedly sits up. We all breathe a sigh of relief—he survives!

Adrenalin is pumping through my body, sweat is beading on my brow, and my heart is beating erratically. I remember my near-drowning incident at the age of three and wonder if Mom experienced the same body reactions. I am on the other side of the fence, watching the drama unfold, and I now have an appreciation of the trauma my mom must have experienced during our event years ago. I totally understand why our parents insisted on us learning to swim at a young age. Swimming is like riding a bike; once you learn you never forget. It is a lifetime skill.

Water incident:

Chris is having a refreshing dip in the dugout. A couple of girls arrive from town. Led by Missy, they stroll with an air of importance to sit by the dugout and puff intensely on cigarettes. They do not offer a cigarette to Chris. Basically, over the years, the candy has morphed into cigarettes.

Chris is not impressed. She is easygoing and mild mannered; however, she has had prior experience with this duo. Chris is not impressed with their haughty attitude. She is perturbed. *Why should they swim in our dugout and use our saltshaker?*

"You can't swim in my dugout," Chris triumphantly announces. Unmindful of her words, the girls wade in and begin swimming. Together they frolic in the water and totally ignore Chris. They avoid splashing water because each of them has their hair wrapped in curlers, prepared for a date that evening. The curled hair must dry on its own for many hours throughout the day. At the time, we didn't have hair dryers; if our hair got wet, we simply had to let it air-dry over several hours.

Chris is exasperated. She gazes at them, perturbed that they are defying her. The more they laugh, splash about, and ignore her as if she is invisible, the angrier she gets. Even the nicest people reach their limit—she is finally bent on revenge.

Chris has a plan. Slipping quietly into the deep water, she dives close to the middle of the dugout to the bottom, which is a good ten to twelve feet. She grabs a handful of mud and proceeds to the surface, to gasp a much-needed gulp of air. Swimming sneakily beside Missy, Chris raises her arm quickly to plunk the muck smack-dab on top of her *dry, curled hair.* A blood-curdling scream shatters the silence.

Missy blows her stack. In a frenzy, she clutches Chris and plunges her head under the water. Chris wiggles, twists, and turns, but cannot get out of her clutches. Chris is running out of air and is overwhelmed with fear. She is oxygen starved and her mind is in a whirl. Without a drop of air remaining, Chris is finally released from the overpowering death grip.

Chris is frantic to breathe. With all her remaining strength, she madly flings her head above the surface to gulp in the precious air. The silence is broken only by her gasps as she breathes deep into her lungs. Aside from panting Chris is silent—she will not give Missy the satisfaction of feeling that she had the upper hand. Missy is thus oblivious to how dangerous the situation was and exits the dugout.

"We need to go. I must wash and curl my hair again," Missy snappishly announces to her friend. They promptly leave without another word.

Crawling out of the dugout, Chris is thankful to be alive!

That evening Chris eagerly prepares for her date – a relatively new boyfriend.

"Tonight, we will be double dating," Chris's boyfriend informs her while strolling to the truck. Chris nods in agreement but upon approaching the truck she ponders the seating arrangement. *We are going to be very snug, sitting all together in the cab of the truck!* Chris lithely swings up through the passenger's door; halfway in, her body comes to a grinding halt. Aghast at the vision, her mouth drops open, and her eyes grow wide. She does not know whether to laugh or to cry. *It is Missy.*

It is a long and very uncomfortable night. Missy and Chris are both embarrassed and it takes many hours before they attempt small talk. Eventually, they discuss the incident and both treat the episode as a prank. Their conversation concludes with the two of them laughing together and brings an end to their conflict in a peaceful manner. They end their dispute as friends.

Chris and Missy possibly wished for a do-over. It is likely that we all have one issue or more that causes a twinge of regret where we would like a do-over.

One instance comes to my mind from our younger days. Charlie, Chrissy, and I are walking to school when Charlie breaks into a run. I dash after him, trying to keep up, leaving Chrissy running quite a distance behind us.

"Wait for me," Chrissy yells.

I hesitate. My mind is in a quandary—I want to wait but I also want to keep up with Charlie. I continue to run. Later that day I am extra nice to Chrissy; however, it does not alleviate my guilt at leaving her behind. I regret my earlier decision from that day forward.

I wish I had followed my instinct. I wish I could have a do-over. In future, I pay attention to my natural intuition.

Boat

Water activities are a part of our family life. Therefore, one spring, Mom and Dad decide to buy a boat. Dad insists on testing the boat in the water before any of us can ride! What a sight, to watch the assessment. We huddle in a small group, observing Dad whip the boat around and spin it like a spinning top. We are in awe to see the boat thrash wickedly in tight circles, then whisk into figure eights, creating gigantic waves. The boat bounces sporadically over the water-rollers, up and down, up and down, up and down. Dad manhandles the boat like a pro! His magnificent maneuvers is proof that the boat is safe!

Patience is a virtue of my dad's. He spends hours upon hours behind the steering wheel, good-naturedly driving while everyone water-skis. He offers and is willing to take anyone for a boat ride or ski—youngsters or adults. Dad is a motivator—if you use two skis, then he suggests trying one ski.

"Always try to do better. If you fall, it's a learning curve," Dad encourages.

Happiness comes in all forms—our parents buy a boat to bring joy to the family.

Chapter 67

Halloween:

It is Halloween night. Charlie, Chris, and I along with a group of friends are either crammed into the cab or in the truck box of Charlie's truck. We are out for tricks and not for treats!

We are cruising–looking for pranks. Someone suggests that we might tip over several outhouse toilets. I spot the ideal outhouse. The tall and skinny rectangular building is outlined against the moonlit sky. This out-house is the perfect target. I pound on the roof of the cab and lean over to shout into Charlie's open driver's window.

"Let's do that one," I shout. We stop and clamber away from the truck and sneakily tread towards our victim – the outhouse.

"Let's check if anyone is inside," I utter quietly. I have heard of an inci-dent where a toilet went topsy-turvy with the owner inside. Therefore, we tap lightly on the door–no response. We line up behind the outhouse and whisper in one voice, "One, two, three, go." In unison, we shove hard, and it topples over with a loud thud.

"Help me! Help me! Help me!" An anguished whispered shriek rises into the darkness. Someone has fallen into the hole of muck.

In the dim light, we gasp in shock at the sight. I can see a shadowy figure in the dim light standing knee-deep in the pile of dung. It is one of the girls. My skin prickles and goosebumps appear on my arm as I gaze at her form. My heart goes out to her being in such a dreadful spot. She had obviously lurched her body along with the outhouse and dropped straight into the waste pit.

"Get me out of here," she whispers loudly in a trembling voice.

Nervously, I shift closer to help with the rescue. Inhaling a deep breath of fresh air, we move as one towards the foul-smelling pit. Extending our arms, we grab onto her raised arms and pull together to yank her out. A sucking sound fills the stillness, and she emerges from the cesspool. She stinks and is covered in slurry from the knees down. A putrid aroma emerges from her body. I feel sorry for her and am eager to calm her down.

"Let's jump into the truck box and go to my house to clean up," I suggest in a sympathetic voice.

We call it a night and go home.

The grapevine tattletales on us. Our parents hear through the grapevine about our trick of the night before. Dad points out that it is not a funny trick and that it is very unfair for the owners to have to struggle to upright the toilet.

"Charlie, pick up some of your friends," Dad instructs. "Go right back to the scene of your crime and upright the toilet." Charlie complies!

Dad's lecture hits us in our hearts, and this is the last time we *toilet tip*.

Chapter 68

Edward:

Edward and I attend school in the same grade from one to twelve. My first recollection of an interaction with him is in grade three, when he chases me instead of the ball during a recess football game. Edward has always been a part of my community; however, we don't interact much together until our latter high school years. Edward is out-going, kind, polite, and generous. He always has a smile on his face—I have never seen him mad or upset. He is dramatic in his stories and his actions. His ideas of fun keep me entertained. Edward's sister Elaine is good friends with my sister Chris, so we spend many fun times together in a group. One time we were having a dance party in their shed-type building which had a huge front window.

"Let's dance in front of the window to look like we are having fun to anyone arriving." Edward suggests. Truth be told it is the simple acts like this that create our fun!

On another occasion, I really needed to study my history. "Come study at my house," Edward suggests. He adds, "I have the latest Beatles album." Edward is the smartest boy in our class, and I do need to study; however, the music is the biggest drawing card! *I love music.* My body automatically begins to sway at the sound of a good tune. The music blares in the background while we attack the history book. This is not my favorite subject. I much prefer English. Although Edward grills me with history questions, we are often distracted. We occasionally break into song and get lost in the pounding rhythmic beat of the music. This is representative of our relationship. He always finds ways to make dreary activities more fun.

A day trip:

Edward enjoys taking day trips in and around our province. And, of course, I am always game to go.

"Let's go to Waskesiu Lake tomorrow," Edward suggests. This sounds like a great idea; the next day Edward, Chris, and I head out on our newest venture.

I am suffering with sharp jabs reverberating through my tummy. This happens once a month. The entire drive there, I lie in the back seat, curled in a fetal position, in agony. Luckily, when we arrive, I am in less pain.

We are strolling along the shore and admiring all the boats tied to the dock.

"Let's hop into this boat," Edward suggests.

"I don't think we should be hopping into a stranger's boat. What if the owners come along?" I reply nervously. I glance around furtively and slowly creep behind Edward into the boat. We position ourselves in the boat and morph into actors.

Julie and Edward

"I'll take your picture," Chris remarks as she aims the camera. We smile, acting as though we own the boat. Thank goodness we do not get caught!

On another occasion, he blithely suggests, "Let's go to Prince Albert to try out my dad's new truck." It is the promise of a good time. Chris joins us and with a loud rumble the truck springs to life as we set off on our day trip. The truck is black, with shiny and cool leather seats. Edward has just obtained his learner's license; since I have a driver's license, he is permitted to drive.

"I am scared to drive in the city," Edward states, as we approach Prince Albert.

"I can drive," I promptly announce. I got my drivers license last December as soon as I turned sixteen years. I love driving any type of vehicle or machinery. I have never driven in the city, but I am confident of my driving skills. I will apply my driving experience along with the knowledge gleaned from my driver's instructor book on lane changes. We enter the city, and I am perched behind the steering wheel. "See, it's easy," I declare. Calculating the left-hand turn in my head, I carefully review the proper lane exchange. Gunning the engine, I move swiftly into the correct lane.

Julie

Suddenly, a lineup of vehicles is driving straight at me. A horrified look of fear is plastered across the closest driver's face.

"You are on the wrong side of the boulevard," Edward screeches in a desperate tone.

I miscalculated! I am going the wrong way on the street. The blood is pumping erratically through my heart, and my hands tremble as I clutch the steering wheel in a death grip. Out of the corner of my eye I spot an opening in the boulevard. Madly stepping on the gas, I whip the steering wheel to the right and swing swiftly through the gap. I do not have time to check for vehicles in the next lane, I just turn into it and throw up a quick prayer. God answers my plea. With a sigh of relief, I am in the correct lane. I lean back and feel some of the tension leave my shoulders. I am driving confidently once more.

"All is okay," I announce with self-assuredness.

Edwards face flushes and his mouth tightens.

"Pull over. I am driving. I can do as good a job as you!" Edward announces in a firm but joking voice. We both laugh as I pull the truck over to the side of the road. Edward and I are best pals.

Play-act:

Edward, Chris, and I decide to stop for lunch at a café in Prince Albert.

"Let's have some fun," Edward suggests.

"What is your idea?" I probe in an inquisitive voice.

"Let's pretend I am the father, Julie, you are the mother, and Chris, you will be our teenager," Edward suggests. His imagination has come up trumps again. Laughing, we agree to the plan—this will be a riot!

We morph into an actor and actresses. For Chris and I it is like our young days of putting on a play with our bed being the stage. Inside the café, we begin to ad lib our skit loudly. We step into our make-believe world. Soon, everyone is staring at us and smiling. By the time we depart to head home, everyone in the café is hooting with laughter.

"Wasn't that fun?" Edward gaily asks. In a fit of giggles, Chris and I agree! We are good friends, creating happiness together.

Traffic Stop:

Upon leaving Prince Albert, Edward, Chris, and I are laughing as we reminisce on all the fun we just encountered. Suddenly, Edward stops laughing.

"There is a police car behind me. What do I do? Did I do something wrong? Do I stop?" shrieks Edward. We are only a couple of miles out of Prince Albert.

"Just keep driving, their red lights are not on," I reply calmly.

"I think I am driving too fast; I will slow down," Edward mutters. He slows down a little, then a little more, then a little more. Soon we are crawling along the road, hugging the centre line.

"Edward, I think this is too slow," I advise with a loud sigh.

"Do you know the speed limit? I do not. They can't give me a ticket for going to slow," he replies, clearly annoyed with me.

Suddenly, the air is shattered by the shrill, piercing whine of the police siren. I crane my neck to peer out the back window.

"The red lights are flashing. Pull over!" I shout.

"Why are you driving so slow?" the policeman demands, as he looms tall and stern at the window. Silence. "You need to travel a little faster, as you can be a menace on the road at this speed." I wonder if we are going to get a ticket and I am too frightened to even give Edward a look of *I told you so!*

"This is a learner's license. Does anyone in this vehicle have a driver's license?" the police officer blurts in a rough tone. With a shiver of apprehension, I promptly pass my driver's license over to him. The police officer glares at me and reprimands me forcefully. "You should be sitting right next to the learner!" Observing the eyes of the police officer on me, I feel the warmth rise up my neck and into my cheeks. Quickly, I scramble with Chris to exchange seats. Thankfully, we do not get a ticket. Maybe Edward was correct!

I am annoyed. The middle seat is uncomfortable; Chris is smiling, happy to get the window seat! We have a fun time together–friends bring joy into each other's lives.

Part Nine

Late Teens
Julie 17 – 18 years

Chapter 69

Education is important:

My parents were forced to quit school. In spite of this, they are avid readers and taught themselves to maintain farm financial books. Mom speaks many times of how she wanted to be a nurse. Dad, on the other hand, never mentions not being able to continue his education; however, he firmly relays his belief that education is important.

"An education is a must," Dad states enthusiastically, many times during our school years. He maintains that an education is a guarantee for a successful future.

Therefore, my grade twelve graduation is a time of great celebration. My *Grad* ensemble is an exquisite,

Graduation, Julie and Edward

knee-length baby blue chiffon cocktail dress, displaying an elegant touch of lace on the blouse and sleeves. My white leather high heels sport peek-a-boo openings, and to complete the attire there is a white clutch purse along with a pair of short white gloves.

The morning dawns bright and clear. However, I am groaning, and my body screams in agony. I am sick—my tummy is jam-packed with sharp pains. Regardless, I am at the beauty salon and suffer in pain through the shampoo and hair dryer.

"I am going to faint," I shout to the hairdresser. I stumble outside moaning, "Why? Why? Why?"

It always happens on special days. I recollect the day Jean acquired her driver's license. She came to take me for a ride, but I could not get out of bed for the pain. And also, that day Edward, Chris, and I went to Waskesiu Lake and I suffered all the way to the lake, curled up in the back seat. It always occurs on a special event. I grumble to myself, *Why today, of all days—my high school graduation!*

"I don't want to go to my graduation," I whimper to Mom. "I am in too much pain."

"We will take you to the hospital for medication," Mom replies.

Best friends, Sandra and Julie

"This will fix you up," the nurse states matter-of-factly while handing me two big white pills. She is correct. The pain soon dissipates; however, I feel very woozy and dizzy.

"I just want to sleep," I whine to Mom.

"You need to get up, Julie. It is your important day!" Mom insists.

In a dazed state I shift my exhausted body—we return to the beauty salon. The hairdresser is not happy to see me. She has a busy day with all her graduation clients, however, she grudgingly finishes my hairdo. My longish hair flips up in a striking wave along my neck—I am pleased. We exit and I inhale a deep breath—an attempt to renew my body and clear my swirling head.

I am on the stage, and I feel better. I am glad Mom forced me to get on with my special day. I sit with an air of importance. Scrutinizing the audience from my upper perch, I search for my parents. They are easy to spot, sitting with an aura of prominence, faces aglow as they smile brightly at everyone. As I stride across the stage to obtain my certificate, I turn to eye my parents, we exchange glances, and it warms my heart to see the look of fulfillment on their faces. They are beaming with pride! I am on top of the world. I know I did them proud.

Our principal, Mr. Wandzura shakes my hand in congratulations, and I begin to reminisce on some of my interactions with him. In one of his earlier classes I had leaned over to whisper to my friend Sandra. I glanced up to see Mr. Wandzura staring at me.

"Julie, what is so important that you must whisper to Sandra? Please tell us all," he voiced. Embarrassed to the core I stood up and mumbled, "I told her that Chris was sick and not at school today." Abruptly I sat down and from that moment onwards I never interrupted his class again.

Edward, Chris, Julie

On November 22, 1963, Mr. Wandzura ushered the entire school into one classroom where we gathered around a small black and white T.V. We were viewing the startling tragedy of the assassination of John F. Kennedy. Mr. Wandzura knew this was a pivotal moment and that his students needed to be aware of this important news.

My most scary moment with Mr. Wandzura was being called into the Principals office. I had been caught playing Hooky.

"Do you not like school?" Mr. Wandzura asked in a caring and sincere tone. My mind was in a whir. *Of course, I like school I had just been swayed by my peers.*

"Yes, I do like school, and I am sorry," I uttered in a low trembling voice. I was not suspended like some of my peers - probably because I apologized. I never skipped school again.

These instances ran through my head as I genuinely shook the hand of Mr. Wandzura. I hope he realized what a good influence he had on my life. He was an exceptional teacher and principal who really cared about all his staff and students.

After the ceremony, a friend wrapped his arms around me in a hug murmuring, "Congratulations."

"I smell something burning," I shout, sniffing an acrid smell.

In the next moment, he is whacking at the back of my skirt. I cannot believe my eyes—in his hand he is holding a *lit cigarette*!!! It burned a hole in my dress. I am speechless and a little sad at my ruined dress.

The next day, Mom performs a miracle and fixes the hole using the tiniest of stitches in the same blue thread. I am pleased, because I will wear the dress to an exciting event coming just around the corner.

Julie, Chris, Dad, Mom

Date Disapproval:

Throughout my teen years I was fortunate to date nice boys who my parents always approved. However, I begin dating a new fella, and after several outings I have a problem. My parents worry that my education and career might be jeopardized with this relationship. Our parents have always emphasized and been adamant that us children need our education in order to be self-efficient.

"We do not want you to date him, we want you to concentrate on your Career," Mom gently informs me. I am not happy. I am angry.

Furious, I turn and stomp out of the house. I stride swiftly along the bush lane and fling myself onto the prickly grass beside the dugout. I stare angrily into the gloomy waters–exactly the same way I feel! Gloomy! I sit and sulk.

Out of my peripheral vision I notice a figure approaching. I jerk my head up to see Dad lowering himself down beside me. We sit in silence for several minutes–you could hear a pin drop! Eventually, in a soft voice, Dad explains calmly that they feel I should give myself some space and seriously concentrate on my career.

"We want you to focus on your vocation. Therefore, in the future you can be independent if unforeseen circumstances befall."

"Those are not valid reasons. I really like him," I state stubbornly.

"When you are eighteen years old you can make your own decision. You can date him then–and if it is real *love*, it will still be there," Dad gently advises. The truth of his reasoning prickles, and I grudgingly agree.

My parents are clever. Almost a year later at eighteen years old my desired date and I get together. After our date, I realize that my parents are right. He is not the one for me. I conclude that sometimes parents know best.

Wedding:

My brother is getting married. We are so excited–Charlie is tying the knot. His fiancé, Nellie, is the most wonderful person. In the yearbook, her quote is, "Can you imagine Nellie not having friends!" She is kind, generous, and the best friend a girl could have–she is my friend.

We are bridesmaids! My sister, Chris, and I have this honor. We are very close siblings and are both friends with Nellie. The bridesmaids' dresses are a baby blue–I will wear my graduation dress. *Thank goodness Mom could repair the damage on my graduation dress*, I muse. Nellies' sister Nettie is the Maid of Honor, and the groomsmen are Glen, Mervyn, and Edward.

We create beautiful flowers from Kleenex. Decorating two wedding vehicles requires many flowers. Assembling the Kleenex flat, we fold accordion-style, tie in the middle, lift each layer and pull toward centre, and lastly separate each layer of tissue. Voila a carnation type of white flower. The church wedding, reception and dance are held in Nellie's hometown, Reserve. It is a joyful occasion, which ends in a night of jubilation with the kicking up of heels on the dance floor.

Charlie and Nellie begin married life on a farm. They purchase the Smith quarter a mile and a half from Weekes and reside in a small one-bedroom house. Ironically it is the same Smith quarter that our parents rented and started married life in a granary.

Julie, Chris, Nettie, Nellie, Charlie, Glen, Mervyn. Edward.
Front: Neil, Barry

Charlie and Nellie in similar steps to Mom and Dad are unified in their commitment to one another to transform their house into a home. With their faith in God, they work together as one to face the challenges of farming while raising two wonderful children.

Chapter 70

Working girl:

After graduation, Edward and I travel to Regina to get a summer job. In September, we will begin our careers. Edward will pursue an accounting career in Saskatoon, while I have been accepted to *stewardess training* in Winnipeg.

In Regina, we rent separate rooms in a boarding house and begin job hunting.

"I got a job," I announce enthusiastically to Edward. "I will work as car hop at Bob's Drive-in."

Working in the bright sunshine outside, strolling from vehicle to vehicle and interacting with the public is very pleasant. I am happy. I obtain the order, pick up the food, balance the tray while striding to the car, and position it onto the open window ledge. This will be a good fill-in job until I start my stewardess training.

A good boss:

At Bob's Drive-in, I am trained in money management. We are taught to count the change to be returned to the customer by starting from the total amount billed and counting upwards. I am very adept and confident handling money. After a huge order of nine dollars and sixty-five cents, I receive a twenty-dollar bill. I hurriedly count back, "Sixty-five," I give a dime and count, "seventy-five," I give a quarter and count, "ten dollars," I give two fives. The sun is blazing hot, and I feel the sweat trickle down my back. I resume calculating the change after being momentarily distracted. I ponder where I was at. *Oh yes, I remember I was at ten dollars.* Out loud, I count, "Ten dollars." I give a ten and continue, "equals twenty dollars."

I hurry back to pick up my next order. Entering the building, the air conditioner is shooting nice, cool air into the atmosphere. The chilly air feels refreshing. Suddenly, I freeze in my spot–I realize my error. I paid out ten dollars too much.

Scrambling madly, I rush to yank open the door, and stomp swiftly towards the parking spot. Shocked, I stop, and my eyes widen in surprise at the unexpected vision. The lonely tray is perched on the cement walkway under the overhang and the vehicle is nowhere in sight. I am devasted.

The shortage of money will come out of my wages. I cannot afford to lose ten dollars. Teary-eyed and with trepidation, I approach my boss to relate my terrible error. He is a nice guy.

"You are allowed one mistake; if it happens again, the money will come out of your pay," he firmly states in a soft tone. I breathe a sigh of relief and stand up to leave the room.

"Thank you, it will not happen again." I quietly express my gratitude. I become an expert money guru.

A few hours later, my shift is over, and I do not have a ride home. Miserable, with aching feet, I stand outside my workplace contemplating the long walk home.

"Do you need a ride home?" inquires my boss, who has suddenly appeared by my side. He is very perceptive, noticing that that no one has arrived to pick me up after work. I am amazed.

"Yes, please," I murmur gratefully. My boss is a thoughtful and caring guy. This is a good job. My residence is a couple of miles from work, however, and transportation is a huge problem. Considering this, I apply for a waitress job across the street from my rooming house.

A few days later, Mom and Dad arrive in Regina. We need to sign the stewardess airline papers. We meet up with the representative from the airline school, review the process, sign the papers, and my parents pay a substantial amount for my course. I am ecstatic to begin my stewardess career in September.

Mom and Dad stop at Bob's Drive-in on their way out of Regina. Mom is impressed at my abilities,

"I can see that you are the best car-hop here, and you are very smart in handling money," is her parting comment. I smile quietly. Her positive encouragement boosts my morale. I do not mention my earlier error. I feel on top of the world. However, I am hopeful for the café job across from my suite.

A new job:

A few days later, I am surprised to hear Edward say, "You just got a job at the café next door." I am puzzled. *How does he know?*

"What do you mean? How do you know?" I inquire, with an expression of bewilderment.

"You got a phone call," Edward replies, with a huge grin. In our boarding house, all the rooms share a telephone located in the hallway.

"Oh, I have a telephone call?" I ask.

"No," Edward replies, with a smug look. "I answered the phone and when the lady asked for you, I pretended I was you."

"I don't believe you. Why would you make such a joke?" I query. A worried expression is etched across his face. Hastily, he averts his eyes. I recognize he is telling the truth. My eyes blaze. "What a stupid prank," I snappily bark. In our house, the "stupid" word was treated like a swear word. Edward knows I never use that word! This is evidence that I am truly enraged. Fortunately, my personality cannot stay in a *mad* state for long. An hour later we are best pals again!

"Your voice sure sounds different between the phone and in person," my boss announces on my first day of work. I am not surprised. I am silent. *What can I say?*

My first day at work goes downhill from there. My co-worker instructs me to take a fifteen-minute coffee break. I eagerly fill my glass with the free Coke and slide onto the cool and slippery bright red counter stool. Raising the glass to my lips, I turn at the sound of approaching footsteps. My boss is marching determinedly in my direction, her face is flushed, and a flash of disappointment flickers across it. *What have I done wrong?*

"Why are you sitting down instead of working?" she demands.

"My co-worker told me to take a break," I mumble nervously.

"You are not entitled to a break yet—you just started work an hour ago," my boss states emphatically. I glance at my co-worker, looking for help; she turns her back and ignores us completely. Stunned, I jump to my feet and furiously begin to wipe the counter. Irritated with my co-worker, I pledge not to take advice from her ever again. I am kept hopping. Serving a table of four businessmen—requesting extra pencils, needing plain paper, ready for more coffee—I am run ragged. Eventually, after one of my many trips to their table, one of the gentlemen leans over in my direction.

"You can expect a huge tip," he whispers quietly. My shift ends while they are finishing up so I depart, knowing that the tip will be given to me the next day. Normally we split the tip if two of us work a table; however, it is obvious the men will soon pack up and leave, so I expect to receive the entire amount.

"What is my tip amount?" I enquire excitedly the next day.

"I get the tip because I completed the service at their table," my co-worker replies smugly. I march swiftly away to talk to my boss.

"My customers were getting ready to leave when I left, and my co-worker finished up. Who gets the tip money?" I question my boss.

"She finalized the provisions at the table, so it is up to her whether she wants to share the tip," my boss answers. Her answer is unacceptable, and resentment burns within–I am not happy. I wonder what amount I lost in my tip money. I am frustrated and stomp home.

"Edward, let's pack up and go home. This is not the job for me," I announce in frustration. "Besides, I need to talk to Mom and Dad. I am having second thoughts about the airline course."

Winnipeg sounds like the other side of the world. I am already lone-some, and I am only a couple of hours away from home. My initial idea of being a stewardess and travelling the world to see different places just does not sound as appealing anymore. I need to rethink my career plans.

Chapter 71

Career:

I arrive home and break the news to my parents.

"I don't want to pursue the flight attendant course; I don't want to be an airline stewardess. Winnipeg is so far away, and I will get lonely," I announce to my parents.

"We have paid for the course already," Dad explains.

"Can you ask for your money back?" I inquire.

"It is non-refundable. Let me talk to your mom," Dad declares. I am worried because I know for sure that I do not want to go! Deep in my soul, I know this is not the career for me—God must have a different plan for my life. Later, I overhear Mom talking in low tones to Dad. Upon detecting my name, I slink closer; remaining unseen, I strain to hear the indistinct words. I lean with my ear against the door jamb.

"... Their daughter went and was so lonely she had a nervous break-down," Mom utters quietly and convincingly to Dad. I gasp and exhale deeply. *I am definitely not going!* I zip back to the kitchen table. My parents return to the room and sit down at the table.

"We have decided you do not need to go to Winnipeg. We will try to get our money back," Dad tenderly informs me. I am thrilled, yet a little sad that I have caused them to lose money over my decision. Dad states understandingly, "It is essential that you have a career; therefore, choose a course in Regina."

I appreciate that my parents understood and took my request seriously and resolved the issue.

Out of the nest:

After a bit of deliberation, my new career plan is to take a secretarial–bookkeeper course at the Success Business College in Regina. I am excited to head into the unknown. Out to conquer the world, I am eager to leave the nest and stretch my wings.

Mom and I strike out for Regina. Clutching a list of boarding houses received from the school, we peruse several homes. After several interviews we choose a house where I receive breakfast, a packed lunch, and supper, along with my room.

Hugging Mom goodbye, I feel a hollow pit deep in my tummy. Unpacking my clothes and organizing my books, I plunk myself on the bed and feel at a complete loss. Nothing is familiar and it is lonely in my tiny, sparse bedroom. It is a relief to go downstairs for a meal and meet my three roommates. They attend the same business school and are very friendly.

I need to talk to Mom. Unfortunately, my parents do not have a phone; I call their friend, Phyllis, to take a message to my parents. After an eternity, Mom calls me back.

"I want to come home," I burst out crying and blubbering upon hearing her voice.

"Why? What is wrong?" Mom asks anxiously. My quavering voice is garbled with wild sobbing. Mom is worried. "Julie, take a deep breath and tell me what is wrong?" I take a deep breath and sniff loudly.

"I am lonesome, and I want to come home," I moan, totally distressed. Distraught, I cry throughout our whole conversation.

"I will talk to Dad and call you back," Mom promises in a worried tone.

I begin to pray earnestly that I can go home. Previously, in my nightly prayers I asked God to help with my homesickness—now I just want to go home. I am used to a houseful of people and communicating every minute of the day. Suddenly I am in room all on my own and too shy to leave my room. I do not like being all by myself—it is foreign to me.

Apparently, their conversation is at odds: Mom wants me to come home, but Dad maintains that I need a career. Dad points out to Mom that there are no jobs in the village of Weekes, that I need an education for my future, and that in all situations I can always fall back on my career. The next day, Mom calls me back and explains all the reasons I must stay and complete my education.

By this time, I have calmed down. I accept the valid reasons and settle into a routine. After several weeks, Sharon, one of the girls at the boarding house, encourages me to come out of my room to sit in her room and chat. We soon become close friends and I begin to feel more at home. All six of us girls gather together and chit-chat every night. On the weekend, Sharon invites me to her home in Weyburn, introduces me to the wonderful taste of pizza and then we chat into the wee hours of the morning. Friends help heal the heart. Life appears much brighter. God answered my prayer after all, just not in the way I expected.

Hair color:

During the previous summer, I dyed my hair black. I am naturally blond; the dark hair drastically altered my appearance.

At that time, Chris and I devised a fun plan: to go into the Porcupine Plain Café and pretend that I am her cousin. I guess play-acting is in our blood – we quite naturally morph into actresses.

"This is my cousin," Chris announces to acquaintances in the Porcupine Plain Café. Instantly, we portray distant cousins carrying on an interesting conversation. It was a riot! We enjoy ourselves immensely, until one of the guys asks me for a date! Chris and I exchange guilty glances and I decide to come clean.

"I am Julie. I have just dyed my hair," I nervously utter. His eyes grew cold, and he stared harshly in my direction. Jumping up from his seat, he stomped out the door. Chris and I exchange remorseful glances. However, on our drive home we laugh uncontrollably. In hindsight, I guess it was a mean trick.

I am ready to return to my natural color. I do a home-dye job at my boarding house–my hair turns a hideous bright orange color and becomes stiff and brittle. I am in a quandary and am not sure what would be the next step. I zip to a beauty salon.

"Can you fix my hair?" I ask. "I want to be blond again."

"You must wait two weeks for your hair to recuperate," is the unfortunate answer.

For that entire two-week period, I am laughed at! People passing me on the street are out-right laughing in my face! I am embarrassed and can feel the warmth creep up to my cheeks. I endure the sly looks in great discomfort.

"I liked your normal black hair," the principal leans in and whispers in my ear at school. I cringe. He does not know that I am a natural blond.

It is a *long* two weeks. Finally, I am blond again.

Stop, Look, and Listen:

Moving to the city was a big change for me, a small-town girl. I felt isolated without my family, and I missed my small town–my community family. The hustle and bustle of the city sounded strange and walking to school, the honking horns, squealing tires, and vehicle noise blended into a blurring hubbub. Not at all like home, with my peaceful walk to school, listening to the birds sing and the frogs croaking. In the city, my one saving grace was that Sharon and I bonded, and I was beginning to feel a new normal existence.

One early morning, Sharon and I stroll together, chatting, on our way to school. We are focussed on our lively conversation as we step into the crosswalk. Abruptly, my body is rammed viciously, and I hurtle through the air. I tumble *topsy-turvy over teakettle.* Landing with a thunderous thump upon the tarmac, my body reverberates with jarring pain. Stunned by the sudden, unexpected assault, I jerk my head upwards. Through my blurred vision, I view the front hood of a vehicle within inches of my frame. Sharon is moaning and sprawled several feet behind me.

What just happened? Why am I sprawled on the road? my clouded brain ponders. Within seconds, comprehension washes over me. *We have been hit by a car!* My mind is in a state of confusion. *Why did the vehicle hit us? Did we not check for traffic?* My frame trembles as I move each of my limbs to assess the damage. No broken bones! I stumble shakily to my feet.

"Are you okay?" a young man asks. He is obviously the driver and concerned. "I didn't expect you to step in front of my car."

"Yes, we are okay," Sharon and I answer in unison. We are embarrassed to be in such a humiliating situation. He gives us his name and number written on a jagged piece of paper.

In a state of shock, we stagger onwards to school. Our bodies suffer aches and pains. I feel like my body has been plowed down by a monstrous work truck. Dazedly, we stumble into school, and I focus on reaching the restroom to orient my bewildered and painful condition.

"It is snowing outside," the principal utters as I bypass him in the hallway. Deciphered, the message is, *Your slip is showing.* I glance at him in frustration. *That's the least of my worries!*

I survive; however, I spend several days in agony. I learn an important lesson: stop, look, and listen!

Chapter 72

Symbol of Flowers:

After my first term at school, the Christmas holidays are finally here. I am anxiously waiting for friends from back home, Jenny and brother John, to pick me up for our trip to Weekes. Jenny and I are friends; we graduated together in Weekes. She has a quiet, gentle, and kind demeaner. She attends a College in Regina and her brother, John, attends College in Moose Jaw. I feel safe with John's driving, and I appreciate the many rides home. John has a friendly, thoughtful, and easy-going personality. As I clamber inside the vehicle, I am not surprised to see Donald W, and he greets me with his usual big smile. He attends the same school as John, and we also graduated together. He is a confident, mature, and outgoing young man. We all get along famously and enjoy each others company which makes our trip home lively and pleasurable.

Squeezing in beside Jenny I notice that she is cradling a bundle of flowers. I shift into my seat and unintentionally jostle against the blossoms.

"Watch out for the flowers," Jenny utters firmly with a frown. I am surprised at her tone. This is highly unusual; Jenny is mild mannered and not one to get upset. I am puzzled.

"Who is the lucky person getting flowers?" I ask and gesture to the flowers.

"They are for my dad; he is very sick," she replies sadly. Her sadness makes me teary-eyed, and I shift away from the precious bundle. I tend to talk with my hands thus my movements again jostles her precious cargo.

I try to be more mindful, knowing these flowers are special and that she is worried about her dad.

Pulling into our driveway and coming to a stop, I am astonished to see Dad waiting in the yard. I hop out of the vehicle and Dad motions me to the house.

"I need to talk to John," he says.

John alights from the vehicle and extends his arm for a handshake in a greeting to Dad.

"What is Dad talking to John about?" I question Mom upon entering the house.

"Dad needs to give them the news that their dad has passed away," she whispers and squeezes my shoulder. I am stunned by this news. I feel my body convulse inside and my mind foolishly thinks, *He will not get his flowers.* I cannot imagine the turmoil my friends are feeling at this moment.

I know our community will rally about with hugs and words of encouragement. That's what our small town does—takes care of one another. The Ladies Club will host a lunch at the funeral, and everyone will come together to give support to the family. Still, I know my friends will suffer the loss of their father. My heart aches for them and I pray for my friends.

We Weep:

Our small town comes to the aid of another family when a disastrous accident occurs. Okley and Ina's thirteen-year-old boy Alvin, while driving a tractor is in a fatal collision. Our families are intertwined with parents being close friends and Alvin's siblings Floyd, Wilmer, June, and Bryon being friends of my siblings and me.

Chris phones me in Regina to relay the news and it hits me like a ton of bricks. I am speechless and listen dazedly as Chris emotionally continues.

"Mom and Ina just engulfed one another in a tight hug and cried their hearts out." I can visualize the scene grasping that *no words were necessary*. Chris concludes, "Many tears have been shed in our household."

I am in a state of shock. It is my first encounter of the death of one so young and to family friends. I stood stock-still in the hallway of my boarding house clutching tightly to the phone. My heart hurt like it never did before. I will always remember that moment – where I was and how I felt!

Chapter 73

Terror Reigns:

I graduate from Success Business School with a good grip on accounting, excellent shorthand skills and a typing speed of sixty-five words per minute on a manual typewriter. My academic success enables me to be employed two weeks later as a receptionist/secretary at the Young Men's Christian Association (YMCA). Mult-tasking is my job–switchboard duties, attend front desk, maintain records, type letters and various secretarial tasks.

Chris is coming! My sister has just completed grade ten and is joining me in Regina for a hairdressing course. I am overjoyed to have my sister in Regina. We scour the newspaper for a suite.

"This place is perfect," I state. It is a third-floor suite consisting of a kitchen/living room with a separate bedroom and a shared bathroom on the second floor. The suite is within walking distance to my new job.

Chris will attend Marvel Beauty School in September. In the meantime, she works part-time at the Golden Mile Café. Quite often, I pop into the café to accompany Chris home. Sipping on a pop, awaiting Chris' shift to end, I am approached by a young fella who is a regular at the restaurant. We chat like old friends.

"Do you want to go to a drive-in movie tonight?" he asks.

"Can my sister come along?" I reply. I maintain that two is safer than one–after all, I only know him from visiting at the cafe. I am still wary from my past experiences.

We are at the drive-in theatre. I cannot concentrate on the movie. I am feeling edgy and apprehensive–my inner instinct is niggling at me. The language is crude, and they are acting a bit on the rough side. I have a growing sense of concern. Chris and I are seated in the front, with me beside my date, the driver. Two other fellas are positioned in the back seat. I nudge Chris, and we glance at each other in silent communication.

"Chris, come to the restroom with me," I utter. We stride quickly away from the vehicle and out of earshot.

"Julie, I feel uneasy," Chris blurts with a worried expression.

"I do too. Let's go home right after the movie," I reply. My sixth sense has kicked in as well.

"We would like to go home," I calmly announce at the end of the movie.

"It's still early, we'll just go for a little drive first," my date replies. Putting the pedal to the metal, we are soon cruising in the countryside. Suddenly, he veers into an open field. Every cell in my body is saying something is wrong. This does not bode well for our safety! Words frantically spin around and around in my inner brain. *Is our life in danger?* I pray, *God, please help us.*

Suddenly, the vehicle plunges to a halt, with wheels spinning rapidly. We are bogged down in the mud. The driver shifts gears, and we rock back and forth, back and forth, back and forth. The guys unsuccessfully attempt to push it from the muck. My stomach is in knots. I know we need to pay attention to our inner feelings. I give Chris an elbow-bump and glance in her direction.

Julie and Chris

"Let's go," I mouth silently.

"We are going to the highway to hitch a ride back to town," I nervously inform my date. Without another word, and not waiting for a reply, we exit the sedan and aim for the highway several yards away. It is after midnight and the highway is desolate. All we can see behind us is blackness. We are a bundle of nerves. We walk and run.

"Julie, I am petrified," Chris mutters anxiously.

"It is a long walk, but we are safe." I speak breathlessly but in a calm tone—I do not want her to worry. I know I must be responsible and take care of my sister.

Suddenly, after trudging a mile, we distinguish headlights emerging from the darkness. We lift our thumbs high in the air. The vehicle slows and stops. The rear door opens, and we are stunned to see the guys sitting snug in the back seat. Our guys have hitched a ride! Gasping in shock, we clasp hands.

"We asked for you girls to be picked up, too," my *date* says. We are afraid not to get in; with a shiver of apprehension, we squeeze inside the vehicle. It is a tight fit, and we are uncomfortable. Once again, our nerves are on high alert. We enter the city of Regina. Our driver offers to drop us off on the main road, several blocks from our house.

"Could you please drive us to our house?" I ask the driver, nervously and hesitantly. Our rescuer agrees—perhaps he can feel our fear. Relief floods through our bodies and we thank the Lord for keeping us safe.

It has been a night of terror. The next day, we relate our scary incident to Mom and Dad who arrived for a visit to inform us about the thrilling news that we were to be Aunties. Charlie and Nellie are expecting a baby. Their news is exciting, our news is not. Our parents are shocked as we re-count the previous nights traumatic episode.

"Girls, in our small town you grew up to trust everyone. In the city, you need to be more discerning," Mom immediately admonishes. Our actions prove her theory regarding our naivety.

The phone rings. It is my ex-date.

"I will pick you up tonight to go out on a date," my ex-date announces on the phone.

"No, thank you," I nervously murmur.

"I thought you had a good time last night. I am coming over," he states firmly.

"It's him. He says he is coming over. I'm scared," I whisper hurriedly to Dad, as I place my hand over the receiver. Dad grasps the phone from my hand.

"This is Dad. If you show up here, I will be waiting for you!" Dad angrily blurts into the phone and hangs it up with a bang. Dad turns to me with a grim expression. "He better not show up." Dad must have scared him good because he does not show up.

Do I believe it was Providence, for the vehicle to get stuck? Yes, I believe God always has His hand in every situation.

Chapter 74

Coming home:

Chris and I go home for a visit. Home still tugs at my heart; visits are special. We especially enjoy hugging and playing with our niece, Charlene who is a loving baby. Snuggling with Charlene we gather around the table and tell stories. This is my favorite moment. It is Barry's turn to relate a story. He eagerly talks about the barn fire incident.

Apparently, Dad created a dramatic scene. The commotion occurred when Dad decided to burn the old barn, on an adjacent quarter of land.

Dad and Barry

Barry relates his story:

"Dad wanted to light the old barn on fire after dark, and sleep overnight in the station wagon to monitor the flames. Mom was not convinced, however, Dad and I persuaded her to tag along," Barry says. "We set off on our adventure with blankets, pillows, and snacks. When the sun set, Dad and I stepped into the pitch-black and crept carefully to the old barn. In the dark, the horizon was obliterated; the sparse beam of light from my tiny flashlight guided our actions. Earlier we prepared the newspaper and kindling. Dad struck a match." Barry grins at this moment; we wait in anticipation for him to continue.

"A tiny flame erupted. In a matter of minutes, the flames hungerly licked at the dry and brittle wood. Soon the fire was ablaze; a red/orange/yellow radiance outlined against the blackness of the atmosphere. The whole sky was illuminated by the massive glow, and the inferno could be seen for miles across the flat land."

Mom and Dad

Barry is out-right chuckling as he continues his tale. "Suddenly, the beam of car headlights turned into the yard. The inside of our station wagon lit up from their brilliant flash of light."

At this moment Barry imitates Mom's frantic voice. "'Shield me with the blanket, I don't want to be seen! Mom shouted.' I quickly tucked the blanket around her and leaned over her. She was hidden from sight."

"The higher the flames climbed, the more the vehicles arrived. Soon the parking lot resembled a drive-in theatre. The atmosphere was shimmering with a bright light that beamed inside all the vehicles. Mom peeked out the window, but quickly ducked down out of sight. Dad and I laughed up a storm and soon Mom saw the funny side of the situation and also burst into laughter."

By the end of Barry's story, we are all howling with laughter. I can see it all happening in my mind's eye. My heart hugs the moment warmly and I know, deep within, that *this is my home, and it will always be my home!*

Chapter 75

Courting:

I am content in Regina. I love my job at the Young Men's Christian Association. My co-worker, Doreen, and I become fast friends. We have similar interests–together we sneakily peruse the gym membership applications of all the young men our age!

One day, my heart is *all-aflutter*. I am serving a handsome young man who is completing his gym application. He returns the application form.

"Thank you," I murmur, in my softest tone, and smile. He smiles and exits.

Immediately I spin my body around to face Doreen. Displaying an excited smirk, I jiggle his application form in the air. Predictably, in a matter

Julie - YMCA Receptionist

of seconds, she zips out of her chair, rushes to my side, and looms over my shoulder. Quickly scrutinizing his documentation, we speedily zoom in on the important information. His occupation is an inspector, and his age is twenty-one years old. Doreen's shoulders droop in disappointment.

"He is too young for me," she sighs.

"He is older than me—he's mine," I state enthusiastically. I am nineteen years old.

I watch for him every day. The young man arrives at ten in the morning and departs around eleven o'clock. We develop a pattern. Upon arriving, he flings the front door open and tilts his head in my direction. He smiles. I smile. Upon leaving, he strides past reception and glances my way. He smiles. I smile.

Am I naïve? Should I be more apprehensive? Mom's recent words, "Be more discerning," reverberates in my mind. I quickly dispel my thoughts.

Several days later, the young man's routine changes. At eleven o'clock he enters the television room instead of departing. I am puzzled. *Why would anyone watch TV at eleven in the morning?*

Fortunately, the television room is in a direct line of sight from my desk. I glance over quite often to keep an eye on him. However, every time I look, he seems to be looking in my direction. I can feel the hot blood creep up my neck—I am embarrassed to be caught checking him out! We spend many days playing this cat-and-mouse game. *Who is eyeing who?*

He is at the reception counter. He appears cool, but charming. My gentleman is with a friend who is obtaining a membership. At the completion of his friend's application, the words from Elvis Presley's song enters my brain: *It is now or never.* I muster up my courage and bravely look *my man* straight in the eye.

"Hi," I murmur quietly.

"Hi," he enthusiastically replies, as his face lights up in pleasure.

The next day, Thursday, it is raining cats and dogs. My fella arrives. He smiles. I smile. At eleven o'clock he is watching television. I shift my attention his way many times—I have trouble focusing on my work. Several times our eyes connect, and I feel ill at ease being spotted spying on him.

In my peripheral vision I note that he is exiting the television room. I plan to casually glance up and exhibit my usual smile. Suddenly, my heart skips a beat–he is approaching the reception counter. I step swiftly up to the counter before Doreen can move out of her chair.

My mystery man from the YMCA

"Can I help you?" I inquire smilingly.

"Are you court-ing?" he asks.

His question stuns me. *Courting?* In my entire life, I have never heard this word used in this context. I take a second to decipher the question. *Does he mean do I have a boyfriend or am I engaged? He must mean engaged.*

"No," I softly reply.

"Can I give you a ride home after work?" he asks.

My brain goes into overdrive. *Dang, I have a male friend picking me up!*

"I am sorry I have a ride home," I reply, mustering up my most apologetic tone.

"How about dinner tomorrow night?" he asks.

My mind is in a turmoil. *Shoot, I have a date already!*

"I am sorry. I am busy tomorrow night," I reply morosely.

His countenance changes visibly–his shoulders droop and his mouth tightens. Slowly, he turns to leave. My breath catches in my throat and my knees feel weak.

"I am free on Saturday night!" I blurt out anxiously at his withdraw-ing back.

He comes to an abrupt halt and whips around. We lock eyes. He smiles. I smile. It is at that precise moment that I know deep in my heart: *He is Mine, and I am His!*

Dave arrives for our date dressed to a tee, in a sports jacket and tie. Am I impressed? You bet your boots I am! We arrive at a fancy-dancy restaurant to our reserved table. My brain swirls in amazement. *This is not my normal dinner date at the A & W.* Suddenly, he pulls out my barrel-type chair. I am in a state of shock. *Who is this fantastic guy? Where did he come from?* The ambience is romantic, with dimly lit candles billowing inside opaque glass beakers on a cozy table for two. Gazing at one another, he flashes me the most charming smile I have ever seen! This fella, Dave, has me in the palm of his hand!!!

The next day we are out and about when Dave orders a Lemonade. He is puzzled when he receives an actual lemonade–he expected a seven-up. All becomes clear when I learn that Dave has immigrated from England, and they use different words for many things. This causes many hilarious moments.

"Would you like to go to the lake tomorrow?" Dave asks. "Do you have a swimming costume?"

A swimming costume. *What is he talking about? An outfit or a swimsuit?* I am in a dilemma, trying to decipher his question. I wear an outfit and quickly discover he meant a swimsuit! Our dating life is kept a-hopping just trying to figure out what he is implying!

Within a couple weeks Dave introduces me to Bill, his boss whom he considers his Regina family. We spend every moment together outside of our work. I am smitten and so is he!

"Let's get married," Dave whispers while snuggling together in my apartment. I am silent. My mind is in a whirl. *Did I hear him correctly? Did he ask me to marry him? We have only been dating three months.*

Dave dressed to a Tee

"Yes," I answer breathlessly. I am over the moon.

"This weekend we will go to Weekes, so I can ask your dad for your hand in marriage," Dave says with a grin. I am surprised and impressed that he values this tradition.

The following weekend we are in Weekes and Dad quizzes Dave.

"What is your job and how solid is your career?" Dad asks.

"We drove here in my X-ray truck; come into my darkroom and I will explain my job duties," Dave replies. They disappear into the darkroom that is mounted on the back of the truck. An hour later, I am getting worried. *What can they be discussing?*

That evening Dad takes me aside.

"Dave is not a farmer, and I don't understand a lot of what his work entails, however, he will be a good provider," Dad announces and smiles. "You will have our blessing to get married."

Julie, Dad, Mom, Chris

The following Saturday night we are seated at our romantic table for two at the same fancy-dancy restaurant of our first date.

"Will you marry me?" Dave whispers with his most charming smile while extending a box housing a diamond ring.

"Yes," I reply knowing full well that he knew my answer before he asked. We decide on an October wedding since,

Back: Charlie, Nellie, Dave, Barry, Mom, Dad. Front: Charlene, Julie, Chris, Barry

sister Chris and her fiancé, Barry are getting married in August. However, Dad has as different plan.

"What do you think about having a double wedding together in August?" Dad asks Chris and me. Our sister bond is close, and this seems a fitting end to our single life. We choose identical wedding dresses, bouquets, and wedding cakes—evidence of our relationship.

Mom and Chris organize the wedding plans while I am working in Regina. I arrive home to attend a wedding shower held in the Town Hall which is attended by most of the women in the area.

At the wedding The Weekes Ladies club serves a hot meal to two hundred and fifty guests—mainly consisting of the community, along with family. Andy MacDonald, a close friend of our parents', who is the nice fella that gave Charlie and I a ride to school one cold winter morning many years ago, gives the Toast to the Brides. Bridesmaids for Chris are her school friend, Lois, and her Hairdressing school

Dave, Julie, Chris, Barry

friend, Sylvia. Groomsmen for Barry are his friends, Norman, and Dave. My bridesmaids are my Boarding house-College school friend, Sharon, and my YMCA work friend Doreen. Groomsmen for Dave are his boss Bill and friend Jim.

Our vows are held in the Redeemer Lutheran Church in Porcupine Plain with Pastor Wanamaker officiating the ceremony. He is a young minister who is nervous because this is his first marriage ceremony and on top of that it will be a double wedding. On our special day all goes according to plan and our vows are completed. Pastor Wanamaker introduces us as newly married couples.

"I would like to introduce Mr. and Mrs. Althouse," he announces waving his hand in the direction of Chris and Barry. After the clapping ceases Pastor continues.

"And I would like to introduce Mr. and Mrs. Allen," he announces with a flair as he waves his hand in our direction. A gasp is audible from the audience, and I smile in amusement. Pastor realizes his error and in a tremulous voice corrects his statement.

"Sorry, I meant to say, Mr. and Mrs. Russell."

Dave and I step outside into the sun's blinding rays to feel the warm heat rise up from the cement sidewalk. Standing arm in arm we shift our eyes to one another and exchange a loving look. He smiles. I smile.

Afterword

My Childhood Home:

Decades later, I return to Weekes.

My first stop is to visit at the Golden Age Club. This is the meeting spot for those in the community to gather for morning coffee. A feeling of warmth overcomes me as I step into the room and see my hometown friends. The years have passed by, we appear older, however, our feelings are the same. We care about one another. Each person is special to me–they are my small-town family.

My second stop is to visit the graveyard. The cemetery and I are at peace. I feel like I am walking into the gateway of home, with so many family members residing in this resting spot. Mom and Dad lie together, side by side. Their entries into Heaven are each a distinct, different, and compelling memorable tale. But wait, that is a story for another day ...

My third stop is to visit our abandoned farm. I gaze sadly at the dull yellow house, overrun with ivy, the wooden sidewalk, sunk into the ground, the row of granaries leaning in disarray, crouching to the earth, and the dugout shrunk and overrun with weeds, it resembles a slough. The ancient cherry tree is bent and twisted at the waist, with its crooked, gnarled arms grasping wildly in a disorderly fashion, its trunks holding a ton of sibling secrets whispered under its umbrella.

In my mind's eye I visualize a house as it existed in the past, with its many changing coats. The colors on the bottom half either a vivid blue, orange, or red, gleaming brightly against the top half of a striking pearly white. The final coat is a luscious sunshine yellow, covering the entire house, signifying the joy within its walls.

I fantasize that the granaries stand ramrod straight, like a row of soldiers attired in a brilliant barn red. Atop are the shadows of us children hopping from rooftop to rooftop, and upon reaching the final granary, leaping into the air to plunge into a huge blanket of hay.

I imagine the dugout clear of weeds, with the wide plank looming out over the luminous blue water. Our special diving board, created out of a huge slab of lumber and held down at the end with a massive rock hauled in from the field. Shadows of us children running, jumping, and diving into the deep waters, squealing with delight.

I shift my gaze to the fields of grain still waving in the wind. I perceive our shadows weaving in and out of the stalks, chasing each other under the hot, blazing sun.

My heart lovingly embraces the past. I know deep within that, *This will always be my childhood home, full of amazing memories!*

In my life I will have several homes; however, within my heart my permanent dwelling is with the Lord. He keeps me safe regardless of my decisions or actions. His words echo in my life with Romans 8:28. And we know that all things work together for good, to them who love God.

Julie's painting of home